Hieroglyph of Time
The Petrarchan Sestina

Published with assistance
from the Margaret S. Harding Memorial Endowment
honoring the first director
of the University of Minnesota Press.

Hieroglyph of Time

The Petrarchan Sestina

Marianne Shapiro
Department of French and Italian
New York University

UNIVERSITY OF MINNESOTA PRESS ● MINNEAPOLIS

Published by the University of Minnesota Press,
2037 University Avenue Southeast,
Minneapolis, Minnesota 55414

Library of Congress Cataloging in Publication Data

Shapiro, Marianne.
   Hieroglyph of time.
   Bibliography: p.
   Includes index.
   1. Sestinas—History and criticism. 2. Petrarca,
Francesco, 1304-1374—Criticism and interpretation.
I. Title.
PN1511.S5   809.1'42   80-10112
ISBN 0-8166-0945-4

The University of Minnesota
is an equal-opportunity educator
and employer.

For Pomme

Contents

Prefatory Note

I owe a fundamental debt to the reference work by Janos Riesz, *Die Sestine: Ihre Stellung in der literarischen Kritik und ihre Geschichte als lyrisches Genus* (Munich: Fink, 1971), which provides a comprehensive survey of the store of available sestinas as well as a summary of literary criticism of poems in this form. Some more recent critical work is cited in my text. The cataloguing and analysis of sestinas in the Slavic languages and of the complete corpus of available Italian Renaissance sestinas has yet to be accomplished.

I have used the English translations of Petrarch and Dante by Robert M. Durling (Cambridge, Mass.: Harvard, 1976).

In the interest of concision I have used the scientific system of bibliographic citation, which obviates the need for footnotes.

The sestina has attracted the attention of numerous Romanists and specialists in Italian literature and is discussed in many handbooks on prosody as well as in histories of national literatures. What is given here of the history of criticism is only what I have found to be of major relevance to the structural and semiotic analysis of the sestina form and to individual poems analyzed. The latter have been chosen from the immense stock of sestinas for their quality or influence; or because they represent the production in a major literary language.

The five sestinas by Petrarch to which I devote an extensive reading and the one discussed in Chapter 7 include poems that generated waves of poetic activity throughout European literature (XXII, LXXX, CCCXXXII) as well as poems that, despite their brilliance and complexity, have received relatively slight analytical attention (LXVI, CCXIV). A number of modern poems are discussed, written often just at the moment that the poets chose to define their voices through close communion with the past. Like the poems of Petrarch, they are works that enter into a complex net of interconnection with other works, a connection that is not chronological but is a kind of relation in which images out of memory are projected as far into the future as the end of time.

During the preparation of my book I had the benefit of a Younger Humanists Fellowship from the National Endowment for the Humanities (1974-75), and of a Morse Fellowship from Yale University. A sabbatical leave from Yale facilitated the writing of the manuscript.

I would like to express my gratitude to John Freccero, now of Stanford University, for his encouragement and thoughtful reading of the manuscript.

Los Angeles, California   M.S.

Hieroglyph of Time
The Petrarchan Sestina

Chapter 1

Introduction

1. Preliminary

This study of the sestina in the context of European and American poetry is also an attempt to reconcile the languages of literary scholarship, that is, synchronic analysis and historical criticism. It is my hope to be able to show that these languages are both valid and that they are the less effective when scholarship tries to make each independent of the other. It is no mere accident that I choose the sestina as my focus of concentration, for the same two fundamental conceptions of time — cyclical and linear — involved in the creation of its form also govern the nature of critical debate about literature and its medium, language.

The sequential reading of a text decrees that it be read as strings of words, but we perceive words as more than sections of a string. Upon reading a text we form new expectations and new recollections, modify our impressions. The material nature of books and their parts furthers a spatial as well as a temporal perception of what is being read. I term the sestina a "hieroglyph of time" while insisting on the metaphorical quality of the space involved. The term "form" entails a spatial status for poems, and this book in turn has a spatial status. This spatial metaphor needs further explanation. The question whether it is possible to compose a history of images addresses the diachronic aspect of this book. In turn, the detailed analysis of a *kind* of poem at any one moment of its evolution is a question that challenges the synchronic bias.

The nonmaterial aspect of the literary "object" heightens the speaking power contained in literary works. Although as an artifact the poem does not propose, does not predict, cannot be verified by evidence, the words in it will not behave accordingly: If a poem is true it is also not false, and a poem (like a picture) may be replete with propositions and predictions of any kind. Finally, it may prefigure them. It is one of my aims to show that the sestina has obstinately adhered to its principal forms throughout its history since the decisive contribution of Petrarch, whose sestina is a poetic manifestation chief among those in lyric poetry, of speculation about the forms of time.

One of my assumptions is that a poem is not a world unto itself, and I hope this book will challenge the synchronic bias in literary studies. I assume that any point that I can raise about a poem has countless points of tangency with other poems and with a host of collateral experiences. For example, once I refer to the lack of a center in the sestina structure, the reference is seen to apply to conditions outside the poem, such as the intense human search for centers as manifested in analogous structures, like those of towns, of Paradises, or of the human soul. I contend in this book that Petrarch's unprecedented mythologizing of an amorous event was the leading condition for a new development for the sestina, whose form presented itself to him as a prior fact. The story, as history imitated in the linearity of poetic process, and the myth, the primordial and primitive origin of an indefinitely recurring theme, meet in this work, and the myth establishes its dominance. This confluence and resolution of two aspects of temporality through the mythologizing of events created a literary symbol that, as such, constantly invites interpretative investigation. At the same time, the verbal recapitulations within sestinas call on the resources of memory, and the reader becomes involved in a spiraling extension of the words, without establishing for any one of them a simple, fixed meaning. The uncentered structure of the sestina is thus carried out in the continuous metonymies created by the rhyme words. In this chapter, I will elucidate the means by which the conditions of formal and semantic openness and closure exhibited by poems and exemplified in the sestina are dealt with so that the poem consistently points beyond itself, toward interpretation.

The organization of the chapters that follow is prompted by the conviction that the structures of form and of content cannot be abstracted from a poem. Nevertheless, not every poem cited or analyzed receives equal space or time. My procedure has been to give each the attention necessary to clarify its relation to the dynamics of the sestina. It will become evident, I hope, that the poems chosen for expanded treatment are fully representative of the body of sestinas available.

Chapter 2 examines the beginning of the sestina's invention in Provençal poetry and studies poems written after the invention of the form; Chapter 3 characterizes the principal changes in the potential of the form as realized by Petrarch; Chapter 4 presents detailed readings of five of his sestinas and one by Dante; Chapter 5 studies the crisis of Renaissance Neoplatonism that surfaces in the French sestina; Chapter 6 explores the intimate connection between the sestina and pastoral poetry as a whole, including a number of pastoralizing commemorative uses of verse that frame it within privileged blocks of time. Chapter 7 is devoted to a functional adaptation of the sestina to a particular kind of allegorical discourse exemplified in Italian poetry, that of the voyage. The Epilogue provides a summary of my theoretical framework and the general premises according to which I have proceeded, in the light of the practical analyses of earlier chapters. Since I have not attempted to make a literary artifact, the reader will note shifts of tone that I consider inevitable concessions to the nature of the material involved.

2. A Symbolic Icon

The tail-biting serpent is a figure of time (Gombrich 1972: 66) that links beginnings to endings and hence signifies eternity. The figure is codified in a host of verbal images, but it is also a living sign, retaining those features of cyclicity first read, translated, and condensed in the process of its encoding. This book will concern a poetic form, the sestina, that involves an analogous concept of ending (closure) and the idea of perpetual rebirth.

To assess the strength and value of an image through a written text is a proposition that takes us far from the purely visual sphere, and I should warn that I will not refer to the serpent-image itself. The visual, hence spatial, metaphor that I have momentarily called to life has its dangers, for the temporality of poetry demands the clear and present dramatization of what in visual art is static: the serpent actually biting his tail before our eyes.

My analogy of the serpent refers specifically to the poetic practice of "head-tailed" rhyme characteristic of the sestina and to its implications of temporal recurrence. I contend that the sestina constitutes Western poetry's most comprehensive use of time as a structural principle, and that it is Petrarch's implementation of this principle that endows his work with generative power. No instance of poetic invention better demonstrates that it is not the inventor, nor the precursor, but the most effective proponent of an idea who becomes the instrument of its fate. The obsessive concern with time that characterizes the content of Petrarch's sestinas is manifested in the "head-tailed" structure.

Much against my better intentions, this spatial metaphor will appear throughout this book, betraying the surface petrifications of language. However, it can follow the erratic, crooked, and labyrinthine paths of actual human desire. Since the sestina itself, especially in the hands of its leading practitioner, manifests the urgent quest for the impossible integration of time and poetic structure, we find distilled in it the quintessence of the poetic function. Here we best perceive what Jacques Lacan called the "metonymic" nature of desire (Lacan 1966), meaning that the object of desire is always irretrievably displaced, so much so that the link between an impulse and its semantic object is available only by rediscovering the incommensurability of desire and object. In poetry, the ontological state of desire surfaces through continguity relationships. For at the instant when an object of desire is named, its uniqueness, even its being as an unattained object, is displaced, and the naming word makes room for another. The revolutions of homonyms in the sestina are uniquely conducive to the reenactment of this quest for the disappearing object, because the circle reproduced in it is never quite closed.

Among the arts, poetry appears, on a continuum tending toward self-reflexiveness, well before music, and after representational painting. In addition to the recurrence inherent in language, rhythm as a sine qua non of poetic structure makes constant reference to *pastness*. Recurrence (*versus*) often means poetry (*versus*), or the main feature of poetry as opposed to prose. The fact of recurrence implies retrospection, the containment of the past in the present, persisting as memory.

Of course poems differ widely in the apportionment and frequency of recurrence. Jakobson's well-known definition of the "poetic function" as a "focus on the message for its own sake" (Jakobson 1960: 359) he and others have refined to salutary effect: Comparing the patterns of equivalence in music with those of poetry, he perceived in their patterning a focus on the *sign* itself ("introversive semiosis" [1971:704]), which is shared in various degrees by all manifestations of the aesthetic function. For most poetry, semantic and referential content supersedes self-reflexive content, making recurrence a subordinate part of content as a whole. In the sestina, compared with other poems, recurrence is codified to the utmost. The proportion of introversive to extroversive semiosis increases accordingly, and *signans* and *signatum* more closely approach fusion. Sestinas are not *about* ideas; they *are* ideas. Their form, more conducive to suggestive juxtaposition than to connected statement, thereby is more able to embody recurrence as process. The stricter the codification of form, the greater the degree of that form's relation to the past, both within the organization of the poem and with reference to its literary, mythological, or historical past. The structural elaboration by the poem of its own, changing frames makes us experience how the interpretation of a sign constitutes yet another sign, which has in turn to be interpreted ad infinitum. Always near and yet just beyond reach, final meaning is the brass ring at the end of the ride.

3. The Sestina Form

The sestina form invented by Arnaut Daniel, and transmitted substantially as he had conceived it, was a play of homonymic equivalences with a concomitant prevalence of semantic signficance over narrow lexical meaning. It is composed of thirty-nine lines: six strophes of six lines each and a *tornada* (or *envoi*) of three lines. The final rhyme-word of each strophe is repeated as the initial rhyme-word of the following one, because the same set of rhyme-words is used in a rigorously determined order in six of the seven strophes. The rhyme-words, numbered 1 2 3 4 5 6 in the first strophe, are reordered to form the sequence 6 1 5 2 4 3 in the succeeding ones, each building from the last. This movement is described in the Provençal *Leys d'amor* (ed. Anglade 1919-20: 106-107), which notes that the rhyme-words rule over the lines, and that rhyme-words orphaned within the strophe of necessity find themselves answered in successive strophes. The formula is invariant for every strophe. The *Leys d'amor* characterizes as *coblas capcaudadas* (head-tailed strophes) all such as these, which repeat the last rhyme of a strophe at the beginning of the next one. The complex itinerary constitutes a dazzling map of variations and permutations of the rhyme-words, but the completed sestina conserves in the entirety of its strophes the memory of the basic feature, which is its first strophe and entry into being.

The procedure, called *retrogradatio cruciata,* is based on repetition and inversion. The first principle shows the utilization of units representative as 1, 2, inverted by the second principle 1, 2 (2, 1).

The layering of the two units 1, 1 and 2, 2 into a crossed figure shows an *emboîtement des structures,* a double dynamic of reversal and layering:

1 2 1 2

This kind of stepped construction creates a simultaneous unfolding and recurrence. Now the two complex units 1 2 3 and 4 5 6 may be perceived as superimposed upon one another in the following order:

6 1 5 2 4 3   (Roubaud 1969: 23)

A triadic component appears in the scheme, but it is ruled by dualism. Insofar as the movement of rhyme-words goes in pairs, the strophe is destined to remain uncentered. The distribution of rhyme-words from alternate ends of the strophe reveals the formation of pairs of digits each with seven as their sum (6 & 1; 5 & 2; 4 & 3) (Fowler 1975: 40-41). In numerology, it is the number of eternity and mutability, of the temporal, sublunary world and the world of the eternal Sabbath.

The poem concludes with a half-strophe that manifests all the rhyme-words, generally but not always in the order of their first appearance.

4. Temporality and Poetic Language

The tacit acknowledgment of temporality is everywhere in the structure of language. Through the four-dimensional continuum of space and time, only the coincidence of two points, *here* and *now,* has a directly verifiable meaning (Wehl 1952). Given the knowledge of four dimensions, it is more difficult to speak even of literature in terms of distance, horizon, landscape, site, road, and dwelling. Literature has kept, however, its compromising conception of space as a particularization of certain points and intervals, the "places" (*topoi*) where it tends to settle. Accordingly, spatial metaphors (the party *line,* the future *perspective,* interior *distance*) constitute an immediately understandable working discourse. The assertion that time and our experience of time as directed sequence originate in the depths of the mind yields Bergson's distinction between spatial time and purely "temporal" time. The time marked by clocks "is a hybrid concept, resulting from the incursion of the idea of space into the domain of pure consciousness." Such time is analogous to the spatial organization of series of lyric poems into syntagmatic wholes. *Temps-*

cadran, the sequence of segments, is not time but space, whereas in *temps-durée,* duration, there would be no enumeration.

A mitigating power is provided by memory, which can confer simultaneity on events of past and present, and it is on this simultaneity that poetry depends for the effect of duration. That desired simultaneity provides a clue to the frequent compulsion to spatialize poetry and to think of the more amenable forms as circular. The relation of simultaneity is thereby imparted to the image of the circle, from time immemorial an image of oneness. Yet the human experience of space is not that continuity by a *number* of points, between which there is nothing. Poetry singles out a few favored points, prompting the discovery of sympathies, imitations, and analogies across the "circumscribed" space of the work.

Changing audiences for poetry throughout the centuries of Western European lyric were introduced to poems variously—by eye, by ear, with or without the accompaniment of music. Aristotle's *mousike* includes instrumental music as well as song (Poetics I, 1). Reading in the Middle Ages was thought of as a fusion of seeing what was on the page and "hearing" it internally (Chaytor 1945: 21 ff.). Emanating from the written letter was a concreteness that conferred power on the very act of writing. The prominent signifying value of the visualized letter produced the pseudo-science of medieval etymology, epitomized in Isidore of Seville's encyclopedic *Etymologiae,* which linked the derivation of words to the images of objects suggested by the dissected verbal entity. (An example would be the adjective *piger,* "lazy," etymologized as *pedibus aeger,* "slow of foot." *Etym.* X 213, PL 82:3890) This is a salient example of the spatialization of language. Another (less important from a global standpoint) is to be found in the *carmen figuratum,* a poem whose "figural" status depends entirely on the faculty of seeing vouchsafed by reading (Zumthor 1972: 215-240). Here, very abstract symbolism is represented pictorially by the image outlined in letters. Every thematic persuasion or linguistic expression (of vocabulary or of syntax), every rhetorical figure is subordinated to the physical shape of the verse.

Poetic spatialization is seen in the modern descendant of figured poems, the shaped poem whose riddle and answer lie within its physical image (such as Apollinaire's *Calligrammes*). Reading these poems becomes a taking-possession that never could be attained through sound or temporality, a simultaneity that challenges the necessarily linear order of letters, revealing first the *number* of lines and their distribution. Of course it can hardly be denied that the relative locations of words in the continuous medium of space operate in the reading of poetry. The silent forms propose a tacit sense that can be articulated as a name and known as a thing or the image of a thing. The written poem is a physical occurrence, and its medium is space. Language cannot, however, be reduced to the terms of space: What we see is never replicated in what we say. "And it is in vain that we attempt to show, by the use of images, metaphors, or similes, what we are saying: the space where they achieve their splendor is not that deployed by our eyes but that defined by the sequential elements of syntax" (Foucault 1966: 9).

Poetic analysis has not deviated from the tendency to posit and fix resemblances by moving through patterned juxtapositions and recurrences to the poem's triumph of self-reference, seeming thereby to close the poem's circle. Inside this network, resemblances are conceived as symmetries, evidence of the unity of the text. Logical relationships drop by the wayside, and spatial relations are seen to reflect the organization of the work. The most systematic study of spatial order in literature, that of Roman Jakobson, has been devoted to the discovery of the disposition of unities within the *space* of the poem on every level, from that of distinctive features of phonemes to grammatical categories and tropes. He has shown that a poem is a complex organism composed of symmetries, antitheses, and parallelisms, as is any spatial structure. Jakobson's discussion is often accompanied by references to geometry. Equivalence then emerges as the constitutive factor of the poetic sequence, relegating to minor status the problem of succession or contiguity. We could argue that both equivalence and succession are spatial, in accordance with the Bergsonian distinction. In the matter of poetic analysis, however, we are left with contrasts of degree.

The fact of recurrence in poetry can verge on a "geometrical fallacy." To recognize the constant irruption of the temporal factor should prove tantamount to asserting the impossibility of total recurrence.

5. Number Symbolism: The Numbers 6 and 7

To understand the structure of the sestina, with its *tornada* in place of the seventh strophe, it is necessary to examine the form in the broader context of number symbolism, specifically that surrounding the numbers 6 and 7. The symbolism of numbers is so striking in the sestina as to become a basic attribute of the poem. In Arnaut's poem and in Dante's we have a foreshadowing of what Petrarch would establish as a structural principle, that is, the tension between odd and even numbers, dyad and triad, 6 and 7. Above all, it is as approximations of time that these numbers receive their significance.

10

In the act of Creation, the number 7 receives the sanction of Jehovah, the biblical story possibly conforming to a Babylonian tradition of the seventh day set apart from normal activity according to the lunar divisions (Hopper 1938: 26). Seven creative acts are specifically given in Genesis, but the last two are fitted into a single day (the sixth). From the belief in the inappropriateness of a sabbatical creative act arose the belief that the Creation prefigured the duration of the world, which would therefore endure for six ages (six days for 1,000 years each), to be followed by the Sabbath of eternal rest. The sixth day, or moment of creation, then, is the last full age. The repetition in II Peter 3:8 of the idea in Psalm 90:4 that a day is with God as 1,000 years illustrates the belief that that interval was the length of an age. Accordingly, Irenaeus and Lactantius agree that the creation of the world in six days foreshadowed six earthly ages. The seventh day of rest symbolized eternal stasis and repose. Still, since there was no evening of the seventh day, the seventh age was timeless. The seventh day is said to culminate in the Judgment and Eternal regeneration of the eighth. Centuries later Thomas Aquinas discusses six in relation to 666, the number of the Beast in Revelations. And in Dante's sixth heaven, that of Jupiter and the Eagle, the sixth age is that of earthly perfection; in this heaven Divine Justice forms its mirror (*Par.* XIX, 28-29). Dante is said to be the sixth of the singers of the Eagle (*Inf.* IV, 102).

The number six, however, emanates from the dyad. Even in its favorable portrayal in the *Comedy,* it reveals itself as an image of the Church-State duality represented in the Eagle. Partaking of the dyad, six represents matter and existence that are eternal but not immutable, since everything divisible is mutable and material. Pythagorean number theory rarely overlooks this weakness of six, even though six is the only perfect number within the decad (its divisors adding up to six itself).

It is proper to conceive of the sestina both as a six and as a seven. As a six, it contains six full strophes of six lines with six terminal words in recurrent arrangement. The strophe and the six strophes (excluding the tornada) taken as a whole aptly describe duality (as we will see in Petrarch). This participation in duality is a sure sign of the instability of six. In Pythagorean terms, the even numbers proceed from the unstable dyad and are called "feminine" because they are "weaker" than the odd. They are empty of a center, whereas when the odd numbers are divided there is always a center. Within the six-line strophe is correspondences, especially when expressed in time values, represent respectively the intelligible and the sensible, the mortal and immortal, day and night, right and left, sun and moon, equality and difference.

Six, then, is a number of limitation. As Durling points out (1976: xxi), Petrarch gave it full figural meaning in the structure of his vernacular poems single and as a whole. The enamorment with Laura takes place on Friday, the sixth day, the day of man's creation and redemption—Good Friday at that! Laura died, as Petrarch lets us know, on April 6, 1348.

Six represents our experience of the created world and of time. Petrarch's commentators generally have been able to link the recurrence of sixes to the soul's entrapment within time. I should like to take issue with this view, particularly with regard to the special status of poetry as envisioned action.

The revolutions of Petrarch's sestinas deal largely with appearances, of which the ever-moving, changing flux of particulars is a part. Such is the illusory world of multiplicity and corporeality, the unreal world of becoming that constitutes the sole field of action for the nonrational part of the mind; the part obsessed with the Laurel, the part that never could, by its very nature, be a source of truth.

The poems are not, however, pure sixes. Tornadas create a seventh entity, a half-strophe that transforms the sestina into a "seven." Thus in its completed form, the poem has an eschatological orientation and a unilateral direction of time. Let us consider the sestina's aspect of "sevenness" within the context of the number-symbol:

The sevenfold incantation of sestinas recapitulates all the ages including the last. The ancient conception of seven as the day creation stopped points figurally to eternity, to life beyond the created world of time. The seven of regeneration is symbolized in the seventh day of God's rest from creation. Because of its uniqueness, it is granted the distinction of absolute isolation and resultant relationship to the monad in Pythagorean number theory. Macrobius calls seven the universal number because of the innumerable heptads in the microcosm and macrocosm.

Augustine dwells on the properties of seven. He explains that it is composed of the first even and the first odd number and is accordingly the symbol of all numbers. Therefore, seven means "perfect completeness." Because seven is the result of adding the triune principle of God and the quadruple principle of man, it is the first number that implies totality; it is the number of the universe and of man, signifying the creature as distinguished from the Creator. Aquinas proves that the number seven signifies universality because the life of man evolves through seven stages; because of the seven gifts of the Holy Spirit; because there are seven churches. Augustine's extended disquisition on seven, through the relation of seven to six drawn by Hugh of St. Victor (seven beyond six = rest after work),

12

medieval thought concurs in allotting to seven (and occasionally to eight) the meaning of completion and eternity: "There is to be a seventh day of rest into which all shall be translated who, during the sixth day of the world's history, are created anew by the incarnate Word" (St. Augustine, *Contra Faustum* XII, 38).

The meanings of seven that display the figural import of completion show how deeply the medieval poet was imbued with this sense. The seventh, crucial, and persistently necessary portion of the sestina bespeaks the figural function of sevenness. In Petrarch's sestinas the seventh part reveals itself in the content as the indispensable conceptual element of closure. As a perspicacious commentary has it, they allude to the intensity of contemplation (XXX), to conversion (CXLII, CCXIV), to death (XXII, CCCXXXII), to the end of time (XXII) (Durling 1965: 67-87). The seventh part of the poem emerges as a statement of vital possiblity and a reaffirmation of living on the borderline of the more-than-possible.

6. The Missing Center

The magnetic force of the triad over the sestina's form (which describes a movement of duality toward the third) is an unbalanced alternation toward the repose of the center. In the six-line strophe, there can be no line equidistant from all the others. Although the lines of the sestina can be perceived as three groups of two members, or two groups of three, participating in a potentially transcendent thirdness, every other feature outranks this triadic aspect. While six is the lowest multiple of three, it is also the lowest multiple of three and two simultaneously. When the order of rhyme-words has progressed in a pincer movement of 6 1 5 2 4 3, having reached the last two terms, the pincer movement closes upon nothing. The rhyme-word 3 is underscored by repetition in the first line of the next strophe, but this emphasis of repetition effects no realization of a triad. It serves only to indicate the generation of a new, centerless strophe.

Contiguity relationships among words dominate the sestina. The rhyme-words demonstrate resistance to being subsumed under one defined and particular meaning. We remember, as we read, the conservation and recycling of form. The exact reproduction of sound serves as the mainspring for the succeeding utterance. Thus the line is constantly reborn from its own ashes. As the accumulation of meaning proceeds, the rhyme-words exfoliate in an ever more inclusive grouping, previous senses adhere to them, and their return is charged with a more portentous content. Against this growth, the center-directed motion of the sestina attests to a continuing metaphysical thirst for stasis at the center, which could be expressed as the world standing still. The scheme of head-tailed chains replicates the eternal enactment of a periodic destruction and regeneration while eluding the temptations of fixed significance. The emergent poem speaks of itself in terms of contiguity and distance. The absence of a center to the strophe and to the poetic whole indicates that the sestina is structured along a continuum of dualistic thought. This principle would seem to encourage the perception of bilateral symmetry (a favorite notion particularly where Petrarch scholarship is concerned), but nowhere as in poems does the metaphor more obviously fail us.

The sestina is a medieval invention, and medieval symbolism accords primacy to the idea of the center: the kernel of meaning within its enclosure of words; the buttressed house of worship; the city center surrounded by its walls. But in providing some idea of the import of centrality we are limited to examining it from an exocentric position. As shown by Eliade (1954), the center is preeminently the zone of Creation and of the sacred in the world, the zone of absolute reality. There exists the ancient conception of the temple as the image of the universe and a recreation of it in small; the Christian tradition sees the sanctuary as representation of the Celestial Jerusalem. Paradise is derived from the symbolism of the center and figures as the center of the cosmos, with Hell as the center of the earth. Since creation is passage from the nonmanifest to the manifest, whatever is created is seen to have its foundation at the center.

Centrality is also associated with the idea of extreme height. As in the concrete world of appearances, cities and sacred places are likened to the summits of mountains; that is why Jerusalem and Zion were not submerged by the Deluge (Eliade 1954: 25). The belief that Golgotha is situated at the center of the world is preserved in the lore of the Eastern Christian. Temples and palaces figure as sacred heights, and the celestial archetype entails the symbolism of the sacred mountain. As with the imagery of the circle, the realized truth of love is found at the celestial summit, which is at the same time a center governed by its own laws and bounded by its own certainty.

The conception of love as the center of the circle is at least as old as Parmenides (Poulet 1961: 30). For the Christian pilgrim coming nearer to the vision of God, Dante envisions a unity of knowing and being that takes place at the center. It is nonrecursive, nondual, and completely self-referential. There knower and known are no longer dual entities but the fused terms of a single act. In this most notable case, the symbolism of the center revealed to the pilgrim incorporates

14

and attests the symbolism of ascent. The quest for the center is invariably evidenced in medieval literary works (Saville 1972). It is present in the idea of the soul as a besieged fortress of guarded virtue. The *Roman de la rose,* whose bipartite structure and different authors still concur in the notion of centeredness, could be viewed as a form of "castle-allegory." In briefer forms of poetry, the lyric of courtly love secularizes the center as the place of lovemaking, reminiscent of the Song of Songs in its evocation of an earthly, paradisiacal enclosure. The beloved herself is seen as a center and height of value. The quest for the center is the passage from the profane to the sacred, from the ephemeral and illusory to reality and eternity, from death to life, from man to the divinity (Eliade 1954: 36).

In versions of the act of Creation, wherever extraterrestrial archetypes exist, a beginning is projected, *"illo tempore* when the foundation of the world occurred" (Eliade 1954: 20) and historical time came into being. Then it is that concrete, measured time is projected onto mythical time, linearity upon cyclicity. Medieval ideologies degraded the value of historical time even as they recognized its indispensability to its obverse, eschatological time. In view of this ambivalence, Dante's lack of interest in measured temporality when he theorizes on poetic composition should not occasion surprise. For the evidence of passing time and of history was eventually to be overcome permanently in the absolute stasis of ahistorical, celestial time.

We know of Dante's interest in a verse-structure that consists of a center member buttressed by two others. But Dante is at once the summation and the preeminent exception of medieval culture. Where poetic form is concerned, we have rather to ask how it was that so few medieval strophic forms displayed topographical centrality, for a persistent antithetical structure informs medieval poetry and points to dualistic schemes. Whether the antagonists are lovers in a courtly fiction, warriors poised for a duel, or the human soul divided between besieging enemies and besieged allies, whether they are contenders in poetic debates or hypostatizations of the will and the intellect, arguers for *sic* or *non,* they are more likely to be competing as potential centers. The contest ranges then as polar opposites, so that the natural forms that represent them are argumentative, agonistically determined and rhetorically based. This fact of antithesis and contention vitiates the possibility of centrality.

7. The Sestina as an Example of Closure

"The sense of closure is a function of the perception of structure" (Smith 1968: 4). I will say much about "closure" in this study, and it is well to make the distinction between *semantic* (conceptual end-stoppage) and *formal* (the end of the poem) closure apparent from the outset. Sestina-writing poets will be seen as operating with the self-imposed constraints of this form to produce, ultimately, a way of achieving emancipation from *semantic* closure. Formal closure, at the same time, must be conceived of on two levels: first, that which attends the end of the poem; second, that which determines its potential as form. The listener or reader of a poem performs a "retrospective patterning" (Smith 1968: 13) that is essentially a response to the formal progress of a poem, the better to perceive it as a formal and conceptual entity. And yet, "closure" (in the sense of knowing when a poem ends) is "secured with reference not so much to the discursive structure of the poem as to the context it implies (Smith 1968: 19).

Even if we restrict ourselves to the recognition of formal closure, it must be apparent that we can never go back again in a poem; we can only repeat it, so that true symmetry in temporally directed art is impossible. The formal structure of a sestina, or of the zodiacal movement that matches its sequence and suggests that the sestina "may be meant to render in its stanzaic structure the sun's annual course around the ecliptic" (Fowler 1975: 40), is circular only in the loosest sense. The fulfilling of *formal* expectations is only one condition for closure.

When lyric was intended for musical rendition, as it was for the troubadours, stanzaic form was the most effective entity the poet could use, supported by musical modification and semantic linkage. For the troubadour, the tornada of the song bestowed integrity on the completed experience of the song. It was normally a half-strophe, addressed to a listener or listeners who might be the beloved, or a patron or patrons. It generally reproduced the rhymes of the second half of the preceding strophe (Jeanroy 1934: I, 93). The Provençal term, which I will retain through my study, was derived from a posited **tornar* (to turn). An intriguing suggestion is that the term alludes to the actual operation of rolling up the parchment after the completion of writing on it; then the action would signify that of closing a poem that was ready for transmission (DeBartholomaeis 1907: 449).

The tornada often had an epigrammatic character that conveyed finality or dismissal. But it could be anticlosural, or affirm nothing but the addressee of the song, a third party removed from its immediate concerns. As this situation suggests, the expressive qualities of such an ending may imply epistemological attitudes that reach far

---

*Provenance uncertain.

beyond the specific universe of the poem. Well after the habitual practice of apostrophizing or simply naming the recipient had ended, the tornada survived in the Italian *canzone* and, more remarkably, in all sestinas written thereafter. While its content could have existed in marked isolation from the rest of the song in general, the sestina through the rhyme-word scheme draws the tornada organically into the rest of the poem. It also establishes precise relations between the tornada and the lines of every other strophe. In the sestina it would recapitulate, contradict, or place in doubt thoughts and rhymes alike.

Since the tornada long ago lost its social and pragmatic function, we must assume that its continuance implies that it is pivotal to the sestina's sense of closure. That it is a half-strophe is instrumental to this sense, signifying an ending but not a symmetry—not a closing of the circle. Moreover, the arrangement of the rhyme-words whose order emerges greatly varied betokens an optional break in the structure. True, the recurrence of the rhyme-words, even in an undetermined ordered and reduced expanse, indicates a sort of reprise. The tornada is related to the *volta* of the Italian canzone, which as Dante states is so named because the poets made it a return to a certain part of the sung melody (*Convivio* II, xii). Whether or not the tornada has the semantic character of epilogue, it remains in some degree the indicator of the ending and a scrambling of the willed order of the rest of the sestina, perpetually interrupting the cyclical order of rhyme-words. Petrarch will use the tornada to concentrate his projections of the "seventh day" or futurity as the final solution to the demands of eschatological time, that is to say, as the marker of openness that is even more semantic than formal.

8. Closure and Openness

The categories I use here are in the province of semantics, and having established that the sestina is a predetermined form, I hope to elicit the understanding that the terms "openness" and "closure" will refer to the semantics of a poem as either distinct from or inclusive of its formal limitations. (I resist the use of "theme" or "thematic" as a characterization of structures: By implication, through association, and in actual practice "theme" is at best a dependent and all too often an arbitrary category. To make time a "theme" of the sestina would be to class a generative principle with frivolous possibilities and ancillary issues.)

Although the events of sestinas are largely interior or psychological, they form an integral structure with respect to time. It is not the formal expectations of a sestina that ultimately determine the perception of that structure, even insofar as these can be projected into the perceptions of countless readers. Whether or not the poet "sets out" to compose a sestina, as the rigors of the form seem to indicate, content informs the otherwise empty vessel of form. They are one when the mold is removed, and this is where the reader comes in.

The concept of time, translated into movement, describe what we can apprehend only as a figure in space, which is primarily linear or primarily cyclical. The direction of the sestina is determined by the order of its six rhyme-words, which in the canon is invariant until the final strophe. The final strophe, the tornada, which is truncated and in which the six words recur in obvious acceleration, provides the listener or reader with a sure signal that the poem is about to end. This feature operates decisively on the semantic and formal temporality of the poem. Since the cycles of words are theoretically and potentially endless, readers are encouraged at first to think of them as closed and as pointing to other closures. The final half-strophe, however, although it ends the poem, or for that very reason, points inevitably beyond the poem. The configuration of the complete poem, then, is a linear progression with infinite extension beyond itself. Within that progression (common to all poems) appear cycles in groups of multiple-groups of six.

Ultimately it is the adherence of the sestina-scheme to the realities of poetic structure that vitiates the cyclical aspect. Thus the formal ending of the sestina functions as an escape route from the infinite cycle in its ordering. Dramatization of the meeting of cyclic and linear time makes the sestina a model of meditation on poetic recurrence. Simultaneously and decisively, however, the event of the poem leaves us an open door. It is to be expected that Petrarch, who invented a poetic dialect that maximized the possibilities of poetic evasiveness, would be found standing nearer to that door than any poet before him.

Petrarch as a Christian writer invariably defended the idea of a created universe, and we may infer that he thought about universal beginning and ending. Any speculation of this kind by a poet would yield the radical contrast between universal as opposed to poetic eschatology. Accordingly, in the sestinas, which turn around the unknowns of universal time, Petrarch expressed the "before" and more often the "after" of human natural cycles with tropes referring to "impossibilities", possible only within poems. They are, however, a strong variety of semantic opening. The poem freely ranges beyond the domain of external, or "natural" possibility, limited only by the necessity of remaining poetry.

Since it deals in so concentrated a form with beginning and ending, recurrence and uniqueness, the cyclical and the linear, the sestina directs its poet to a position on a continuum extending from translation to imitation. The historical contingency consists chiefly in Petrarch's appearance on the scene, but it is a pretext. Of course, awareness of the existence of the form amounts to knowledge of poetic tradition and probably of other sestinas, and the force of recurrence as poetic tradition invites a number of sestina-writers to comment upon them. Yet among a host of fixed poetic forms, the sestina displays an unusually high degree of speculation on the past. This feature cannot be explained further by allusion to its sheer difficulty or complexity, which contrasts radically with the sequential forms of most contemporary verse. We must recognize the unique aptitude of the form for meditation as recapitulation, because of its inherent pattern of recurrences. It is so treated by the modern poets who write in it, of whom W. S. Merwin and John Ashbery will be represented here (Chapter 6) in some detail.

Viewed either as a continuum or as a string of discontinuities, poetic tradition is an open structure, a structure of historical or linear time. If sestinas tend to appear somewhere near the midpoint of their creators' careers, this may well be because they point beyond themselves.

Cyclical movement and movement that is directed toward a formal end contend with one another in the sestina so that the formal dismissal in the tornada nevertheless betrays an open-ended doubt, tentativeness, or rejection of the absolute and unqualified assertion. These attitudes we know as otherwise characteristic of Petrarch's semantics, which question the possibility of unassailable statement and the legitimacy of the final word, insofar as humanity can conceive it. The historical line leading into the moment of this very writing has no natural termination. By comparison, as regards poetic form we have only to summon to mind the seemingly enchained linear progress of Dante's invention, *terza rima,* and be tempted to declare it potentially endless, though centered. But the centered universe it creates for us has so high a proportion of coherence, and its evasions are so matter-of-factly put in abeyance, that we may read the *Commedia* persuaded of its symmetries. Petrarch does not allow for panaceas of this kind: His often-cited "symmetries," coordinates, synonyms, and repetitions are temporal extensions substituted for semantic coherence. That they can often be paired shows us no true semantic closure; for that, once would be enough, were we able to discover a center of repose. The quandary as Petrarch saw it is still very much with us.

The social familiarity among the members of Petrarch's lexicon easily became a focus of parody, for the word play is often carried to the utmost and it is the extreme that is most easily parodied. But parody was inevitable in view of the plethora of imitation and repetition that Petrarchan poetry accommodated, and in view of the sheer proliferation of poetic matter, few Italian courts of the Renaissance, for example, being without their Petrarchino. It is as though repetition alone could provide magically the incantatory and propitiatory power attributed to composed words. We know this phenomenon of repetition, too, to have no point of semantic closure as long as poems continue to be written, and no point of ultimate corroboration.

For past and future always exist only as signs. Their perception in the present moment of reading exists insofar as they become part of the poems' signs. The lyric poem, of necessity, speaks not in a perpetual present but in a directed consciousness of time. When a poem refers to events beyond the margins of known past and imagined future, it confers an eschatological function on these events. History, limited to human and lineally perceived time, receives a context not through the poet's awareness of living in an eternal present but through his anticipation of its abolishment in the future.

9. Myth and Poetic Process

The Petrarchan sestina has its matrix in the poet's fictionalized version of the myth of Apollo and Daphne. The implications for lyric poetry are enormous: Henceforth it will lay claims to a perennial truth through its reconnection with an immortal story. Petrarch's innovation resulted in the linkage to myth through his series of 366 poems, one for each day of the year (cf. Roche 1974), with a condensation of the concept of metamorphosis and petrified human desire that was initially conceived by Ovid (*Met.* 451 ff.) and to which Petrarch's astonishing contribution ushers in nonmedieval forms of expression.

It is imperative, however, to think of the *Canzoniere* as a retelling, not only in its recurrence to Ovid's, but also in its myriad forms of repetition, substitution, inversion, and experimentation with the then recent past. Petrarch took ample cognizance of memory as the mother of all the Muses. In a wider sense, Mnemosyne is the patroness of poems, in that orientation toward the past unites cultures of all types (Lévi-Strauss 1962: 24). She is at the same time the opponent of Messianic hopes, for she metonymizes all in a ritual process that depends on the reenactment of events from the mythicized world. The separations, transitions, and reaggregations involved in the individual instance of reenactment presuppose a lost, primordial time that was not strictly a beginning but "begins each day anew" (Corbin 1957: 161).

Myth as eternally revived in memory achieves no conclusion. According to its pattern, time turns around endlessly, and myth has little to say of final time. Magical language is its accomplice. The relation it draws between man and the ends he desires is distinctive. As "symbolic action," magical language like that of poems seeks ways to possess objects of desire. As the outward sign of contemplation, it seeks to enjoy the knowledge of these objects even while fulfillment is deferred. This formulaic binding of action and contemplation comes to designate poetry a separate mode of activity. Poetry, in affirming itself as a whole and an absolute (while belonging to a system of wider and complex relations), arouses the tendency to perceive a world in a lyric, the "sensation d'univers caractéristique de la poésie" (Valéry 1958: 1363).

The metaphoric aspect of myth has often been emphasized in the interest of showing how the principle of similarity encourages the translation of myths into poetic material. Anthropologists also have stressed the "symbolic" character of myths, which they often seem to equate with metaphor in that myth is seen as a figurative or indirect mode of discourse (Turner 1968: 675). Petrarch, in apparent support of this emphasis, translates the facts of the myth in occasionally startling flights of fantasy to the new givens of his love for Laura. One of these instances occurs, as it happens, in a sestina (XXII): May his lady be with him forever, the lover wishes, and never transform herself into a green plant, as once she did when pursued by Apollo!

The pursuit of Daphne and her transformation into the laurel are taken to be the prior, primordial, and "primitive" origin of something that could recur indefinitely. Petrarch translated into his needs a structural model in which first and second enactments constitute one another in a kind of mirror reversal. The primary scene is posited temporally anterior to his "now" as the foundation of the present — that is, of marking the unspecifiable point of origin. Temporality becomes a metaphor for an anteriority that is structural and logical. The myth of origin mirrors the impossibility of origin; it contains its own negation, its own death, and therefore speaks a kind of double language of time. One aspect segments time in some quantifiable sense, and another is the paradoxical language of *durée*, which inverts the diachrony of the former into vertical stillness and silence. The episode represents a semiotic transformation of myth into the syntax and semantics of desire. By diverting the Apollo-Daphne myth to the

21

new context, Petrarch showed unprecedented awareness of the semiotic work of myth. For what he does is indeed a diversion: The dramatic setting, the images, the switches and reversals, the inhabitual associations constitute a secondary elaboration of the myth's semiotic system. To read this figure as a metaphor for his own story of Laura is to recognize only his accomplishment of cultural integration without perceiving the concomitant of irony that illustrates the intersection of mythical (cyclical) time with linear time. His view of the myth is not holistic as far as his own poem is concerned; the path from Daphne to Laura displays incongruity rather than congruity, displaces more than it aligns, and therefore upsets the coherence and unity of the mingled narrative. In so doing, it emphasizes contiguity rather than similarity.

The establishment of semantic distance and the simultaneous reduction of it is worked out throughout this poem and the others, in a process of semiotic indirectness that supercedes each individual meaning of a rhyme word. A psychoanalytic reading (of a kind I will not attempt) would most certainly show repressed content. I have raised the issue to suggest that the sestina, which is based to an extreme degree on contiguity relations, is particularly hospitable to Petrarch's rendering of myth. For Petrarch displays the intersection of the two conceptions of time—cyclical and linear—that uncovers the sestina's full potential.

10. The Rhyme-Word: Metonymic Progression

Linear and cyclical time correspond to the dual process of selection and combination by whose means all linguistic signs are formed (Jakobson 1960: 1971). Selection is likened to the directionality of cyclical time, insofar as it draws from preexistent paradigms of language, subject to manifold uses both in and out of poems. Combination is more manifestly akin to linear time, insofar as the words are syntagmatically linked in a contiguity relation.

Even on the level of selection, each line of a sestina is determined by the context of the rhyme-words. This principle of composition demonstrated the transformability of contexts and their successive action upon a verbal sign that is mnemonic in that the unchanging sounds of the rhyme-words orient each manifestation back toward the previous one. The memory involved in recapitulation is in charge, as far as the poem is concerned of storing the fundamental "codes" that rule over the poem's language, values, and practices. For meaning is immanent in the controlling relationships among the rhyme-words. Meaning is more emphatically rendered by some words than

22

by others, and when a word attracts attention to the rhythmically dominant places in a poem, and binds together the whole poem as a unit of interstrophic composition, describes limits, and defines endings, it has a special retrospective connotation. Accordingly, rhyme-words contract relationships among themselves, generally forming into twos or threes (contrasting or complementary pairs having common reference to time may be counterposed to threes having reference to space or topography). Equivocation and polyvalence may depend on the syntactic function of a word.

The linguist Karl Bühler characterizes the "word-sentence," such as a child's first words, as having the value of an entire sentence in pointing to the expression of a desire (Bühler 1934: 72). William Empson compares the "inner" grammar of complex words to the "overt grammar of sentences" (Empson 1964: 253). Beyond these points of value, the grammatical function of a word determines a fundamental part of its semantic relations. The predominance of nominal rhyme-words in sestinas contributes, for example, to their illustration of "essences" and "ideas."

Metaphor in rhyme-words is an extreme case of violence and tension in sestinas, forcing a search for the completion of meaning outside the poem. While identical rhyme participates in aspects of punning, which is a linguistic metaphor, the force that causes the intuition of the relationship between the parts of a metaphor supersedes the phonic resemblance of the pun. It has been correctly observed, however, that both pun and metaphor are rare among rhyme-words in a sestina (DiGirolamo 1976: 159). The poets are more likely either to produce oscillations of meaning by maintaining lexical constancy and altering the context, or to introduce semantic nuances that transgress but do not obliterate boundaries. The association the reader has to form between sound and sense accordingly develops cumulative meaning, abetted by the restricted possibility of varying the rhyme-words by addition before the final accented vowel (example: rested/arrested).

In turn, even a *near*-perfect reproduction of meaning is discouraged by the predominance of the contiguity relation. It may well have been this limit on semantic variation that made the sestina inhospitable to the conceits and feats of metaphor's daring that became typical of baroque poetry in those languages that had first propagated the sestina form. Although it was through a predilection for equivocal rhyme in his other poems that Arnaut Daniel arrived at rhymes constituted by the same word, Petrarchan practice, following Dante, swiftly drew the language of the sestina definitively toward the metonymic pole. Metonymy there rises to the status of a means of signification that shapes the poem. The delineation of metaphor and metonymy furnished by Jakobson (1971: 345-59) shows the latter trope to be dominated by the contiguity relation. Negation (for example, "the Infinite") is quite possibly the ultimate or quintessential metonymy, since its particpation determines both identity and distinctness. And the crucial relevance of negation, which is the point of departure of symbolic language (including its theological variant), is that it governs the ceaseless search for repose manifest in the sestina. Since the negative entails, or includes, the positive term of an opposition (such as any of the fundamental Petrarchan ones), since the negative term of an opposition necessarily makes reference to the positive term, there being no negatives in nature (whereas the positive term only implies or makes covert reference to its negative opposite), the positive is included in the negative; the latter is a specified absence of the former. This obligatory, overt inclusion of the positive in the expression of the negative is what renders the negative a metonymy of the positive and demonstrates the ultimately inclusional nature of metonymy. That is why on reading one of Petrarch's sestinas, it is possible to read desire and its interdiction simultaneously, as they are implemented by a controlled but extremely rich spectrum of means.

Sestina poets generally avoid using verbs and adjectives as rhymewords. The latter would encourage a far greater semantic variation in the nominal context; the former would narrow the context dramatically, as it does in the example of Michelangelo (Chapter 7). The cumulative meaning stands to the single one in an oblique, not a contrastive, relation along lines determined, at least in Petrarch, by his assemblage of strongly determined semantic fields. In his work, intersections of words from a given field can be made to render only one general meaning, one previously connected with a single feature (*ombra*, for example, for "Laura"). Any component of the field can come to be a metonymic substitute for the field as a whole.

If poets tend to preserve the predictable direction, it is in deference to the predominance of the linear over the recurrent in poetry, as exemplified in the complex structure of the sestina. The "subordination of the semantic to the syntactical field in language" (Kurylowicz 1975: 92) reveals the whole rather than the separable part as the object of comprehension.

The example by Hjelmslev (1961: 13) happens to provide a model of the chains of contextual association initiated by translations of *selva*, a favorite Petrarchan term:

1 wood	legno	Holz	1
2	bosco	Wald	2
3 forest	forests		3

Beyond this set of given lexical contexts in which a word may appear, however, there is what Kenneth Burke (1966: 359) terms the "non-verbal or extraverbal context" that infuses a word with "some 're-pressed' or 'forgotten' context of situation." If this superseding context is transposed to the crux of the Petrarchan situation, the result is the displacement of meaning as in metonymy rather than the translation of meaning as in metaphor. Like the translation example, the sestina creates a web of organization showing the impossibility of absolute reality. And in accordance with the quasi-mythical status of Petrarchan language, its metonymies constitute both a splitting and a uniting mechanism, both severance and bond repesented in the displacement of referents. The semiotic result is the establishment of boundaries that keep self and world at a reflective distance. It also makes sure that the movement toward the center, or toward repose or self-possession, sustains its momentum by constantly dispossessing itself.

Petrarchan quasi-myth presents desire as the search for the center of an earlier Paradisiacal state of things, but this state is an anteriority that cannot be accounted for in time. It has to be seen as the reverse (up to the unknown instant) of the way things are now, as in the *adynaton* or impossibility-figure, which is in turn the poetic presence of an external absence. For external reality is not amenable, finally, to any specific semiotic formulation; a thing exists in context and in relation to other things. In poems, language alone has it both ways: All that is negated, or metonymically juxtaposed, on one level can be affirmed on the other. Now what is too often conceived of as the inability of language to speak univocally may be understood as a strength that allows new meaning to rise metonymically to the surface.

11. The Sestina: Diachrony

The inherent formal limitations and possibilities of one literature are never quite the same as those of any other. Not only the towering example of Petrarch but the abundance of rhymes in the language, especially of feminine rhymes, contributed to the proliferation of sestinas in Italian (as well as to the tendency, established as a quasi-rule, to use bisyllabic rhymes). It was the Venetian cardinal Pietro Bembo in his *Prose della volgare lingua* (1525) who spearheaded a regeneration of interest in the form, describing it as "un ingenioso ritrovamento de' provenzali compositori" (an ingenious find, from Provençal inventors [ed. Marti 1961: 326]). It is noteworthy that Bembo, who composed two sestinas, singularized the form for the interstrophic pause created by the "head-tailed" sequence of identical rhyme-words:

> più grave suono rendono quelle rime che sono tra sè più lontane . . . per chè gravissimo suono da questa parte è quello delle sestine, in quanto meravigliosa gravità porge il dimorare a sentirsi che alle rime si risponda primieramente la legge e la natura della canzone variandonegli . . . Il riposo che alla fine di ciascuna stanza è richiesto, prima che all'altra si passi, tramette tra la continuata rima alquanto spazio . . .
>
> (ed. Marti 1961: 326)

(Rimes that are distant from each other yield a graver sound . . . therefore in this way a most grave sound is that of sestinas, in that it is primarily the law and the nature of the song that answer to the rhymes, varying them . . . The rest that is called for at the end of each strophe poses some space between the rhyme and its continuation.)

The programmatic recognition awarded to the sestina by Renaissance poetics bridged divisions between form and content in their theoretical conflations as well as their poetic production. It is clear that a sense of genre dominates the blending of statements on semantics and syntax in such a view as Antonio Minturno's (1564, ed. 1971: 236):

> Chè si describe nelle Sestine? Qualche stato del viver nostro all'humane passioni, & a gli accidenti della fortuna soggetto. . . . Come si descrive? Con allegorie, con metaphore, e con dicevoli comparationi.

(What is described in sestinas? Some state of our life which is subject to human passions and to accidents of fortune. . . . How is it described? With allegories, metaphors, and telling comparisons.)

For the Petrarchist, the sestina became an obligatory and a nearly academic pursuit. The work of discovery is, however, far from complete. Even the most industrious historian of the sestina would find further employment in documenting the plethora of sixteenth-century Italian sestinas. The long arm of Dantean influence extends over much of it. Beyond this reach, the poets of Provence returned to a place of honor after a long silence, through the devoted amateurism of Bembo, who collected the old songs and was joined by a number of other translators and editors. Arnaut Daniel's poem was translated by Bartolomeo Casassagia (Contini 1946: 142), who was the grandson of the poet known as "Il Cariteo" (Benedetto Garret). But sestinas on the Petrarchan model proliferated so as to eclipse any rival strain. These poems have in common the explicit semantic connection of the poem with problems of time and of will. The known catalogue of authors includes nearly every Italian poet from the fourteenth century forward. We have the fragment of a sestina by Boccaccio (preserved by Giangiorgio Trissino [1529] 1969), another tantalizing fragment by Michelangelo besides the complete one available to us, a sestina by Pico della Mirandola, an encomiastic one by Girolamo Benivieni, and two by Torquato Tasso (Riesz 1971: 245-247). The eventual decrease in production coincided with a diminishing interest in collection. Such curiosities as a sixfold (37-strophe) sestina (by Agostino Torti) or a mock love-poem by Andrea Calmo portended the decline of the sestina as a principal poetic form, a decline that lasted for another two hundred years.

The two poems by Pontus de Tyard and one by his contemporary Pierre Le Loyer (1550-1634, in his collection *L'Érotopegnie,* Riesz 1971: 129) continued as the sole representations of the sestina in France until the work of Ferdinand de Gramont (1872). In view of the lack of interest in the form and the distortion of it into canonically rhymed verse, it is odd that Gramont's debut occured in Balzac's *Revue parisienne,* where Balzac's remark penetrates to the knot of will and desire, closure and openness implicit in the form:

> Dans ce petit poème, la pensée doit se montrer aussi libre que si elle ne portait pas un joug pesant et gênant; en un mot, la fantaisie des poètes doit danser comme la Taglioni tout en ayant des fers au pieds.
> (Revue parisienne 1840, cit. Riesz 1971: 31)

(In this little poem, thought has to show itself as free as if it bore no heavy, hindering yoke. In a word, the poets' fantasy has to dance like [the ballerina] Taglioni though it wears irons on its feet.)

Ezra Pound, himself the composer of a sestina, improved upon this view, calling it a "dance of the intellect among words" (Pound 1954: 78).

In languages that more durably absorbed the Petrarchan tradition, sestinas were composed, under highly varied circumstances, but evincing the bond of the form with problems of spatial and temporal closure. These include so far-flung a pair of examples as a sestina in dialogue by the Christian Socialist Niccolò Tommaseo, in which pre-Christian myth struggles with historical, linear progress, and Rudyard Kipling's "Sestina of the Tramp Royal." These compositions display the structures of recapitulation contending with change and draw their urgency from a preoccupation with eschatological time.

27

Some two hundred years of neglect of the sestina were interrupted by the researches of August Wilhelm Schlegel. His revival of medieval, specifically Provençal, studies and his interest in the Spanish Golden Age stimulated his preoccupation with versification. Against competing notions of poetry as the product of a necessarily easeful genius, Schlegel's work marks the only brilliant critical mind at work on the sestina during the nineteenth century. He translated one of Petrarch's sestinas (*Canzoniere* CXLII) and found in it an ideal adapted to speculative imagination. Moreover, he recognized the sestina as a genus to be characterized in the terms of its poetic life. Taking poetic expression as maximally distinct from nonpoetic expression in much the same sense as Russian Formalism often did later, he found the sestina to be the form "according to which poetic expression distinguishes itself from ordinary life as much as possible" (cit. Wellek 1955: 299).

Schlegel's writing on the sestina eclipses any other theoretical work I have been able to discover. He noted the fundamental coherence of all features of the form—the revolutions and permutations of the rhyme-words, their "yearning mood" (*sehnsuchtige Stimmung*) that may be seen as evidence of the quest for the center, and the cardinal importance of the number six. He views the strophic scheme as an emancipation from the tyranny of canonical rhyme and notes that "the strophes rhyme with one another," settling the question of the validity of identical rhyme. He characterizes variations on the form according to their languages and invites German poets to experiment with it, noting the success of poetic principles having little to do with canonical rhyme in a number of languages. The semantic associations among the rhyme-words are explored, together with the play of identity and difference among them. The art of the sestina consists in varying their contexts. Each of the six strophes frames one of the six rhyme-words into a beginning or an ending. They are six because it is the multiple of the smallest even and the smallest odd integer. Schlegel's description takes account here of the sestina's components of dualism and triadicity.

Having characterized the sestina in its textual materiality, Schlegel proceeds to speak of the mental processes whose representation it is. His conception is evidently part and parcel of a sweeping Romantic manifesto; nevertheless it retains critical power and appropriateness. The sestina is "a fantasy of fantasy making, a dreamlike representation of dreaming"; there imagination "immerses us in the universal, in which [the imagination], like an enchanted realm of endless transformations where nothing is isolated . . . moves within us" (cit. Riesz 1971: 27, tr. mine).

Romantic theories of the imagination aside, this view may surprise the reader who is primarily aware of the closed aspect of the sestina, its formal constraints. Progressing from that point, however, we must note the astonishing aptness of Schlegel's remarks, for he adumbrates the processes that set in motion the semiotic transformations whereby the repetition of an entire linguistic sign appears as the symbolic presence of an absence, as does a dream.

Before turning to the sestina itself, in connection with the resemblance of its content-form to dream and myth, I wish to note the experiment of the twelve-tone composer Ernst Křenek, who supplied an actual sestina to go along with his composition entitled "Sestina" (Riesz 1971: 220). Křenek fits the poem to a twelve-tone row divided in two groups of six that undergo permutations according to the movement of the poem. He concludes that "necessity streams into the unforeseeable reality of the process of the living" (cit. Riesz 1971: 220), the aleatory poured into the mold of form.

> Vergangnen Klang und Klage, sanfter Strom,
> Die Schwingung der Sekunde wird zum Mass.
> Was in Geschichte lebt, wer's nur ein Zufall?
> Verfall, Verhall, zerronnene Gestalt?
> Die Stunde zeitigt Wandel, wendet Zeit,
> Das Vorgeschrittene ordnet sich der Zahl.

(Past sound and lament, gentle stream, the second's vibration becomes a measure. What lives in history—decay, decline, melted form—was it only change? The hour brings change, time's turning. The elapsed part of Number orders itself.)

Finally, the result of form is still also the product of chance.

Chapter 2

Arnaut and Arnaldians

1. Arnaut Daniel: "Lo ferm voler"

The hermetic troubadours of Languedoc and the French southwest provinces brought to vernacular poetry the notion that artistic creation is the result of the contention against semantic inadequacy and formal limitations. As maker and shaper, the poet or singer was conceived as determining the conditions of meaning. Their brilliant moment occurred during the inception of troubadour poetry as we know it, as a phenomenon of its beginnings. Unlike more demotic colleagues, they found maximal freedom in the awareness of an intellectual definition, sometimes corroborated by a heightened sense of aristocracy in concert with their patrons. For these poets, the fit of complex forms with a subtlety of content underwrote the spontaneity of creation. Arnaut Daniel, early distinguished as the most fruitful artist of the middle period (c. 1150-1200), was remembered by his trademark, a *labor limae* not his alone but particular to him in degree. Dante knew him as the "best craftsman in the mother tongue" (*Purg.* XXVI). To Arnaut he accords the last word of any vernacular poet in the *Commedia*. In Paradise, Arnaut declares in the Provençal dialect, perpetual joy will replace the concealments of earthly poetry; all will be open and known.

Meanwhile, a love-poet could be perceived as a sage wise in the ways of men and things, a bridge-builder between the natural world and the force of mutual attraction. At the same time, he did his work in a sort of carpentry shop, shaping, refining, and polishing. The risks of poetic reification are dealt with, often transformed into metaphor, and the narcissism endemic to formal closure is threatened with its occupational hazards. Certain troubadours claimed the distinction, however, of gaining self-knowledge and completion from the experience of loving, composing, and singing viewed as an inseparable unity. Gnomic poets feared the falsification or vulgarization of their songs in performance, and their fear of the familiar could be compared with the drive toward defamiliarization (that we think of as peculiar to the Russian Formalists and the Prague School).

Obscurity was not necessarily a defaming charge. It could be caused by the lack of perspicacity on the poet's part or by ignorance on the reader's. Tortuous syntax could be a cause; more often, lexical rarity. The hermetism of troubadour song, as it developed during its period of productivity, emanated, as well, from the very generality and multiple meanings of single words appearing in the songs. Above all, hermetic poetry depended on the supposed power of individual words to control the texture and "color" of a poetic image. Whether or not these troubadours, sometimes said (like Arnaut) to have studied their *letras* or Latin grammar and composition toward a clerical career, actually were scholars of rhetoric as well must remain unknown, together with the great part of their lives (but cf. Paterson 1975). Their use of rare and *rarely situated* words and the use of these words in new senses were the elements most clearly isolated as "closure." Arnaut went so far as to provide a signature in a number of his poems, in addition to the mention of his own name, by following a certain image from song to song. Provençal was not codified as a *grammatica* until well after his time (fl. 1180-1200), but Arnaut's experiments with the limits of poetic language strained what we know of the *koiné* of troubador poetry, including neologisms such as we will note in the sestina.

The troubadours often recognized the unit of syntactic function and referential meaning. Yet the discussion of function usually takes place on the level of the single word, approaching a realist view of the signified as meaning that is immanent in words. Although troubadour poetry was intensely self-conscious, it generally veiled its speculations in any references to love. The courtly love adventure could easily comprehend the experience of love as internal distance and detachment. Long after it became a poetry of defiguralized commonplaces and buried its traditional connections with performance, the

31

songs show the escape from the violence of erotic experience in an accession to another order of things. The frame of the song remained an unchanging and permanent love, and the fusion of the will to love and the will to compose remained an ideal well after the execution of desire was detached from it.

The expression of poetic language, sounds, written signifiers, the movements of articulation, were made the topic of poems. A cultist position was established that was associated with intellectual or social prestige. Poetic "understanding" could be perceived as a means of fixing and establishing hierarchies of generosity or intellect. Experimental poetry found stimulation in the poet's will to impose his private, singular creation on a social collectivity of distinction. The use of words based on the realization of the disjunction between a word and its referent could dominate the organization of ideas. According to the poet's genius and his will to abide by self-established conventions, it was his prerogative to designate the disposition of things in his poem as opposed to any "natural" order of succession in external reality. In such cases, even the linear succession of time could be thought of not as a faithful representation of a stable reality but as an illusion, and truth in art as resident in the perception of a transcendental order, microcosmically immanent in the creative mind. Even as love drew from a supernaturally derived constancy of "will," the canso ("song") or quintessential poem of love, war, or virtue (as Dante's later summary has it) was itself an act of will. In the case of trobar clus, ("closed poetic") this willed artifact, intended to be as beautiful as the "spirit" that moved the poet to create it, could ultimately suffice as a desideratum in itself.

Not only the high quotient of narcissicm in the troubadour situation but the intensely conventional character of song in an essentially oral culture made the aesthetics of memory the accomplice of the canso. Inevitably repetition and recurrence functioned as mnemonic aids to the listener and probably conspired in the easy memorization of a song by jongleurs and audiences. It is no wonder that a number of poets strove to escape from the singsong of the self-contained, hence movable, interchangeable, and misrepresentable strophe toward the ideal of a seamless poem. For the soul of the canso is the strophe, Dante's stantia (De vulgari eloquentia II, 2 ff) or "room" inhabited by rhyme, meter, and melody. The strophic formula of a canso must be identical, and we have no poem containing a marked enjambment from strophe to strophe. Each strophe was an autonomous unit, producing the danger of rearrangement in poems with but one logical sequence. The strophe was the support-system for rhyme, word play, etymological figures, assonance, alliteration, and even internal rhyme—all part of a fundamentally communicative act and representation that sought nevertheless to exact its strictures, fix its limits, and arrest its indiscriminate and undiscriminating use.

Stanzas were based on rhyme. To "speak" in rhymes for a troubadour was tantamount to composing in hexameters in classical Latin. In ever-varying combinations, rhymes determined the frankly spatialized scheme in which rhythmical series were delineated. Troubadour poetics knew no certain distinction between rhyme and rhythm. Rhyme called attention to the rhythmically important places in the poem, which were synonymous with meaning. If the rhyming sound included a whole word, then the replication of sound with an added sense multiplied the possibilities of play. Generally the troubadours eschewed identical rhyme, but an early example of it is the refrain-word taken up from strophe to strophe. The increase in the number of refrain-words per strophe encroaches upon canonical rhyme, substituting for it a new liaison of senses, and considerably emphasizing the contexts fashioned to fit it.

Since the choice of a rhyme-word presupposes recognition of unequal semantic factors, its uses reiterate the nonexistence in language of strict synonymy and the asymmetrical relationship between words and referents. Simultaneously, the rhyme-words can reiterate a persistent striving toward impossible harmony or centrality. Always they function to bind together larger units of interstrophic composition. Homonymic equivalence, instituting a balletic interchange of identity and difference, reveals a predominance of semantic significance over lexical value. Compound rhyme, in which words differ in their prefixes, and derivative or grammatical rhyme, in which they differ in inflection or in their suffixes, may encourage the formation of neologisms. A line of Arnaut's sestina shows the enveloping of one unit by another: "C'aissi s'enpren e s'enongla/Mos cors en lei" is a dynamic that compares the passionate heart to the improbable "fingernail" in their common property of tenacity. The completed metaphor is "explicated" by the immediately following nonfigural simile, "cum l'escorssa en la verga," which fixes the end of the progression.

In that they impose special constraints, rhyme-schemes may be thought of as closed. It was natural under these conditions for hermetic poets to seek out acoustic, semantic, and rhythmic complexity as an individual form of expression. Not all rhyme-schemes showed complexity of design, but often the simplest are distinguished from each other. Although treatises on poetic composition postdate the far richer periods of creativity, they provide retrospectively a reliable sense of what poets came to think of as the tools of their craft, and the terms in which these are described appear occasionally within the songs themselves. The *Leys d'amor* ("Laws of Love") provide a number of such descriptions. In order to knot strophes together, they could be *capfinidas:* A word or phrase in the last line of a strophe, or a word derived from the same root, is repeated in the first line of the succeeding strophe. Among the other linking methods that could spur the memory of the listener was making the first line of each strophe rhyme with the last line of the previous one, the strophes then being known as *capcaudadas* ("head-tailed"). If the same head and tail rhymes were used throughout the poem but in different order in different strophes, the song belonged to the category of the *canso redonda* (redundant). Now the tail-biting serpent could display the colors of its scales in varying, shimmering combinations.

Another way of welding strophes together was to use *rimas dissolutas,* rhymes that find no answer in their own strophe, but keep the ear waiting until they are answered in the same position within each subsequent strophe. A poem could consist, like a number of Arnaut's, of *coblas estrampas,* in which all the rhymes are *dissolutas.* Often the orphaned rhyme-words tend to seek support outside of conventional rhyme. The listening ear deprived of its expectation likewise sought out significant phonetic recurrence, which generally consisted of assonance or alliteration. These were expedients of Neo-Latin verse and as such a constitutive element of a poetry still largely dependent on the decoding of acoustic images. Alliteration and assonance furnished a contiguity-relation on which such comprehension could rely, although the punlike relations so contracted could function as independent of sense.

Repetition and inversion, once we accept the principle that true repetition is impossible, may be seen as the moving forces of troubadour rhyme. A brilliant song by the noble Raimbaut d'Orange develops the topos of the world upside-down in six strophes of eight lines, each ending in a refrain-word. It is easy to understand the sestina as a development of this procedure. Raimbaut's rhyme-words are identical from strophe to strophe, and the second half of each strophe presents its rhyme-words in identical order. The second and third lines of every strophe, however, proceed in inverted order:

> Ar resplan la flors enversa
> Pels trencans rancx e pels tertres,
> Cals flors? Neus, gels e conglapis
> Que cotz e destrenh e trenca . . .
> (Strophe I, 1-4, cit. Pattison 1952: 49-50, XXIX)

(Now shines forth the reversed flower among the sharp rocks and the hills. What flower? Snow, ice and frost that cut and destroy and burn. . . .)

> Quar enaissi m'o enverse
> Que bel plan mi semblon tertre,
> E tenc per flor lo conglapi,
> E.1 cautz m'es vis que.1 freit trenque

(For so do I reverse it that gentle plains seem hills to me, and I take the ice to be a flower, and it seems to me that the heat cuts through the cold.)

It is a poem about contrariness and autonomy; the lover declares his independence and physical detachment from the external world both of natural cycles and of linear progress. He reverses his "flower" through an act of will that determines the poem's entire direction. In concert with his statement of reversal, each even strophe reverses the rhymes of the previous one in the third and fourth lines or as he approaches the center.

"Closed" poetry reveals itself here as far more than the interweaving of complexities. It is the unification of form and meaning where the form itself is an image of the meaning. Even where the troubadour's technical activity is not a topical focus of the song, distinct layers of meaning come to be woven inextricably through one another. The tornada of another song (Pattison 1952: 23-24, X) demonstrates this sense of binding, analogous to the actual fastening of a parchment:

> Mos vers, qu' enaici s'estaca,
> Volgra que.m fos portaz segurs
> A Demoniad'e quel fos grams.
>
> (Strophe VIII)

(My verse, which is fastened up this way, I wish carried safely to [the lady] Demoniac, and let it be grim for her.)

The "closed" poem, because of its extreme formal constraints, was hospitable to the treatment of the topic of secrecy. Earlier in the same poem, Raimbaut, for example, makes it a rhetorical premise to the guarded revelation of whatever he has to impart:

> Mas aura ni plueja ni gel
> No.m tengr'ieu plus que.1 gen temps nou
> S'auzes desplejar mos libres

De fag d'amor ab digz escurs;
So don plus Temers m'essaca
Qu'ira.m fes dir midons e clams;
Que mais d'amor don m'estaca
No chantari' ab nulhs agurs
Tro plais vengues entre nos ams.

(Strophe II)

(But I would not care any more about wind or rain or ice than about the gentle new season if I dared to unfold my books of love-deeds in obscure speech. Fear draws me back from this all the more, because my lady made me voice anger and complaints. So never again should I sing of the love with which she transfixes me—under no conditions—until some truce be made between us.)

Whatever the contingencies that forbid the lover to express himself more openly, the convention of timidity or docility in love-service admirably suits the play of concealment and revelation dramatized in hermetic poems.

In many kinds of hermetic troubadour poetry, and in many non-hermetic poems as well, a complicated rhyme-scheme appears in a relatively simplistic context. One of the latter is Guilhem Peire de Cazals' *canso redonda,* noted by the pioneering Romance scholar Diez as a midpoint between the sestina and the "round" (Diez 1883: 103). The poem has five strophes of six lines and a tornada of three. The second strophe repeats the rhyme-words of the first in inverse order, the third those of the second, and so on throughout the poem. Thus the movement of inversion meets that of repetition. When Arnaut composed his sestina, the only technical divergences from this earlier scheme were the use of *retrogradatio cruciata* (crossed retrogression) with its greatly enhanced complexity and the reappearance of all six, not only three, of the rhyme-words in his tornada (Davidson 1910: 19). Regardless of its tenuous genetic importance, Peire de Cazals' otherwise undistinguished poem combines with Raimbaut's sparkling songs to show the climate of growth and challenge that proved favorable to the sestina.

Although it involves a use of language strongly attached to the conventions of troubadour discourse at its most frankly sophisticated, the sestina recalls such ancient forms as anagrams, acrostics, and palindromes, in announcing its own sufficiency and giving retrospective coherence to every element in it. It involves the isolation, framing, and classification of otherwise common words. Neither irony nor ambiguity suffices to describe its evasions of committed speech. As in many modern poems, the occasion of the poem is the acknowledgment of an ultimately unresolvable process, and semantically its conclusion is a question rather than an answer, although the tornada end-stops the force of continuation. We are led to understand its specificity as reflecting the characteristic inner life of the lover who speaks. Thus particularities of time, place, and circumstance are as vague as they are in any troubadour poem, hermetic or not. The argumentative lover is ostensibly concerned only with the eventual response of his lady, whom he invokes as an absent addressee. She in turn may well be suspicious of the persuasive resources of his rhetoric. But any reader will respond to the poem—not to its persuasiveness but to its expressivity.

I. Lo ferm voler qu'el cor m'intra
No.m pot jes becs escoissendre ni ongla
De lausengier, qui pert per mal dir s'arma;
E car non l'aus batr'ab ram ni ab verga,
5   Sivals a frau, lai on n'aurai oncle,
Jauzirai joi, en vergier o dinz cambra.

II. Quan mi soven de la cambra
On a mon dan sai que nuills hom non intra
Anz me son tuich plus que fraire ni oncle
10   Non ai membre no.m fremisca, neis l'ongla,
Aissi cum fai l'enfas denant la verga,
Tal paor ai que.ill sia trop de m'arma.

III. Del cors li fos, non de l'arma,
E cossentis m'a celat dins sa cambra!
15   Que plus mi nafra.l cor que colps de verga
Car lo sieus sers lai on ill es non intra;
Totz temps serai ab lieis cum carns et ongla,
E non creirai chastic d'amic ni d'oncle.

IV. Anc la seror de mon oncle
20   Non amei plus ni tant, per aquest' arma!
C'aitant vezis cum es lo detz de l'ongla,
S'a lei plagues, volgr'esser de sa cambra;
De mi pot far l'amors qu'inz el cor m'intra
Mieills a son vol c'om fortz de frevol verga.

25   V. Pois flori la seca verga
Ni d'en Adam mogron nebot ni oncle,
Tant fina amors cum cella qu'el cor m'intra
Non cuig qu' anc fos en cors, ni eis en arma.
On qu' ill estei, fors en plaza, o dinz cambra,
30   Mos cors no.is part de lieis tant cum ten l'ongla.

VI. C'aissi s'enpren e s'enongla
Mos cors en lei cum l'escorssa en la verga;
Qu' il m'es de joi tors e palaitz e cambra,
E non am tant fraire, paren ni oncle:
35   Qu' en paradis n'aura doble joi m'arma,
Si ja nuills hom per ben amar lai intra.

VII. Arnautz tramet sa chansson d'ongla e d'oncle,
A grat de lieis que de sa verg'a l'arma,
Son Desirat, cui pretz en cambra intra.

(ed. Toja 1960: 378-9)

(I. The firm will which enters my heart no slanderer who damns his soul by tale-bearing can destroy with beak or nail, and since I dare not beat him with branch or rod, at least in secret where I'll have no uncle, I'll delight in joy, in orchard or chamber.

II. When I remember the chamber where, to my detriment, I know no man enters, but rather all impede me more than a brother or an uncle, there is no part of me that does not tremble, even my nail, like a child before the rod—so much do I fear that I am hers too much in soul.

III. Would that I were hers in body, not soul, and that she concealed me, consenting, in her chamber! For it pains my heart more than the blows of a rod that her own servant cannot enter where she is. Always I will be with her like flesh to fingernail, and pay no heed to chastisement from friend or uncle.

IV. I never loved the sister of my uncle more or as much, by this soul! For if it pleased her, I would be as close to her chamber as a finger to a nail. The love that enters my heart can do more with me, at will, than a strong man with a weak rod.

V. Since the dry rod blossomed and nephew and uncle issued from lord Adam, so fine a love as that which enters my heart, I think, never was in body or is in soul. Wherever she may be, out in the plaza or in her chamber, my heart and self do not leave her by so little as a nail's space.

VI. For so does my self press and en-nail itself into her, just like the bark in the rod. For she is to me joy's tower and palace and chamber, and I do not love brother, parent or uncle so much. And in Paradise my soul will have double the joy, if ever any man enters it from loving well.

VII. Arnaut sends his song of nail and uncle for the pleasure of her who holds the soul of his rod; his Desired One, whose chamber value enters.)

The nominalism that generally came to govern Provençal lyric, especially *clus* poems, radically distinguishes names from things and sumultaneously yearns for the opposite of that distinction. The reception of Arnaut's poems reflects a mediate step in that direction. A well-known satire on troubadours known to him and written in 1195 by the versifying Monk of Montaudon accuses Arnaut of a "fals motz c'om non enten" (false *mots* that no one understands)

38

(cit. Hill and Bergin 1973: 143). The compiler of his capsule bio-
graphy (*vida*), writing about a century after his death, describes him
as an incipient cleric turned troubadour, or at any rate one who had
learned his clerical course of letters. Both Dante and Petrarch elevated him to high places in their hierarchies of poets, and according
to the view of *Purgatory* he was the best *fabbro,* or craftsman, "in
the mother tongue" (*Purg.* XXVI 117). Unlike Bertran de Born, the
other troubadour of Provence represented in the *Commedia,* Arnaut
is allowed there to speak in Provençal. In the course of his treatise
De vulgari eloquentia, Dante cites the debt of his own sestina to
Arnaut's poetry, although to the mystification of many a reader, he
bypasses the sestina for another canso as a term of comparison.

This concentrated, dark poem declares interdiction to be at the
core of its motives. Since he cannot beat off slanderers, the lover will
meditate and delight in secret upon his love. Never addressed directly,
the beloved is invoked through a veil of polysemous words. The
larger interdict of sin hovers around the construct of "tale-bearers"
so that lyric impetus is never far from ironic pause. The rhyme-word
verga (rod) is variously the weapon forbidden him and the one with
which he imagines himself beaten. Dante, confronting the long-
absent Beatrice in Purgatory, recalls this simile of a child trembling
before punishment (*Purg.* XXX, 43-5) when the pilgrim turns to
Virgil for comfort. Sin as pleasure and as interdict are concepts latent
throughout the metamorphoses of *verga* from the simple rod into the
Dry Tree of Christian myth. The image of original sin and its ultimate
fruitfulness is subjugated to the uniqueness of one love in one poem.
This paradoxical view of sin and redemption, however, is balanced
by a story of vision and blindness.

Assonance tends to supplant rhyme. The four tonic assonances
(Arma, cAmbra, Ongla, Oncle) and two atonic ones (intRA, cambRA)
concur with a full complement of consonantal alliteration (oNgLa,
oNcLe; veRga; aRMa, caMbRa). The first rhyme-word, *intra,* establishes that the poem is to be about barriers. It is the single verbal
rhyme-word and remains in the same mood and tense. The lover who
dares not face nay-sayers or the beloved herself head-on, situates her
in an indeterminate medium colored by a range of negative emotion
from fear to anger. The poem replaces action, transforming the
"slanderers" into strange birds (reminiscent of such images in the
work of other troubadours such as Marcabru and therefore pointing
toward the universality of his predicament). The division between
physical reality and its transfiguration, between the place of the lover
and the *cambra* of the lady, is also the delineation of the poems'
contraries, as the lover contemplates a world of seeming contra-

39

dictions and generalizes them into his entire environment. The very anticipation of fulfillment increases appetite for itself, so that he can never turn back. Union with the beloved constantly reappears as as possibility, rehierarchizing the places of every other individual related to himself. The recurrence not only of *oncle*, but brother and parent, recapitulate those relationships of blood renowned in non-amorous poetry. The barrier between the lover's chosen world and that of epic poetry is near and palpable. The poem reveals itself as a place of internal distance and otherness, therefore containing the germ also of irony and even parody.

"Tower, palace, and chamber" of desire, the lady easily takes her place outside the poem as its missing center. She is persistent as an image of closure and ennobled like her lover by a sense of the inevitable. Whereas semantic import (as of the rhyme-words) fluctuates, the presence of meaning is guaranteed. To this expansiveness and yet certainty of meaning a large number of readings continue to testify, in their very divergences. Existing within the limitations of incomplete opposites like those in the near-pun of *ongla* and *oncle*, this lover's ontological instability is nevertheless apparent. If he is nothing to her, the lady will never take her place at the center, and this possibility haunts the poem's revolutions—the idea that her lover is indeed speaking into a void without issue. Metaphors for centeredness abound. The absent point of repose is allegorically interchangeable with every structure connoting value: The poet's soul *(arma)* is occasionally paired, perhaps, with a suggestion of his sexual organ (*arma*); the earthly paradise of fulfillment, the castle tower and palace, are opposed not only to the chaotic and careless tongues of slanderers and the lesser affections proper to relatives, but also to the surrounding corruptibility of the external world. By the mere transfer of otherness, the passage through the barrier from externality toward the internal center of value is achieved.

Although the melody for the song was passed down to us (Beck 1908), we can only conjecture the sound that listeners must have heard during the enjambment from the first "ongla" to its complement "de lausengier." That tiny suspension of sense is maximally associated with the words *ongla* and *oncle*, which are in turn part of Arnaut's name for the poem. More than the ambiguities of *arma* and *verga* or the relatively forthright interiority of *cambra*, their play of sound and meaning, partial homophony and nonpolar resemblance, reflect a contiguity association among words in time that gives us a fleeting glimpse of the atomistic nature of resemblance. It is in the same interest that paronomasia and other structures of near-repetition function in the pattern of the poem. "L'amors qu'*inz* el cor m'*intra*," for example, in moving from the passive adverbial to the active verbal relation, both intensifies and activates. Similarly, the construction of *jauzirai joy* lingers lovingly over the rich word, juxtaposing active and passive forms. In the *Commedia* Dante recalls this poem to signify a definite and foreseen futurity. (There Arnaut declares, "vei jausen lo joi qu'esper denan": Rejoicing, I see before me the hoped-for day.)

At its inception, the sestina contains the tendency to widen spirally. Another example: In recurring to assonance as compensation for the lack of canonical rhyme, Arnaut actually reenacts the reversal of time figured by the tail-biting serpent. Historically, rhyme had superseded the supplanted assonance, leaving assonance in the virtual, inferior role that had come to be associated with "popular" verse (Frank 1955: I, xxx). In the case of the rhyme-words, however, an entirely counter-logical premise subtends their association, so that the poet must do away with even minimal appearances of symmetry. Even canonical rhyme in troubadour poetry is a kind of mountain-climbing, with the most expressive syntactic element at the end. But where the poet shows how erotic dialectic can counteract the most familiar lexical functions of a word, in transgressing static unity of the whole word, the act of binding the song together surpasses its origin in antithesis and internal contradiction.

Hence *verga* can be the instrument of interdiction (strophe II) and of liberation (strophe I), in either case subject to the reference of will. The alternation gives way to the notion of punishment (strophe III), succeeded by the comparison of the lover dominated by Love as a fragile rod by a strong man. This simile in turn leads to the crescendo of generalization attached to *verga* as interdict. The tree of good and evil with its ramifications in the Christian tradition of spiritual "fruitfulness" is *la seca verga*, the only one that miraculously blossomed again with the birth of Mary from the seed of Jesse (Kaske 1971: 79-81). Now the dry "rod" becomes the absent center of concentric structure tantamount to paradise. The poet figuratively celebrates a rebirth of love signifying also the redemption of the fallen human nature that ushered sin into the world. Nature is in medieval terms a reflection of hidden truth and moral order, and biblical exegesis has made tree-imagery into a major commonplace in the measurement of value. The tree is the symbol of good and evil, and of life at its center. Its generative virtue, however, is the main feature in the hierarchy suggested here, since the praise of the beloved and the restatement of faith in her are assimilated to it. What could be a mere introjection amounts to the joining of one miracle with another, from two universes of discourse often perceived as rivals.

The troubadour remakes the universe into the background of his love. Adam receives the honorific *en* (roughly "sir" or "lord"), and it is in this medieval dress that he is conceived as the initiator of the masculine line *(nebot ni oncle)*. Although included within the precincts of the courtly universe, he is politely cast out of the second paradise, which might be characterized as a feminine one.

Indeed, the missing feminine element corresponds in several ways to the imagery of the center: The six feminine rhymes of the poem occur in word of masculine gender, which has a less prominent place in love's hierarchy, namely *oncle,* in its extended meaning of "kinsman" (Farnsworth: 1913). Once more a lover had been persuaded to relinquish earthly ties for potentially paradisiacal ones. The circle around the missing lady is formed within the wider one of Christian reference, closer to the desired center and dependent on it. Through a similar impulse, Dante's Francesca will lend courtly meaning to God as *re dell'universo (Inf.* V, 91), which *Paradiso* corrects in direction and value when amorous terms are applied to St. Francis' Lady Poverty *(Par.* XI, 58 ff.). In vision and safety, wherever the lady is, she is a tower, palace, and chamber, a center within a center, encircled by adoration, as is the *cambra* that metonymizes her.

The dynamism of love "entering" the lover's heart reveals a movement of regeneration, subject in turn to linear directionality. Creation apart from nature emanates from the new being at the pinnacle. Constituted by the song's will, the linear succession of time, analogous to the experience of temporality on earth by the devout Christian, can no longer be thought of as a faithful representation of reality but is itself an illusion, subject in turn to a transcendental order. The lady is a paradise of joy and plenty surrounded by the fallen world of suffering, and endowed with a directed movement strangely parallel to the dismal succession of masculine descendents. Imagined as a place of closure, she can only be conjured in secret and in the mind. Hence there can be no semantic closure with her as referent, even as no formality forces the closure of the song. Where the lover will at last be unobserved is "lai on n'aurai oncle." Thence comes also chastisement and patrilineal descent. The referent *oncle* also conveys the suggestion of a subversive maternal element that functions both as a provocation and a taboo. May we not view *la seror de mon oncle* as more than a stretching for the brass ring of the rhyme-word? It is no wonder that the rhetorical stance is that of preterition: The neutralization of the masculine and feminine polarity has among its multiple connotations a near-feminization of the masculine self, a fragile rod in the hand of a strong man. *Amor* has his will of the lover.

42

In view of this peril of surrender, the lover's timidity, consisting for the reader largely in his convention of outward silence and inner turmoil, has a special function. He is not sure whether his persistence in devotion will commend him to God. His statement of double joy in Paradise for lovers contains a conditional "if," gazing beyond death. Dante will correct and explicate it for the character Arnaut in his *Purgatory*. Having abjured lust, he is reconciled with his "uncles" and allowed the incremental gains of disembodied love. In the sestina and as a living poet Arnaut knows the regeneration of the "dry tree" through the impetus provided by the beloved, a result that has been conducive to a sexualized reading of the whole poem. The child facing the rod can see beyond punishment to fulfillment in the future, in the conception of ultimate union of the body with soul.

Note the sequence of events in the sixth strophe. There the flowering of the dry rod is *followed* by the descent of men from Adam, so that the tree makes its first appearance in the poem already redeemed. The lover becomes a kind of new Adam, his story next in the linear progress that contends with recurrence and recurrences. The play of secrecy and revelation finds its semantic correspondent in the poem in the tension between closure and openness. Analogously, as in troubadour lyric generally, the identity of the lady is concealed, her lover's desire revealed. *Intra* often marks the advent of change: First it is the impulse to desire, then alternately denotes closure and blockage (with reference to the room no one enters). The fourth strophe shows a reentry of love in fuller strength, and the fifth dubs it *fin amor,* or noble. In the sixth the place of entry is Paradise, the full ascent in status accomplished.

Although the whole unfolding is attended by marks of fear and withdrawal, the poem gravitates toward an absent center. Arnaut, whose persona in many songs also loved a "Laura" upon whose name he embroiders from time to time (ed. Toja 1960: IX, X, XVI), provides for the Petrarchan sestina not only a historical beginning but a poetic bridge. His refusal to capitulate to semantic closure, even as its delights might suffice the lover, are answered by the poet's invention of a song that builds constantly out of itself. Petrarch's sestinas will openly discuss broad perspectives of temporal development and make this strength the linchpin of the sestina. He will not use a verbal rhyme-word as Arnaud did; rather, the unfolding of the poetic argument will take place through internal action on nominal rhyme-words, far more amenable to contextual change. Petrarch's recognition of the primacy of contiguity relations in the sestina and of sequentiality in human events, however, actually bring him closer to the origins of the form and to the climate of Arnaut's composition than to the mediating one of Dante. Arnaut's lover has no history; in Petrarch the lover is the subject of a patterned sequence imposing its own stresses upon the individual work. The psychic constants of the sestina are inherent, however, in Arnaut's invention. Dante and Petrarch will use the tornada to signal formal closure and semantic continuity in a way that the Provençal poet of occasions could never know. But they will retain the strophe as chamber of form, the wound of interdict (closure) and escape (openness), the ambivalence of will and desire; and the yearning for the center and the immanent structures of regeneration that underlie the retelling of the story.

The two sestinas in imitation of Arnaut composed in the Provençal literary language are both *sirventes*, (the genre-name roughly translatable as "servants' poems") songs on social and political topics easily adapted to satire written from the stance of a faithful and truth-telling servant. The first, to be analyzed here, is by Guilhem de Saint-Grigori, a quotidian versifier. The second belongs to the canon of poems in Provençal by the Venetian merchant Bartolome Zorzi (b. 1230-1240). It displays the cross-pollination of Provençal genres as defined by purpose, function, and semantic content. Containing marks of amorous and moral poems, the canon betokens an effort to reconcile currents that had helped to define the antitheses on which Provençal lyric had based itself and from which it had largely drawn its power. This phenomenon attended the destruction over some fifty years of the society that had underwritten the brilliant songs and waves of poetic activity ushered in by the first known troubadours. The two poems, one a near parody, use Arnaut's rhymes and strophic scheme. In Zorzi's sestina we may easily discover embedded shreds of phrases and ideas from the source, but it is a philological parlor game, yielding little more than a heightened sense of how poetic language fares under the pressure of business practice.

2. Guilhem de Saint-Grigori: "Ben granz avolesa intra"

Parody is an unfit vehicle for the recovery of information about originals. The very intelligibility of its content depends on the reader's acquaintance with the original that leads to awareness of the discrepancy between them. The parody of Arnaut Daniel's sestina by Guilhem de Saint-Grigori participates in the retrospection that is peculiarly proper to the sestina in general, as it looks to a model in the past. At the same time, the pervasiveness of external reference adding itself to counterlogical prior meanings creates a poem that belongs to the marginal realm of poetic commentary.

44

The sestina had juxtaposed terms that were incongruous in an amorous context, stretching the accepted limitations of polysemous association, and in a strophic scheme that brooked no departures. Now the parodist playing with this equilibrium depends, for his communicative effect, on perfect adherence to the strophic scheme of the sestina and to the order of its rhyme-words:

I. Ben grans avolesa intra
A N'Aesmar entre la charn e l'ongla
E a.n pres luoc inz el cor iosta l'arma
E malvestatz bat l'ades de sa veria
5   Mal resembla al bon Prebost, son oncle
En cui bons pretz fai per soiorn sa chambra.

II. N'Aemars fai lum en chambra
De sef ardent quant a privat se.n intra.
Anc re non tais al bon prez de son oncle,
10   Que cors e senz l'es partitiz totz per l'ongla.
Vist agues eu mesurar d'una veria
Lo vas on fos lo cors que destrui s'arma!

III. Eu non plaing lo cors ni l'arma,
Mais la terra on bos pretz pert sa chambra,
15   Qe N'Aemars l'a tant batut ab veria
E degitat de toz los locs on intra,
Q'ab lui non pot metre ne pel ni ongla,
Mais ben floris e miels gran' en son oncle.

IV. Per bon e per ric teing l'oncle,
20   E.l neps es tals qe no.i a res mas l'arma,
Flacs e volpils del cim tro bas en l'ongla,
E malvestatz es sa corz e sa chambra.
Ha, Coms savais, cel q'en grant amor intra
De ren ab vos, es tochaz d'avol veria!

25   V. Be.m segnei ab bona veria
Lo iorn qu' ieu vinc al bon Prebost, son oncle,
E s'ieu intres sovent lai on el intra,
Mais en valgra toz temps mos cors e m'arma;
Q'ab ferm voler met bon prez dinz sa chambra
30   Et es ab lui aissi cum charns et ongla.

VI. Lai vas Mon-Berart vir l'ongla
Q'anc non batet ni feri de sa veria
Pretz ni ioven ni.l gitet de sa chambra,
35   S'ab ferm voler de tot bon dreit non s'arma,
Plus perdutz es q'arma qu'en enfern intra.

VII. Sirventes, faz per ongla e per oncle

45

A n'Aesmar, per veria e per arma,
E al Prebost, per chambra e per intra.

(Bertoni 1917: 34-6)

(I. A great vileness finds its way into Lord Aesmar, between fingernail and flesh, and has found its place in his heart next to his soul. Evil constantly beats him with its rod. He resembles not at all the good Prebost his uncle, in whom every good quality sojourns as in a chamber.

II. Lord Aesmar, when he furtively enters his chamber, lights it with a burning torch. None of this goes for the fine traits of his uncle; it is Aesmar who has lost his valor and sense through the fingernail. Oh, if I could only see them measuring the coffin for his body, that is destroying his soul!

III. I have no pity for his body or his soul, but for the land where valor is losing its dwelling-place. For Aesmar has beaten it so and cast it from every place it enters, that in him, Aesmar, it can never find skin or nail though it bears flower and fruit in his uncle.

IV. I judge the uncle to be good and generous, and the nephew is so empty that he has nothing in him save his soul. Weak he is, and cowardly from head to foot, and malignity is his court and his chamber. Ha, miserable Count, anyone who enters into intimacy with you is touched by a mean rod!

V. I certainly crossed myself with a fine rod the day I went to the good Prebost, his uncle. And if I often "entered" where he does, I'd be worth more myself. For with a firm will he brings valor into his chamber and it stays with him like flesh near a nail.

VI. I turn my steps toward Mon-Berart, who never struck a blow against valor and joy, nor banished them from his chamber. And I remember well the goodness of his father and uncle. If he does not arm himself with all righteousness, with a firm will, more is lost to him than one soul entering hell.

VII. I make this *sirventes* for Lord Aesmar with "nail" and "uncle," and for Prebost, with "chamber" and "enters.")

Guilhem tells us that he is changing topics, which in medieval poetics is tantamount to a change of genre. The atmosphere is now imbued with the battle cry of a wronged "servant" rather than a lover's complaint. We might well ask where the parodistic aspect lies, were it not for the persistence of Arnaut's formal scheme transposed to the unexpected context. Even this aspect existed in abundance within troubadour poetics; it was common for poets to adopt one another's rhymes and meter even in altered contexts. What makes the capital difference is the fact of identical rhyme and the full-scale transposition of entire words. Arnaut's famed sestina dictates its "terms" to the parodist, who retaliates by choosing terms of opposition. The subject is male, not female, presented *in malo,* not *in bono.*

46

The immobility of rhyme-words is challenged by their use and reuse within lines. Once the code of the sirventes (or politico-moral polemical verse) is understood as bearing reference to the new double-subject "uncle/nephew," with "uncle" tauntingly echoed in the persistent denotation of the rhyme-word, the meaning of the poem appears fully only through reference to Arnaut.

The poem hovers between the projection of ridicule, owing to its meticulousness of imitation, and ridicule of the model itself. Hurled from its preeminence in Arnaut, *ferm voler* reappears in Guilhem's fifth strophe, to be repeated in the sixth, each time within the context of masculine morality. Buried puns usher in the displacement from her pedestal of the absent beloved as object (Arnaut: "ferm voler"; Guilhem: "avolesa"). Homonymy approaches the pun, introducing the formally embodied recollection of referents outside the poem. The new, masculine object exists as a foil for the term *oncle,* compelling emphasis on the denotative aspect of the rhyme-word. The comical discrepancy between the model's hermeticity and the trifling object is complemented by the presence of two objects (noble uncle, vile nephew), carrying the dyad of model/imitation into the heart of the poem, its genre. The word *c(h)ambra,* once the beloved lady's chamber, occurs only in its connotative sense, as the figural locus of Prebost's good qualities and of Aesmar's "entry" into trouble or in apposition to his evil, finally achieving juxtaposition in the tornada to *intra.* This echoes Arnaut directly ("cui pretz per cambra intra") but simultaneously manages to attenuate its grammatical integrity and reveal its disembodied function of reference to Arnaut, pure and simple. The play with *intra* underscores that loss. Seeming to retain its former status in the first line, it enters into grammatical word-play in the second (*intra/entre*), then progresses further away from its secret sharer, *chambra,* to be coerced into reunion with it in the grammatical chaos of the ending. Similarly, the strained contexts of *oncle* in the original, which already called for a high degree of metaphorical elaboration, melt into simple referentiality. The interstices between strophes become filled with tenuous shifts of reference metonymizing Arnaut.

It is as though the mere reproduction of formal features makes their exaggeration or condensation in parody unnecessary. Arnaut's homonymy, clearly distinguishable from polysemy in his use of *arma,* is faithfully recalled. Used in the meaning of "arming oneself" it occurs in the same line as the final reference to *ferm voler,* now turned definitively from the topos of love to that of arms. This is the only figural transformation of the original. For the rest, Guilhem is content with the defiguralization of Arnaut that culminates in concluding desemanticization, as the tornada detaches sound from sense. Within the poem, denotative senses prevail, but all connote Arnaut outside the poem.

Guilhem created a third presence, bringing together Arnaut and implicit comment on him. Imitated for their invariability, Arnaut's forms of expression are revealed as movable, transferable. The transmission of form to the new context results in a contest between the denotative and the connotative aspects of words: in the search for closure, stasis, safety characteristic of medieval hermeticism, and of the sestina in particular, is shown the lability of the individual signifier, with respect to subject, and concomitantly, genre. The sestina, which catapults recurrence into the forefront of consciousness, now gives us the result of figural loss in the heightening of merely phonetic emphases. Not by departure from the courtly code (of lady-worship) but through expression of a different part of the same code (virile virtues and vices), Guilhem transmits his sirventes through the metonymic filter of Arnaut, taken as the ground common knowledge and awareness. The topic of statis and firmness flows in the reversed tributary of the imitator-parodist, the centerless poem functioning as his "center." Recurrence depends on that crucial shift of reference as within the sestina itself. However, it may urge a return to Arnaut's poem, for the parody forms a surreptitious new context for both poems.

3. Ezra Pound: "Sestina: Altaforte"

This poem by Ezra Pound is included among the "Arnaldians" partly because Pound is able to perceive the sestina from the model Arnaut provided, using neither a narrowly philological nor a Petrarchan stance. Like Arnaut, Pound does not initiate a discussion of temporality, but allows awareness of temporality to consist in the song's own recurrences. Finally, his "Sestina: Altaforte," while not a translation from Provençal, displays a number of important features—lexical, syntactic, even ideological—that emphasize the strength of this poem as homage.

Ezra Pound's activities in music received a powerful thrust from his poetic concern with Provençal verse. He looked with nostalgia and envy at the troubadours and what he saw as their fusion of words and music. In his critical writing on music, Pound seems to have been chiefly concerned with rhythm, calling what he liked "pattern music" (Schafer 1977: 76 passim) and preferring long-term, seamless effects achieved by continuity of tempo to the frequent slackening and quickening of romantic interpretation that seemed to

him to have the lulled the Victorian ear. Clear limits, the "beat . . .
a knife-edge and *not* the surface of a rolling-pin," his claims for
music converge with those he made for the constituent elements of
poetry and their ability to alter one another. Poems such as the one
to be analyzed here follow a deeply embedded pattern of recurrence.
To liquidate the massive and suffocating presence of the nineteenth
century, he recurred to certain features of it, its "medievalism," for
example, as a ground for change.

Pound's sestina, loosely constructed by comparison with the
troubadour model, turns on the search for centrality, now desired in
the exhortation to battle. The imagined "center" of action is the
battleground, the natural meeting ground of masculine and feminine
principles, of swords and "broad fields," the space between contenders:

Sestina: Altaforte

I. Damn it all! all this our South stinks peace
You whoreson dog, Papiols, come! Let's to music!
I have no life save when the swords clash.
But ah! when I see the standards gold, vair, purple, opposing
5   And the broad fields beneath them turn crimson,
Then howl I my heart nigh mad with rejoicing.

II. In hot summer have I great rejoicing
When the trumpets kill the earth's foul peace,
And the lightnings from black heav'n flash crimson,
10   And the fierce thunders roar me their music
And the winds shriek through the clouds mad, opposing,
And through all the riven skies God's swords clash.

III. Hell grant soon we hear again the swords clash!
And the shrill neighs of destriers in battle rejoicing
15   Spiked breast to spiked breast opposing!
Better one hour's stour than a year's peace
With fat boards bawds, wine and frail music!
Bah! there's no wine like the blood's crimson!

IV. And I love to see the sun rise blood-crimson,
20   And I watch his spears through the dark clash
And it fills all my heart with rejoicing
And pries wide my mouth with fast music
When I see him so scorn and defy peace,
His lone might 'gainst all darkness opposing.

25   V. The man who fears war and squats opposing
My words for stour, hath no blood of crimson
But is fit only to rot in womanish peace
Far from where worth's won and the swords clash

49

<pre>
              For the death of such sluts I go rejoicing;
30   Yea, I fill all the air with my music.

              VI. Papiols, Papiols, to the music!
              There's no sound like to swords swords opposing,
              No cry like the battle's rejoicing
              When our elbows and swords drip the crimson
35   And our charges 'gainst "The Leopard's" rush clash.
              May God damn for ever all who cry "Peace!"

              VII. And let the music of the swords make them crimson!
              Hell grant soon we hear again the swords clash!
              Hell blot black for alway the thought "Peace"!
</pre>

(Pound 1957: 7-9)

Here is another case of *translatio*. The poem could properly be termed a composite "imitation," for it encompasses the formal scheme set by Arnaut viewed through the wrong-ended telescope of cultural distance and the war-topoi of his litigious contemporary, Bertran de Born, singer of war. Its meter juxtaposes occasions of the Arnaldian initial octosyllable with leisurely expanses of Italianate hendecasyllable and punctuations of the old Romance epic decasyllable, the very flexibility of metric organization bringing the inflexible forms to mind.

Like Guilhem's little poem, this is a sirventes, so determined by its topic. Bertran de Born, the "headless trunk Dante meets in Malebolge" (Pound 1952: 45), his deepest Hell, is the one to enunciate the principle of *contrappasso*, the counterpass of punishment to sin. Given this function in virtue of the tireless advocacy of war in his songs, Bertran even as warrior-poet had to frame his love of strife within the limits of lyrical pleasure. The poem Pound echoes in strophe IV bears an eerie resemblance to songs of the genre known to Provençal poetic treatises as the *plazer*, a simple enumeration of things the singer likes:

<pre>
              Be.m platz lo gais temps de pascor,
              Que fai fuolhas e flors venir,
              E platz mi, quan auch la baudor
              De.ls auzels, que fan retentir
5   Lor chan per lo boschatge,
              E platz mi, quan vei sobre.ls pratz
              Tendas e pavilhos fermatz,
                  Et ai gran alegratge,
              Quan vei per champanha rengatz,
10   Chavaliers e chavals armatz.
</pre>

(Hill and Bergin 1973: 115)

50

(I love well the gay springtime that brings leaves and flowers, and it pleases me when I hear the clamor of the birds that make their song resound through the wood, and when I see tents and pavilions spread over the meadows, and it really makes my happy to see, ranged over the country-side, knights and horses in arms.)

Once the poem as symbolic action is taken for granted, it compels awareness of itself as production. The same reality is taken into account by Pound's martial music. In amalgamating Arnaut's forms with the war topoi of Bertran, its mortar is Pound's use of archaic words (destriers," "vair," "stour," carrying the poem nearer to Romance) or alterations such as the contraction "heav'n" that negates "feminine" endings. The spectrum of rhyme-words encompasses the sun and nature; all of its elements seen in strife. Pound characterizes nature as being in a state of war, its contrasts ranged in battle-order, tense between movement and stasis—"opposing" as a statement of position against the active "rejoicing"; "peace" against "clash." "Crimson" continually refers to the flow of blood (I, III, IV, V, VI), "music" to the flow of sound, ambivalent terms bracketed within the larger battlefield. The final music of swords grows out of a chiastic meeting. Battle is the stage of centrality the poem seeks, and yet it involves a dualism instrumental to its continuance. In this dependency lies the raison d'être of the feminine element.

Arnaut's imitators discard his love-poem or transform it into some other exhortatory variant—a call to virtue, as in the case of the Venetian troubadour Bartolome Zorzi (Riesz 1971: 62-63), an extended vituperation for Guilhem de Saint-Grigori. Androgynous characters ("sluts") passively challenge the warriors by their inertness; these are cowards who "rot in womanish peace," peace that is also termed foul and stinking. Pound words with accumulations more than progress, his absorption in the exhortatory argument positing a perpetual anticipation in a static present. The poem's means of organization is conflict envisioning conflict but supported by no dialectical movement; the speaker goes to a predialectical historical moment to make his points. Recurrence of Arnaut/Bertran disinters a hybrid creature latent in courtly ethic. It is nearly always swords that clash (strophes I, II, II, V, VII), and even "opposing" is neutralized into adjectival status ("gold, vair, purple, opposing"). The materiality of the poem resides firmly in names and things. There is the odd trace of still other troubadours such as Marcabru in its speaking of squatting cowards, inviting pause in the enumerative discourse. If the successive phases of the sun are conceived of as in antagonism, masculine openness against the feminine darkness, even here little hint of true succession exists but a simultaneity evokes Romanesque

51

visual narrative art. Pleasure truly lurks in the corners of this call to war. Revealed as the product of the poet's stay-at-home thoughts, music signals his openness to external forces ("Let's to music" changes to the passive "the fierce thunders roar me their music", to "pries wide my mouth with fast music", and to a final falling into step). In alternate strophes music is creation ("I fill all the air with my music," "the music of the swords"), the alteration in rhetorical stance underlining the duplicities of arms and letters as practiced by the same man.

The binary character of the sestina is the aspect most hospitable to its depiction of static conflict or chiasmus. Pound is able to synthesize dramatically all the luxury and indolence of court life by entering his poem in medias res and implementing the word-bound conditions of that life.

At one moment only, Pound overruns the sestina's boundaries, abandoning the convention that has all rhyme-words repeated in the tornada. He omits the two verbs "opposing" and "rejoicing," thereby eliminating the markers of conflict and looking towards eternity ("Hell blot black for alway . . ."), praying for the obsolescence of his own pre-text. For the existence of the poem depends on unbroken tension. When war becomes a permanent state, the song will be understood. In anticipation of a disruption already missed, Pound's poem emerges as little more than an artifact of museum quality.

Chapter 3

Concepts of Time
and the Petrarchan Sestina

1. Time and the Heavenly Bodies: Plato, Aristotle, St. Augustine

A brief review of formative conceptions of time known to Petrarch is pertinent to the examination of his poems. Plato's *Timaeus* had a decisive influence on medieval conceptions of time. It enunciates the idea of a gulf between Being and the created universe. Time is characterized as "a moving likeness of eternity . . . a likeness moving according to number" (37b). The Body of the Universe, that is, the celestial sphere and its revolving rings, and the Soul of the Universe, the motion represented by those rings, had already been created. Time came into existence to enable the cosmos to resemble even more the pattern after which it was created. The regular movement of the stars gave rise, says Plato, to "the invention of number . . . [and] inquiry into the nature of the universe; thense we have derived philosophy, the greatest gift the gods have given or will ever give to mortals" (47b-c). In the motion of the stars man discerns the pattern of reason, and by following reason man can join in the nature of the gods.

What is eternal suffers no change, but the stars and the sensible world are in motion and, therefore, in the process of change. Nevertheless, in the unfluctuating duration of change time resembles the

53

permanence of eternity: "So time came into being with the heavens in order that, having come into being together they should also be dissolved together, if ever they are dissolved" (38b). Time itself does not belong to becoming and change; rather it is the *measure* of that becoming that has been ordered. It is simultaneously the eternity of becoming and the means by which the eternal is discerned on earth.

When the Demiurge ordered the heavens, he created time. In Plato's text, time is constituted by the revolution of the eight spheres of heaven. The sun, the moon, and the planets "came into being to define and preserve the measure of time" (38b-c); and time exists insofar as the movement of these bodies measures it. In the universe the measurement is of two kinds: the movement of the circle of the Same and the movement of the circle of the Other. The first kind of motion, which is the circuit of the fixed stars, is uniform and regular. The motion of the Other comprises the diverse movements of the seven planets. The revolution of these seven around the earth gives rise to Plato's statement that time proceeds according to number. For if the revolution of the sun around the earth establishes one number or measure, then the revolution of the moon establishes another, so that in the diversity of their movements the planets establish all the numbers that measure time. As the circuits of the sun and moon around the earth are fundamentally unique, each "guards" as its own the number determinative of time that it establishes. It is this establishing and guarding of number that Plato calls time.

The *Timaeus* contains the germ of the idea that time is the medium through which the divinity is understood in the world. Augustine was to develop it in the direction of the soul's individual perception. He drew in part from the less expected source of Aristotle's *Physics.* In the fourth book of his *Physics,* Aristotle argues that time does not exist apart from motion but *cannot be motion itself.* Nor can time be the revolution of the planets, for a part of the revolution of the sun is also a species of time, and the sun does not complete its revolution in that time. Nor is time the motion of the sun, while time is everywhere the same and present to all things. Motion, unlike time, can be faster and slower. If you wish to know where an object moving along a path is, you can find it only in the present moment, as it is no longer where it was and is not yet where it will be. In this respect the present moment is continuous and the same; as such it measures motion, which is also continuous. Here Petrarch parts company with Aristotelian ideas. Linking time and motion, he asserts that since there was always time, there was always motion; thus there must be time beyond the furthest extremity. It is interesting to note that

Aristotle (*Physics* IV, 267b) finds the ultimate cause of time in the unceasing motion of the first heaven, motion which is effected by the influence of the first mover being exerted as the heavens' circumference. Both Plato and Aristotle, then, determine that the motions of the heavenly bodies are an integral mechanism of time.

Yet the difference of attitude in the two philosophers is profound. Plato approaches the problem of time metaphorically and Aristotle physically, through the study of nature alone. In defining time as relative to motion, Aristotle regards the present moment as the end of the past and the beginning of the future, for which reason there is always time. For Plato, as later for Augustine, the present moment is the moment through which the future hurries into the past. It is thus Aristotle's idea that permits most explicitly the *marking* of time by measures of motion. The question then arises: How can time, which (as Aristotle says) is everywhere the same, be the measure of all motion if some motion is regular and some irregular? Aristotle's definition tells us what time measures (motion) without telling us what time is. The measure of planetary motion, for example, then has a reality apart from time.

Aristotle confronts the matter of essential time as it is related to the perceiving soul; posing the question whether, if the soul did not exist, time would exist (223a). He concludes that movement may indeed exist but cannot be measured or numbered without the soul. Since time is the measuring or numbering, it can only exist insofar as the soul exists to do the measuring. We can recognize the effects of this and similar ideas on Augustine's evolving interpretation of time.

Augustine asks in his *Confessions* (XI, 22): "I once heard a learned man say that time was nothing but the movement of the sun and the moon and the stars, but I did not agree. Would it not be more likely that time was the movement not only of the heavens, but of all other bodies as well?" This is clearly reminiscent of Aristotle. However, Augustine continues, as we call a day the total orbit of the sun, from the time it arises in the east to the time when it sets in the west, is this "day" the movement of the sun, the time needed for the completion of its orbit, or a combination of both? These ways of measuring exclude each other: If the day were the motion of the sun, there would be a day if the sun moved around the earth in only one hour. If the time the sun actually needed to complete an orbit were day, it would not be day if the sun rose and set in one hour, for there would have to be twenty-four revolutions of the sun to make one day. If day were both the motion and the time the motion requires, there would be day neither if the sun orbited the earth in one hour nor if the sun remained motionless for twenty-four hours. Time, therefore, is not the movement of any body.

Augustine does not even consider the view that claims that time is constituted by the motions of the heavenly bodies (time = pure motion). Rather, he interprets this suggestion to mean that all intervals of time (among which are days and years) are dependent *for their existence* on heavenly motions, whereas it is the soul that measures intervals of time and motions by means of time. The Scriptural account (Exodus 11:23) of the sun's standing still for the Victory of Israel may not have been unimportant in prompting Augustine to consider time as independent of the motions of heavenly bodies. Augustine comes to regard time as a kind of distention, since the battle, for example, took place in time. However, he does not deny that the motions of the heavenly bodies provide convenient landmarks for charting time's course.

2. Man and Time: Christian Conceptions

The ground for the Christian poet inquiring into the mysteries of time is established by meetings of concepts of time and the functional compromises that result from them: poetry is also an activity of the mind that measures motion, one that the poet exalts to a position of preeminence from which the external world is surveyed; and yet the temporal landmarks with which he is provided are no more than convenience, the calendar man substitutes for the understanding of altogether different laws of operation.

Virtually all of Western literature from the Norman conquest to the Renaissance was written in accordance with Christian cosmology. The mainstream of this literature assumes, at least as background, a divinely ordered universe all of whose parts are ultimately related. Man, the microcosm, was understood to be correspondent with the universe, the macrocosm. The great majority of poets wrote of an anthropocentric world, and accordingly, of the human experience of time, understanding man as a traveler in time. An important definition of self-comprehension (Corbin 1957: 116) asserts that for man "falling back to the farthest limit of the dimension of his present . . . is to understand."

On the occasion of the new year we are wont to experience the effective cessation of a time, the beginning of another, and the abolition of the past. European literature since Petrarch abounds in "anniversary" poems that mark such a reified time. We know that unlike European peoples there are those who have not objectified time, for example the Hopi Indians, for whom time is a separate dimension in a language that agrees strikingly with that of modern physics: The Hopi cannot speak of "ten days" in the same way as of "ten chairs" (Whorf 1950). The language of our literature, however, persistently measures time. Two distinct orientations toward the meaning of man's time define themselves early and continue to prevail: cyclical time, periodically regenerating itself ad infinitum, and finite time, a fragment (itself containing cycles) between two timeless eternities. The dialectic of the two conceptions has been thoroughly studied with respect to archaic and primitive cultures by Mircea Eliade, who elucidates the means whereby "archaic man tends to set himself in opposition . . . to history, regarded as a succession of events that are irreversible, unforseeable, possessed of autonomous value" (Eliade 1954: 195). By no means, however, is the conscious disregarding of history to be seen as peculiar to primitive peoples: The eternal repetition of the fundamental rhythm of the cosmos, its periodic destruction and recreation, has often been thought of by historians as a beginningless, endless cycle "from which man can wrest himself only by an act of spiritual freedom" (Eliade 1954: 115). In that conception, both the entire cosmic process and the time of the world of birth and death develop in cyclical pattern, in the course of which nothing is created and nothing lost, and there can never be a beginning or an end. The world has always moved in circles and is eternal.

Certain thinkers of late Antiquity—Pythagoreans, Stoics, Platonists—went so far as to maintain that within each of these cycles (*aiones, aeva*) the same situations perpetually recur, so that no event is unique. Any creation or consummation of the universe would then be inconceivable. We find the Christian poets, Petrarch early among them, reiterating the Creation and strenuously attacking the eternity of the universe. The passage of time in the universe can never be represented by a straight line with an initial and a final event, nor can it have an absolutely defined direction, a "before" and an "after." This in broad outline is the Greek conception of time and its consciousness of history, which views history as part of a perpetual cosmic order.

A central reference point defining and orienting a historical past and future was provided by Christianity, which colligates its own innovation in time with the Creation and the continuous, directed action of God. Time unfolds unilaterally, beginning at one source and building up toward a single goal, oriented in a line from the past to the future. A straight line, finite at its extremities, willed and governed by God, contains the total history of the human race. The direction of time is irreversible; the world is created within time and must end in time, beginning with the launching point of the first chapter of Genesis and ending in the eschatological resolution of the Apocalypse. This eschatological end orients the past toward the future and binds the two together in such a way as to make the unilateral direction of time a certainty. Western historicism as it proceeds from the Christian standpoint underwrites the assurance of the uniqueness of the individual. History no longer appears as a cycle that repeats itself endlessly, but as a line governed by a singular fact. The destiny of mankind, as well as the particular destiny of individual human beings, is likewise enacted only once and for all and draws its meaning from an invisible end. The magnetic power of this end draws time forward as the medium of constant progress, now given its full import, orientation, and intrinsic meaning. Prior to this solution the Romans, continually preyed upon by the idea of the end of Rome, constantly sought systems of renovation. St. Augustine defended the idea of a perennial Rome "solely to escape from accepting a *fatum* determined by cyclical theories" (Eliade 1954: 133), taking the position that no one could know just at what moment God would decide to put an end to history. With time viewed as dictated from Providence, the enactment of history came to be interpreted as the "conflict between the love of God and the love of self." This essentially Augustinian interpretation became the moving force of the personal "histories" created by Christian poets such as Petrarch, whose immense popularity, paradoxically, did much to emphasize for poetry the privacy and integrity of the person.

Under the pressure of linear progress, the medium of time becomes understood as connected, bringing with it the appointed tragedy of the historical moment that heralds the final catastrophe. Nor does the man undergoing the experience of linear time perceive it less in terms of moments. For as the past announces the future and the future explains the past, earlier events are moments, types, and prefigurations of subsequent events. Monotheistic revelation takes place in historical duration, in time, when Moses receives the Law at a certain time and place, and thereupon faith is revealed progressively in a series of theophanies, each with its own value. The conception of a series of moments definitely situated in time applies to humanity; only God's time is eternal. But it is only in linear time that God is vouchsafed to man and that human experience is perceived. Only by virtue of a temporal sequence do actions assume meaning with respect to God's timelessness. When Augustine asks what relationship is possible between God's timelessness and man's time, he can answer only by internalizing time as a reality of the mind related to the everlastingness of God as human knowledge is to omniscience.

It was possible, then, for the Christian poet writing nearly a thousand years after Augustine to represent the moment of his enamorment as the beginning of his measuring of time. Petrarch's meeting with Laura on Good Friday is a privileged moment precious *for its very irreversibility* as historical event. It draws upon the tensions that characterize the predominant conception of time, and on a deeper stratum, on the theory of cycles and/or astral influences on human destiny that in the Middle Ages already had begun to hold sway over speculation on history and eschatology. It must be acknowledged that the Christian conception of time did not abolish circularity: Events are to be repeated in a "new time," for Paradise after the Second Coming was to be reestablished as it had existed in the beginning. Time is perceived in moments, evidence by events disclosed to man under the eyes of death, as segments on a line. On the other hand, a quotient of metamorphosis survives the establishment of Chrisitan order based on time. In poetry it is reflected, for example, through the minute interest in the "reincarnations" of Ovid's *Metamorphoses* by medieval poets and theoreticians. It was also poetry's task to create a present in the memory that would enter into a dialectic with the outer world of change. The retelling of the myths is in part a revolt against historical time, or at least an attempt to restore it to a cosmic, infinite place.

If we study poets who conceived of time primarily as the measure of motion or change, then the retelling of myth emerges as something quite different. Petrarch uses the linear segmentation of time not only as a horizontal pretense for story-telling but as a sign of its own rhythm, much in the way that the careful and proper segmentation, or rhythmicization, of breathing is said to provide psychic illumination. The value of his strategy of repetition emanates most convincingly through a poetic form such as the sestina, in which the segments of time are continuously redefined by each other.

3. Petrarch's Sestinas and the Problem of the Center

The formal complexities of the sestina are intimately related to rejuvenation, to beginnings and endings. Time measured from Aristotelian limitations—through the study of nature, its beginnings and endings—propels forward the consciousness of *new times,* new beginnings. Insofar as time consists in the awareness of a new time defined by its environment past and future, the passage from strophe to strophe always marks a new time. Consonant with the deeply rooted temporal suggestion of the end of one "thing" being the beginning of another, the particular kind of strophic enchainment typified in the sestina should come to embody the consciousness of a new time.

For the poet following Augustine, time is in the soul. But the universe of changing things is encompassed in time, while God is in eternity. He has knowledge of the world without distention of any kind, for the entire course of time is known to him at once. The soul of man, on the other hand, is obliged through the threefold activity of anticipation, attention, and memory to participate in the flux of motion itself. Man's perception of motion and the measuring of it are accordingly in flux (Augustine XII, 15); hence the necessity to grasp and record the succession of motion in piecemeal fashion. The soul must use time because it has been placed in a universe of change and succession, subject to the dispersion of a temporal existence.

Petrarch's sestinas constitute his most poignant and searching exploration of the poetic consequences of this position of Augustine. Most are structured on terminal words that record the passing of time intervals or that are metonymies of these. The alternations of "night" and "day," "evening" and "dawn," broken only by the act of spiritual freedom epitomized in the tornadas, reflect man's capacity for measuring time. Man, in the midst of God and the rest of creation, represents the futile marking of time that is the lot of all who live in the eternal present, on the verge of something more. Restlessness is elevated to a metaphysical principle segregating man, for good and evil, from his fellow animals (as in sestina XXII) through the uniqueness of desire winged by imagination. The temporal plan of Petrarch's sestina tends to recapitulate the yearly cycle sketched by the poet and reminds us—as does generally the schedule of 366 poems—of the cycle of the Christian year. The immediately perceptible externals of the sestina form) the recurrences of terminal words—replicate cyclical motion. But in his using the only measures accessible to him, the inadequacy of such measurement and the apartness of man are emphasized. Sestina XXII meditates on the possibility of an eternal light of love, analogous in process to the stasis of the sun at Jericho, and concludes that such a thing is possible only in eternity, which we are incapable of comprehending, when day and night are fused together ("e il giorno andrà pien di minute stelle").

4. Excursus: Lorenzo de' Medici

Imitators of Petrarch show an awareness of the structural similarity of the sestina form to temporal mimesis. In the Italian Quattrocento

60

there is the prominent example of Lorenzo de' Medici ("il Magnifico") who composed five sestinas. The first (XVII in his *Rime*), begins on the familiar Petrarchesque lament:

> Quante volte per mia troppa speranza,
> da poi ch'io fui sotto il giogo d'Amore,
> bagnato ho il petto mio d'amari pianti!
> E quante volte, pur sperando pace
> da' santi lumi ho desiato vita,
> e per men mal di poi chiamato ho morte!
>
> (ed. Cavalli 1958: 20)

(How many times, through my excessive hope, since I was under the yoke of Love, I have bathed my breast in bitter weeping! And how many times, still hoping for peace from the holy lights, I desired life, and then for better called on Death!)

The poem turns on the axes of the terminal words. Two are markers of time (*vita, morte*); one (*Amore*) fulfills the function through which time is here measured (in tears, *pianti*); and, finally, the counterposed *speranze* and *pace* echo the first pair, life and death. The poem concludes with an anticipation of eternity in the tornada ("aspetterai per miglior vita morte").

The second sestina (XXXII) is a meditation on memory. *Tempo* is a rhyme-word together with the *mente* in which it is created, as are *Amore, pianti* (a virtual metonymy of the preceding), *vita* (the human substance of time), and *libertade*. Gathered into the constellation of Petrarchesque idiom, the words contract relationships of reference among themselves and with other, less regularly recurrent terms (*perso:* strophes II, V, VI, VII) that bespeak a primary Fall. The tornada refers to the first loss of liberty and conjures up the eternal present of bondage.

The third sestina (XLVII) retains the rhyme-word *tempo*, and the lament for lost "time" recurs in every strophe. The marking of time is the quest of the poem, which displays the impossibility of measuring:

> Le nostre passion quanto sien vane,
> quanto il pianto e il dolore è fermo e certo,
> e quanto è invano ogni mortale sdegno,
> quanto è perduta ogni umana fatica,
> mostra quel che a fuggir mai non è stanco,
> che ogni cosa ne porta e fura, il tempo.
>
> (ed. Cavalli 1958: 44)

(How vain are our passions, how firm and certain are weeping and grief,

how vain all mortal disdain, how wasted every human effort, is shown by
that which never tires of fleeing, which takes and robs everything: time.)

In the fourth sestina the meditation on time is presented in the
guise of the myth of Diana. Petrarch's imagery of his Sun now combines with the potency of myth to connote chastity and permanence.
It is an eternal Sun ("nè però il foco del mio chiaro Sole/ scema");
similarly green thoughts of love may be perpetually reborn in its light
(II). By contrast, the hunting art of Diana cannot appease the fire
within; as long as there is sun, the lover will follow his chaste beloved (VII).

Lorenzo's last sestina (LXIV) explicitly refers to Petrarch's first:

> Pria che si muti il mio fermo disio,
> frigide lascerà mia membra morte . . .
>
> (ed. Cavalli 1958: 61)

(Before my firm desire changes it will leave my dead limbs cold.)

The poem is a restatement of "firmness" in love, to which it recurs
again and again in the commentative *regge,* referring externally and
at various times to the actions of God, the beloved, Hope, and finally
to Desire itself. The polysemy creates an iridescence of meanings,
viz. "dominate," "rule," and "support"; yet all of these suggest a
stasis that opposes the mutable world. On the verge of eternity, the
poet suggests that desire can, in the process of final mutation, be and
act alone, disembodied:

> Nè mai per morte cangerassi l'alma
> se dopo lei il disio forse si regge.
>
> (ed. Cavalli 1958: 61)

(Nor will my soul ever change through death, if ever desire can last, after
it.)

The Petrarchan questions are brought to the fore in these sestinas
principally by the poet's awareness of poetic forms as a means of
articulating the measure of time. Art would triumph psychologically
over death and even over life itself, surmounting their futile confrontation. The surrender of self to a beyond that is a domain of
peace would constitute a transcendence of man's fate and a resolution
of the "duality" between death and transcendence. It is Lorenzo's
gift to have recognized the sympathetic network between the tensions of the sestina and the counterposition of two temporal conceptions.

5. Time, the Pastoral, and Petrarch

The preoccupation with analogy and contrast between the forces of nature and human mortality is embedded in the design of Petrarch's poems. Out of the solar cycle of the day and the seasonal cycle of the year he weaves a single pattern of meaning that informs the *Canzoniere*. (Scholarship has even been prompted to correlate each poem painstakingly to a day of the year [Roche 1974]). The events of psychological time are presented as inherent in biological time, understandable as measured by an internal clock conditioned by the sun's cycle. Accordingly, the rhyme-words of the sestinas include terms with explicit reference to periods of the cycle. Petrarch's cyclical arrangement tentatively bridges the chasm between the mundane and the transcendent, and makes out of nature a voice that transmits the assimilation of an earthly vision to a supernatural one. The symbolism of periodic regeneration is to be found both in the imagery assigning archetypal meaning to the poetic rite, and in its explicit association with myth. The yearly round is the ground of Petrarch's analogy: fictionalized time. It is the special province of Nature, while the speaker concerns himself mainly with the smallest version of the cyclic pattern, the daily epicycle in which man toils and rests. For the speaker, the day is the unit of time that gives his poem form. Earthly creation and agriculture, then, are only one of the planes on which the symbolism of recurrence and regeneration is applicable:

> A qualunque animal che alberga in terra
> Tempo è di traveagliare quanto è il sole . . .
> (XXII, 1-2) (see translation Chapter 4)

Man is included among the animals who retire when the sun sets and are reawakened by its rising. A bit later in the poem, we are given to understand that the poet stands outside his cycle, unmoved and unmovable. This difference is not the only point of contrast in the poem's temporality. The other, encompassing, antagonism is that between historical and mythical time.

In Petrarch's first sestina there is no recognition of a uniformly perceived cosmic situation that would clearly imply a metaphysical position. It would be insufficient, however, to ascribe this lack to Petrarch's fabled "evasiveness" (Contini 1973: 408) and thereby to decline to plumb the poem's authentic meaning.

Unlike animal species, the speaker is out of equilibrium with, although still in, the created world. We distinguish him first simply as the speaker, for speech is both the consequence and the maintainer of this disequilibrium. The only possible speaker has to be a guilty descendant of the lost Edenic past. This awareness alone would appear to invalidate the hope of human alignment with any nature-opening. The question arises whether it is feasible to attain the genuine integration of the speaker into the diurnal and seasonal cycles.

The possibilities of myth now enter. As the poem develops, the negative analogy of Petrarch-Laura to Apollo-Daphne increases in prominence. The creation of the anterior story which took place *in illo tempore,* at a beginning, is actualized again. Petrarch's use of tenses sweeps across cosmogony and anthropogony by the sheer force of ritual:

> et non se transformasse in verde selva
> per uscirmi di braccia, come il giorno
> ch'Apollo la sequia qua giù per terra.
>
> (XXII, 34-46)

(and let her not be transformed into a green wood to escape from my arms, as the day when Apollo pursued her down here on earth!)

The speaker becomes the contemporary of the mythical pattern, projected into the epoch of the beginning, walking (as Petrarch suggested in a different connection) "forward into the past." In the example of Apollo-Daphne resides a magical power, an "idea of primordial time, not as a time very remote in the past, but rather . . . a prototypical time. . . . Primordial time is creative; it creates what happens today" (van der Leeuw 1957: 330). Both stories would be enacted as the same mythical instant of the beginning, thereby suspending the profane duration of time. It is, then, through imitation or repetition that fallen man might be projected into the mythical epoch in which his archetype was first revealed.

While the analogy of Laura to Daphne is valid and successful, there is at the same time no identification of the speaker with Apollo. The asymmetry of the analogy manifests itself on both the conceptual and the verbal levels. The myth aids in constructing Petrarch's central and personal story. Simultaneously, however, it particularizes the contrasts between iteself and the appearance, increase, waning, and summation of human life. In time as the locus of transience, only life can come to an end; only for man can biology, through a process of self-revelation and commentary, become history.

In pastoral escape, the avoidance of historical time is accomplished. We have an abundance of Petrarchan examples that enrich our understanding of the collision of temporal conceptions in his sestinas. One of these is in sonnet CLXXXVIII, which I cite in full:

64

Almo sol, quella fronde ch'io sola amo,
tu prima amasti: or sola al bel soggiorno
verdeggia e senza par, poi che l'addorno
suo male e nostro vide in prima Adamo.

5   Stiamo a mirarla: i' ti pur prego e chiamo,
o sole, e tu pur fuggi, e fai d'intorno
ombrare i poggi e te ne porti il giorno,
e fuggendo mi toi quel chi'i' più bramo.

L'ombra che cade da quell'umil colle
10   ove favilla il mio soave foco,
ove 'l gran lauro fu picciola verga,

crescendo mentr'io parlo, agli occhi tolle
la dolce vista del beato loco
ove 'l mio cor co la sua Donna alberga.

(ed. Ponte 1968: 150)

Life-giving sun, you first loved that branch which is all I love;
now, unique in her sweet dwelling, she flourishes, without an
equal since Adam first saw his and our lovely bane.

Let us stay to gaze at her, I beg and call on you, O sun, and you
still run away and shadow the hillsides all around and carry off
the day, and fleeing you take from me what I most desire.

The shadow that falls from that low hill where my gentle fire is
sparkling, where the great laurel was a little sapling,

growing as I speak, takes from my eyes the sweet sight of the
blessed place where my heart dwells with his lady.

This poem affirms the significance of myth for the light it throws
on the structure of time, and on Petrarch's recognition of difference.
At first glance it would appear that both metamorphoses (Daphne
and Laura) were enacted together within the framed narration that
privileges its own temporality. Petrarch's beloved "frond" was once
loved by the sun, and it is the same (going back to *illud tempus*).
Petrarch, however, introduces an ambiguity in his use of *sola*, which
exploits its phonetic relationship to *sol*, pointing explicitly to the
detachment of Apollo's Daphne from his own Laura. The first *sola*
is a bridge to the "solar" analogy that the second *sola* destroys. Now,
he continues, the frond is without peer since Adam first sighted *his*
beauteous evil. The "laurel" incorporates features of both Daphne
and Eve, who would have challenged her. The ultimate connection
forged in the strophe is the Christian one between Laura and Eve.
The syntactic ambiguities that facilitate the intuition of subconnec-
tions include the placement of *suo* (and *nostro*) well before *Adamo*

so as to create doubt as to its referent: It could, after all, refer to the *fronde*. Such a reading would name Petrarch's beloved as the primary source of his fall (and ours).

Petrarch achieves a dazzling network of temporal linkages; yet these connections ultimately do not cohere. It is the incompatibility of two kinds of time, one mythical and atemporal, the other (as far as Petrarch is concerned), historical and linear, with a familiar eschatological burden. The strophe embodies conflicting dreams that are ultimately irreconcilable. It is in the plenitude of that knowledge that the poet addresses the Sun: Let us stop and gaze at her, he pleads, but the sun has already "moved," taking with it the clarity of the beloved image, the shadows "crescendo mentr'io parlo." The poet had emended the line from "crescende poco a poco" to the final version so that the present might become past in the saying, as if to echo and resonate to the primal experience of metamorphosis incarnate in the myth. Against the paragon of the evergreen laurel, however, we explicitly recall our mortality. The anguish of the speaker is due to his understanding that if the past (as Augustine has it) is everpresent (*praesens de praeteritis*) as memory, yet time as linear progress toward an end dominates the poem, and to such a concept of time Petrarch must adhere.

Petrarch argues (as might be expected) for the Platonic-Christian conception against all natural philosophers who would propound the eternity of the world (in his *De sui ipsius et multorum ignorantia*): "They would not shrink from assailing not only the fabric of the world of Plato in his *Timaeus* but the Genesis of Moses and the Catholic Faith and the whole most holy and saving dogma of Christ" (Cassirer and Kristeller 1948: 93). His authority is unquestionably Augustine, from whom he draws a Christian citation of Cicero: "There was . . . an eternity measured not by any limit of time; but in terms of space it can be understood how it was. For it does not enter in the least into our thoughts that there was a time when there was none" (Cicero, *De natura deorum* I, 9:21). It is the eschatological conception of time in its two essential moments, the creation and the end of the world, that dominates Petrarch's attempt to reconcile the "two antiquities." The structure of the *Canzoniere* as a whole and in its parts rests on the revelation of the irreversibility of the events. Death is realized as the end of living things, is knowable in life through the frailty of the living substance. The evergreen laurel, however, provides a catalyst for the cyclical ideology that survives beside the principle of linear progress. The laurel helps to explain the periodic return of events, the recurrence of "configurations of content which in turn reveal a certain temporal Gestalt, a coming and going, a rhythmical being and becoming" (Cassirer 1955: 18). By the fact of narration, profane time is symbolically eliminated: Narrator and audience are projected into mythical, sacred time.

In the syntax of the sonnet, the two kinds of time are again juxtaposed. The syntax changes radically after the first strophe, which is constructed in a pattern of retarding inversions, the first of the two main ones ending in *amasti,* the second in *Adamo.* Bridging them is a proposition whose semantics is made perfectly clear in the unfolding. The rest of the poem mimes the linearity of continuous time. Only the two propositions that speak of the two antiquities are inverted, suspending the transference of force from agent to object. Each inversion betokens an avoidance (though not an exclusion) of the verb, a procedure that has long characterized Petrarch for modern readers. Petrarch describes the continuing present in linear terms. But myth is given over to experimentation with the dialect of death and continuity implicit in the creation of all human cultural forms.

Petrarch's laurel is literally a tree, and his search for her can be epitomized in the circling in its shadow of sestina XXX. Here, however, he is more interested in depicting the possibility of the laurel's own development in time. The reference to her birthplace in the first tercet "ove 'l gran lauro fu picciola verga" is juxtaposed to "crescendo mentr'io parlo" in the next tercet. The positioning aligns the idea of ceaseless growth with two possible referents, Laura and the shadow that comes from her original home. With the syncretism of symbol and referent proper to the medieval spirit, the laurel also remains Laura and, therefore, subject to death. The persistent asymmetry of Petrarch's analogies points to contrasts as well as to similarity and displays more than the relation of complementarity or split personality that is generally supposed, for the movements of same and other proceed dialectically. The fable of Apollo and Daphne, then, is the recounting of myth dressed as allegory.

Petrarch originates for modern poetry a fundamental stance: That in order to deny his death man must reject his "creatureliness" and set himself apart from other animate beings. The animalistic impulses Petrarch acknowledges with respect to his feeling for Laura as woman only underscore the distance between such nostalgia for dramatic action and the limbo of disarmed reality.

Transformations, magic spells, and manifestations of obscure divine and demonic forces, such as those operant in the metamorphoses of Petrarch's "song of the visions" (XXIII), are recurrent in pastoral. It would appear that the conditions for pastoral are present as well in the poet's expressed dream of a happines to be gained without effort, of an erotic bliss rendered absolute by the lack of consequence. It is the task of pastoral "to overcome the conflict between passion and remorse" (Poggioli 1975: 65), and this Petrarch clearly does not accomplish. Exaltation of the pleasure principle even where it occurs thinly veils the awareness of death and retribution. Through this aperture in "pastoral" consciousness, knowing his death remains the privilege and the fatality of the speaking man confronting creation.

The superficial layer of pastoral in Petrarch corresponds to the self-contained appearance of his sestinas. Their form would at first seem to realize the sufficiency of pastoral worlds—secluded, enclosed, replicating everywhere the mutual dependency and external independence that is the "ideal of the tribe, of the clan, of the family" (Poggioli 1975: 5). The economy of the sestina does otherwise (as we shall see) lend itself admirably to pastoral material, though at some cost to the attainment of perfect coherence between form and meaning.

The pastoral embodies conflicting dreams that are ultimately reducible to the desire for innocence and for knowledge. The evasiveness and breadth of Petrarchan semantics facilitate the necessary vagueness of that sort of world. In Derrida's words, "l'absence de signifié transcendental étend à l'infini le champ et le jeu de la signification" (the absence of a transcendental signifier extends infinitely the field and the play of signification [Derrida 1967: 411]). We are not, The absence, however, is not total: The ultimate referent of Petrarchan signification is too often discoverable—in the recurrence of mythical event, that is, in repetition itself.

For this reason repetition, which replaces rhyme in the sestina, emerges as the quintessential means of Petrarchan signification. Here we approach closely the cyclical view of time against which all of his discursive production argues. It is in pure repetition, that of a fundamental poetic rhythm, that periodic destruction and recreation are concretely experienced. Whereas the poem itself has a limited duration, traces of the periodic regeneration dominate its form by projecting concrete time into mythical time. The recounting of the Apollo-Daphne myth simultaneously admonishes and consoles us. When it is commingled with the unrepeatable story of Adam (as in the cited sonnet), only then is it subordinated to eschatological time. Otherwise the fact of repetition transfigures the individual myth into one of a category, thereby recapturing for it an ontological status of permanence.

Only truth functions toward the "staticization of becoming, toward annulling the irreversibility of time" (Eliade 1954: 125). Even the perfection of classical poetry and the unparalleled glory accruing to the poets are drawn into the realm of possibility and doubt as regards the future, since the *Parnasia laurus* is evergreen (unlike its human namesake). In these implicit comparisons resides the Petrarchan dialectic that reveals itself as movement in the poems. What Eliade calls "profane time" can be thought of for Petrarch as equivalent to linear time. At essential moments, however, the poetic rite encourages the momentary projection—through imitation—into the mythical epoch in which the poet's archetypes were first revealed. The anteriority of myth guarantees the fundamental truth of what Petrarch has to say about love; and in the spirit of emotional veracity he defends his "spirante Laurea . . . cuius forma captus videor" (*Familiares* II, 9, cit. Ponte 1968: 628). The conflict that arms his religious consciousness against his love for Laura is in large measure a conflict between conceptions of time. The lover depicted by Petrarch tends to become engulfed by mythical time. No new *illud tempus* awaits him, nor a series of events to present theophanies, but a potential of infinite, cyclic repetition.

Petrarch conceived of himself as burdened by the times in which he lived and expressed more than once his consciousness of living on a descending trajectory. It was in this awareness that he admonished students of classical letters to walk forward into the past, yet the scheme of his *Canzoniere* mimics the temporality of monotheistic revelation. That moment between God and Moses remains a limited moment, as does the event of Christ's crucifixion, on whose anniversary Petrarch situates his meeting and enamorment. Since such a moment does represent a theophany, it acquires a new dimension. I It becomes "previous" in itself because of its irreversibility as a historical event. Thus in his utilization of the two antiquities Petrarch inserts linearity into myth. He is reluctant at best to relinquish in turn the myth's cyclical temptations, since they are instrumental to keeping death at bay. And yet the end of time cycles, as they operate at every level of his experience, promises both the end of his plight and a reward for resisting misfortune with a firm will. It is in this anticipatory spirit that the speaker of a sestina often releases us from the poem. Meanwhile, its body affirms a metaphysical thirst for the permanent ("sol una notte, et mai non fosse alba"). From the point of view of the infinite, the *becoming* of things that perpetually revert to one sole state is implicitly annulled. Nevertheless, Petrarch detaches his own wish-dream from myth ("et non si transformasse in verde selva"). It emerges that the pure reenactment of myth would be unsatisfactory. The desired event is one that would either create a new myth or supplant it as a single occurrence in linear time. The genesis of Petrarch's mythical analogies may be discoverable in cyclical concepts of time, but it can be demonstrated that at every critical moment the Christian poet takes over and forges the analogy into a new event. A form rooted in ritual, releasing the need for rhythm, for alternation and contrast, may thus come to a climax and an unfolding in full richness. The Petrarchan sestina thereby reasserts the characteristic capacity of the human spirit to invent and to develop within the temporal flow forms of expression that, in their aesthetic autonomy, triumph over time.

6. Tornada and Adynaton: The Problems of Repetition and Rhyme

The tornada embodies the end of the poem's world, that is to say, of a particular historical cycle translated into its known expression. Beginnings and endings have such strong cognitive significance in poetry (as in all species of aesthetic knowledge) that they tend to be set apart whether or not they are verifiable with respect to external reality. The poet readily accords himself the right to pluck a supposed sequence out of an unknown flux of time. The conventions of Petrarchan beginning help us understand a lyric poem as immune to subsequent disproof and prepare us, through a prior estrangement from literal truth, for a cognitive revelation given sequentially.

In the sestina the recurrent pattern of rhyme-words is often emphasized by end-stopped lines, and cognition is to a large degree the *re*cognition of sequential measurement. We may think of this as commonplace in all poetry, but since in the sestina the syntagmatically progressive order of words is undermined by maximal emphasis on recurrence (*versus*), the poem's drive toward its end is semantically both encumbered and accelerated by the reader's expectations. Temporal consciousness proceeds (as elsewhere) to a directed consciousness of limits and the awareness of death as a threat.

The six rhyme-words of the strophe are brought together in the tornada in pairs per line, but with no prior set order among them. The simultaneity of time may be said to have achieved its most convincing representation in such apparent chaos, where all modalities are conflated and the principle of sequence established previously by the rhyme-words is shaken to its core. Final time, indeed, revolutionizes the course of the poem: A hiatus is declared. Though natural imagery may continue to serve as measure, the event falls out of the cycle. The eschatology of the poem lies in the tornada; for that reason it survived all other medieval functions of the tornada as an inalienable part of the sestina's structure.

The developing response of the reader to the words as they succeed one another is shattered at the poem's end. The catastrophe that puts an end to the poem's history is at the same time judgment of that history. Cyclical time had unfolded irreversibly, hence the apparent despair accompanying the ending with its anticipation of the last day. The motif of "eternal return" has decisively ceded to the motif of "the end of the world."

The powerful sense of catastrophe as regards the formal properties of the sestina is evinced by Petrarch's frequent practice of conferring on the tornada (a formal entity) the semantic function of the figure adynaton. We shall note the presence of adynata—"impossibility" figures—elsewhere in his sestinas, as five of the nine contain them. In two sestinas the tornada is occupied by an adynaton (XXII and CCXXIX); in another the adynaton occurs in the two lines preceding the tornada (CCXXXVII). Petrarch utilizes the "impossibilia"—a daylight filled with stars, breezes gathered in a net—to affirm the fixity of desire over and above external obstacles (the cruelty of Laura); and his imitators were generally inclined to follow suit. The figure occurring in the final position refers to a moment impossible in time, that is along the trajectories (cyclical and linear) of the remainder of the poem:

> Ma io sarò sotterra 'n secca selva,
> e 'l giorno andrà pien di minute stelle,
> prima ch'a si dolce alb 'arrivi 'l sole.

(XXII, 37-39)

(But I will be under the earth in dried wood, and the day will be lit by the tiny stars, before the sun arrives at so sweet a dawn.)

The irreversibility of time here finds compensation in the limitation of events to time. In final position, the adynaton effects a magical invocation to history to abolish itself *in the future.* Final time, after all, begins in the midst of historical time. In the New Testament it is announced to the people via adynata prophesied as wonders to come. In prophecies of the end of the world, it is announced that as the end approaches the year will be shortened, the month too will diminish, and the day will contract. There chaos is to be expected. We are familiar with the notion, from the fishes that remain hanging on the limbs of the trees in the myth of Deucalion, to the mountain that is transplanted into the sea in the Sermon on the Mount of Olives. It must be recognized, however, that in the eschatological context the impossible *becomes possible,* that its "impossibility" must be viewed only as "improbability in nature." Secular imitation of the eschatological use of the adynaton accordingly makes excellent use of the residual implications. This "end" will be survived by the stasis of desire and the constancy of the lover. The adynaton invokes the realization of the impossible. Dante is capable of asserting in an amorous context the impossibilities that ensued upon Exodus. When Israel came out of Egypt, "The sea saw it and fled; / The Jordan turned backward. / The mountains skipped like rams, / the hills like young sheep" (Psalm 114).

> Ma ben ritorneranno i fiumi a' colli
> prima che questo legno molle e verde
> s'infiammi, come suol far belle donna, di me . . .

(But the rivers will return to the hills before this tender green "plant" will burn, as beautiful women do, for me . . .)

Exodus taken in itself and as a type for redemption by Christ is to be understood both as unrepeatable as single event and to be awaited as type, a "natural impossibility" that is nonetheless realizable outside nature. What does not change is the fixity represented by the firmness of a lover's will. Corresponding love and reward could only be entailed by the conflation of all forms in the abyss of another beginning. The adynaton serves to describe present forms by implication of that opposite chaos. It can be a means of describing the actual; the world of chaos (dream, madness) then appears like the reflection or the double of the natural world—the same but reversed. A tension emerges between the ubiquitous consciousness of the possible alterity and the powerlessness to conceive of difference in any way but as a reversed identity.

It is paradoxically only a linear concept of time that makes death a true threat and thereby delineates the human being (the poem's speaker) against the world and the chain of generations. For the medieval poet the vegetable, animal, and human stages of organic life represent three distinctly separate modes of temporality or finiteness, only the last and highest of which actually discloses the relationships of time to death. Natural catastrophe in such a scheme has the significance only of a partial destruction; something of man survives it.

History is abolished in the future, and in Christian terms we cannot speak of "impossibilities," for not only are they possible outside of nature but are awaited by Christendom. Since we conceive of difference by way of identity, the imagery is borrowed from nature: Day and night, summer and winter. But the prophet Zacharias can say that it will be light at eventide in describing a future regeneration of time. For *illud tempus* is situated not only at the beginning of time but also at its end. The paradox of the possibility of the "impossible" suffuses the Christian adynato with a potentiality that exceeds the denotational or referential context.

72

The envisioned end of linear time would bring with it the resorption of opposition, the disappearance of antithesis (expressed along the lines of Laura's love), magically projected into a dimension of futurity. Life *in time* compels the postponement of that union, whereas the end of time would entail not a stoppage but a reversal and recommencement of activity (rivers would flow backward, night become day, light pass from the moon to the sun [CCXXXVII, 16- 18]). An actual regression of forms, no mere chaos, would lead into mythical nonelapsing time. From that point we can imagine only a new linear path, and it is clear that the implication of such a series belongs essentially to cyclical time. However, the possibility of reversal is repeatedly invoked by adynata, implying a twofold motion.

The notion is by no means confined to a Judaeo-Christian context. Plato found the cause of cosmic regression and cosmic catastrophes in a twofold motion of the universe:

> Of this universe of ours, the Divinity now guides its circular revolution entirely, now abandons it to itself, once its revolutions have attained the duration which befits this universe; it then begins to turn *in the opposite direction*, of its own motion.
>
> (Plato, *Timaeus* 38b)

This change of direction is accompanied by gigantic cataclysms: "The greatest destruction, both among animals in general and among the human race, of which, as is fitting, only a few representatives remain." This catastrophe is followed by a paradoxical "regeneration": "The white hair of the aged darkens, while those at the age of puberty begin to lessen in stature day by day, until they return to the size of a newborn infant"; then finally, "still continuing to waste away, they wholly cease to be." Upon this phase ensues the birth of the "Sons of the Earth" (*gegeneis*). During the age of Cronos there are neither savage animals nor enmity among animals. Plato gives a description of the golden age otherwise renowned in pastoral: The fruits of the earth are taken in abundance, the Sons of the Earth sleep naked on the soil with no need for beds because of the mildness of the seasons. In other words, cataclysm is followed by the myth of the primordial paradise. This scheme corresponds to the lover's wish expressed in two of Petrarch's sestinas by adynata (XXII, CCXXXVII).

Apocalyptic prediction, however, determines the consistent futurity of Petrarchan adynata and places them decisively within a Christian framework. To be sure (as Curtius points out), the Virgilian adynata were know in the Middle Ages. In an especially well-known example a shepherd who has lost his beloved declares: Now may the wolf of his own free will flee the sheep, the oak bear golden apples, owls compete with swans in song, . . ." (*Ecl.* VIII, 53-55). The directness of futurity that we find in Petrarch's adynata is missing here. Although he, like Virgil, utilizes the figure to comment on an adverse present, the tone is predictive as well as incantatory:

> ch'allor fia un di' Madonna senza 'l ghiaccio
> dentro, e di for senza l'usata nebbia,
> ch'io vedrò secco il mare e' laghi e i fiumi.
>
> Mentre ch'al mar descenderanno i fiumi
> e le fiere ameranno ombrose valli. . . .

(LXVI, 22-26)

> (for one day my lady will be without her inner ice
> and without her outer customary cloud —
> when I shall see the sea dry, and the lakes and the rivers.
>
> As long as the sea receives the rivers
> and the beasts love shady valleys,)

Again:

> Allor saranno i miei pensieri a riva
> che foglia verde non si trovi in lauro;
> quando avrò queto il core, asciutto gli occhi,
> vedrem ghiacciare il foco, arder la neve. . . .

(XXX, 7-9)

> (Then my thoughts will have come to shore
> when green leaves are not to be found on a laurel;
> when I have a quiet heart and dry eyes
> we shall see the fir freeze, and burning snow;)

As these examples show, Petrarch did not necessarily situate the adynaton in the tornada. Nor is it always clearly distinguishable as a figure from the antithesis in general. The line between paradox and reversal is sometimes blurred; here it is to be discovered in the active future tense (*vedrem*), which implies a palinodic process realizable in the imagination and hence not entirely "impossible."

We are so informed when in sestina CCXXXIX Petrarch declares the autonomy of poetry: "Nulla al mondo è che non possano i versi." (There is nothing in the world that cannot be done by verses.) This sestina contains the single example in the nine poems of an adynaton not given in the future tense. Petrarch here draws on a metaphor of Arnaut Daniel that became Arnaut's hallmark through its recurrence in three of his eighteen known cansos. It is transposed into the context of the sestina's tornada, anticipated by the last line of strophe

VI ("'e col bue zoppo andrem cacciando l'auro" [we shall go with a lame ox hunting the breeze]):

> In rete accolgo l'aura, e 'n ghiaccio i fiori,
> e 'n versi tento sorda e rigida alma,
> che ne forza d'Amor prezza ne note.
>
> (CCXXXIX 36, 37-39)

(In a net I catch the breeze and on ice flowers, and in verses I woo a deaf and rigid soul.)

Arnaut identified himself with this image in one of the relatively rare instances of troubadour signature:

> Leu sui Arnautz qu' amas l'aura,
> e chatz la lebre ab lo bou
> E nadi contra suberna.
>
> ("En cest sonet coind'e leri," 43-45)

(I am Arnaut who gathers the breeze and hunts the hare with an ax and swims against the tide [current].)

Petrarch uses *l'aura* "breeze" for a word play on the name of his beloved, and his pun extends to the *rete*, "net," that would form the second and third syllables of Laura's name (in Provençal, *Laureta*). The borrowing from Arnaut, whose imagery in a number of songs including the "chansso d'ongla e d'oncle" must have seemed to Petrarch like a huge adynaton, adduces literary authority (albeit in the form of the vernacular) to argue for the limitless powers of verse.

The metaphors from Arnaut that appear in this sestina are developed and flanked by analogies in a sonnet:

> Beato in sogno, e di languir contento,
> d'abbracciar l'ombre e sequir l'aura estiva,
> nuoto per mar che non à fondo o riva,
> solco onde, e 'n rena fondo, e scrivo in vento;
> ....
> ed una cerva errante e fugitiva
> caccio con un bue zoppo e 'nfermo e lento.
>
> (CCXII, 1-4, 7-8)

(Blessed in sleep and satisfied to languish, to embrace shadows, and to pursue the summer breeze, I swim through a sea that has no floor or shore, I plow the waves and found my house on sand and write on the wind;

and I pursue a wandering, fleeing doe with a lame, sick, slow ox.)

It is important to note that the "impossibility" quotient of the images is considerably diminished in the sonnet, although here too the Catullan allusion to writing in the wind heightens the atmosphere of privileged literariness. The source of the diminution is to be found in the qualifying *in sogno* "in dream," as well as in the numerous adjectives Petrarch adds to the "ox" image and in his transformation of Arnaut's hare into a deer (suggesting that the objects alone would lack sufficient paradoxical value). Whereas the sonnet posits a special realm of dreaming, the sestina accords privilege to "verse" itself, explicitly describing its Orphic aspect ("e li aspidi incantar sanno in lor note," line 29). The allusion ot the miraculous power of poetry is again drawn directly from the matrix of Virgilian adynata, the *Eighth Eclogue*. In accordance with Orphic legend the pattern of reversal found in the adynaton would operate in its most extreme force, as Petrarch says in his double sestina (CCCXXXIII), the one most overtly concerned with pure form:

> Or avess'io un sì pietoso stile
> che Laura mia potesse torre a Morte
> come Euridice Orfeo suo senza rime.
>
> (CCCXXXII, 54-56)

> (Would I had so sorrowful a style
> that I could win my Laura back from Death
> as Orpheus won his Eurydice without rhymes.)

A number of elements in the passage call for comment. Not least of these, together with the implicit statement of the power of song to realize impossibilities, is the comparison of the poet with Orpheus and Laura with Eurydice. It is the linkage of mythical possibility with human, historical possibility that renders impossible Petrarch's wish. In the suggestion of the deed of bringing back the dead, the idea is beyond the pale of reality. Within the freedoms accorded by poetry, however, Petrarch is indeed returning Laura from the dead. In the poem all is possible, even to the point of realizing the virtual aspect of his Arnaldian pun: *In rete accolgo Laura* (CCXXXVII).

More than this is implied, however, by the link with myth. We have to take into account the far-reaching and diverse connotative power of Orphic legend for Petrarch. In Virgil's *Eclogues,* Orpheus represents, together with the poet Linus, the tradition of antique poetry that Virgil, poet triumphant, will surpass:

> Non me carminibus vincet haec Thracius Orpheus,
> Nec Linus, huic mater quamius atque, hic pater adsit
> Orphei Calliopae, hinc formosus Apollo
>
> (*Ecl.* IV, 55-57)

In the *Georgics,* on the other hand, Orpheus is transformed into a symbol of defeat for the poet. There the passage substitutes for an earlier one that had dealt with Egypt and its first governor under Rome, Virgil's dear friend Gallus, who being suspected of disloyalty to Augustus, took his own life. The eulogy of C. Gallus, then, influenced Virgil's treatment of the myth. By placing Orpheus at the end of his *Georgics,* Virgil situated him at the symbolic center of his work, between the *Bucolics* and the *Aeneid:* "Orpheaque in medio posuit" (And he placed Orpheus in the center [*Buc.* III, 46]).

The tradition inherited by Virgil had emphasized, in the Orphic cults, the descent to the underworld, but it was Virgil's innovation to judge the incantatory power of his poetry as overcoming both Hades and love. In the *Bucolics,* Orpheus emerges as the ideal poet whom Virgil aspires to imitate and surpass: the pacifier of nature personifying the cosmic power of poetry. Included within this large charcterization is the definition of the poet's function in terms of the erotic quest.

From his point of view, we can extrapolate the ambiguous state of Orpheus as a representation of the power and also the defeat of poetry (a function similar to Dante's interpretation of Virgil in the *Commedia*). Virgil emphasized the mortal element of Orpheus, his fragility and imminent destruction by dismemberment in the *Georgics,* and in the Bucolics gave a triumphant version, from which the Middle Ages chiefly derived their interpretations of the myth. For Augustine, and still for Thomas Aquinas, Orpheus is a philosopher as well as a poet. St. Thomas links his name to Linus (based on the reference to the *Fourth Eclogue*):

Orpheus fuit unus de primis philosophis qui erant quasi poetae theologi. . . . Et iste Orpheus primo induxit homines ad habitandum simul . . . ita quod homines bestiales et solitarios reduceret ad civilitatem. Et propter hoc dicitur de eo quod fuit optimus citharedus in tantum quod fecit lapides saltare, destita fuit pulcher concionator quod homines lapideus emollivit. . . .
(St. Thomas, *Commentaries on De Anima,* I, lect. 12)

(Orpheus was one of the first philosophers who were like poet-theologians. . . . And this Orpheus first induced men to a similar life . . . in that he brought bestial and solitary men back to civilization. And on this account it is said of him that he was an excellent player, for he made the stones leap, and an excellent singer, for he softened men of stone. . . .

This role of mediator between man and civilization has its source in Ovid's *Metamorphoses* (X, 1-85). It is Ovid's version to which Dante refers in his *Convivio* (II, iii, 3). Dante follows Thomas Aquinas in making Orpheus and Linus poet-theologians. They are coupled

77

again in the *Commedia*, where we find the single mention of Orpheus' name (*Inf.* IV, 140), and there, as the context of Limbo tells us, he is a man and a pagan whose fate and fame depend on his poetic accomplishments. The literary figure emerges denuded of religious or miraculous powers, conferring his influence on future evocations of Orpheus.

Exegesis has always demonstrated the elasticity of the myth, nowhere more evident than in medieval iconography. On one hand, a monotheistic Orpheus is to be found in the *Testament of Orpheus,* a poem which makes him into a devotee of one deity who is at once Zeus and Jehovah (Friedman 1970). The same Orpheus, disciple of Moses, appears in the writings of early Christian apologists (who seek to prove thereby the anteriority of Judaic to Hellenic culture). Early Christian funerary art yields numerous examples in stone and mosaic of a Christ-Orpheus, *pastor* of souls. Within this comparison there would appear the contrast between Christ (more than man) and Orpheus; yet apologists concede that Christ completed the work of the explorer of Hades, thus making Christ into a new Orpheus.

On the other hand, it is hardly possible to recapitulate here the mass of allegorical interpretations that followed on those of Boethius in the *Consolatio philosophiae.* This is the first Latin writing that develops an ethical interpretation of the story of Orpheus and Eurydice in the underworld. Its interpretation struck a vein, however, that would determine much of the structure of the *Rerum vulgarum fragmenta.* For Boethius, Orpheus attained a degree of supernatural light but was irremediably attracted by material objects and therefore arrested in his spiritual progress. From this Platonic perspective the misadventure of Orpheus reveals the threatening power of the passions over the superior aspect of the soul.

The Platonistic exegesis of the myth is taken up by Boethius' medieval commentators—Rémy d'Auxerre, Guillaume de Conches, Nicholas Trivet—who add their variants, including details taken from Virgil's *Georgics* and subjected (in their turn) to allegorical interpretations. It is possible for Pierre Bersuire to discover a recapitulation of Christian history in the story of Orpheus and Eurydice, drawing on the continuity of Neoplatonic tradition. The legend is explained by Guillaume de Conches in terms of a conflict between Orpheus, who embodies the *nous,* and Eurydice, who embodies the powers of the passions (*epithymia*). At the same time, Nicholas Trivet emphasizes Orpheus' eloquence as a cardinal feature of his *sapientia.* The ambivalence of the tradition becomes apparent as regards Orpheus the singer. It is less so in the case of Eurydice, who emerges in Boethius and his commentators (and in clerical tradition generally) as the incarnation of concupiscence opposed to reason.

A reciprocal influence of the two main strains of interpretation is certainly to be discerned in Petrarch. As is usual for him, allegory is perhaps honored more as a hovering absence. Yet the cited passage goes further. It stresses Orpheus' eloquence, which could reverse the process of death (or expunge adynaton) while coupling the name of Laura yet again with a projection of the lover's desire ("Laura *mia*"), which easily surmounts the obstacle of her death. The aspirations of the wish, however, go beyond these conventional limits, as we read *rime* in its combined medieval acceptance of "poetry" and "rime." The analysis of the entire poem invites understanding of its polysemy: *rime* is twice opposed as poetry to *versi* as Latin is contrasted with the vernacular (strophe I, III); in cases other than the cited passage it is bound to generic adjectives or simple prepositions. However, when Petrarch speaks of his *roche rime* "raucous rhymes" (line 32), it is a reference to the unity of form and content familiar to readers like Petrarch, of Dante's *petrose* and of Provençal lyric. Commentators have generally understood *senza rime* to mean only "unrhymed poetry" in the fashion of the Greek verse. The distinction between Latin and vernacular poetry is made in the first strophe:

> . . . . i soavi sospiri, e'l dolce stile
> che solea resonare *in versi e'n rime*. . . .
>
> (CCCXXXII, 3-4)

(and gentle sighs and a sweet style that used to resound in verses and rhymes.)

If we read the Orpheus lines on this level, what emerges is a wish to bring Laura back to life in free verse, that is, in a style that presumably would convert its immanent obstacles from rhyme to meter. If we read *rime* as "poetry," however, the multifold meaning gives us "without poetry." The impossible would, then, be accomplished not even by poetry but by an act of overreaching resolution, the arrow of desire hitting its mark without any mediate impediment. Language would be separable from being, and in that ultimate impossibility the poem would achieve the realization of what holds sway over the poet, though it could not be expressed in words.

The comparison of Petrarch/Laura and Orpheus/Eurydice proclaims a reversal of time analogous to natural cataclysms. The Christian poet must write in the ever-present awareness that outside the fabulous precincts of classical myth, resurrection will ensue only upon catastrophe. Petrarch's renowned "ambiguity" operates in his chosen optative form of verbal expression, "gaining time" (as it were) in the mediating zone of fantasy.

79

An instance approaching adynaton is introduced indirectly into a single sonnet (CCXVIII) that anticipates the death of Laura and assimilates it to natural disaster. A personified Love speaks of the age of Laura as synchronic with the life of virtue; and predicts that on her death his reign will cease. Petrarch elaborates:

> Come natura al ciel la luna e'l sole,
> a l'aere i venti, a la terra erbe e fronde,
> a l'uomo e l'intelletto e le parole,
> ed al mar ritollesse i pesci e l'onde:
> tanto e più fien le cose ascure e sole,
> se morte li occhi suoi chiude ed asconde.

(CCXVIII, 9-16)

> (As if Nature were to take away the sun and the moon from the heavens, the winds from the air, from the earth grass and leaves, from man intellect and words,
> from the sea the fish and the waves: so dark and darker will things be and deserted, if Death closes and hides her eyes.)

This is—with the exception of the Arnaldian allusion of sonnet CCXIII—the single example of Petrarchan adynaton that does not occur in a sestina. A far more frequent and somewhat allied figure is oxymoron, which entails opposition rather than reversal. Oxymoron provides a purely formal solution to the discord of opposites. Departing from canonic oxymoron, Petrarch's verbal oppositions are not necessarily polar: *dolce nemica* (CLXXIX, 2) is a possible, albeit elusive conjunction; *un'uom di ghiaccio al sole* (a man of ice in the sun [LXXIII]) is also possible though short-lived. Sometimes an etymologically motivated opposition will increase the degree of polarity; thus *umil fera* (CLII), where the secondary meaning of *fera* "fierce" brings the coupling of terms into a higher degree of privative opposition. Temporal stasis is entailed, evading a substantial rapprochement of the terms. However, the chasm between oxymoron and adynaton, which are figures allied by their articulation of "impossibilities," is not merely formal. The adynaton is to be understood from the standpoint of form as not expressing impossibility, for its temporality easily allows of a graspable sense. With regard to substance, the "impossibility" quotient of adynaton can be determined only through a hypostasis of the "present" in time. As has been noted, Petrarch's *impossibilia* have their precedent in apocalyptic prediction. The "end of the world" or "the world upside down" are, by contrast with the terms of oxymoron, easily imaginable.

Other Petrarchan paradoxes clearly stand apart from adynaton. The frequent image, the light emanating from Laura *che fa sparir il sole* (makes the sun disappear), along with other hyperboles, cannot be confused with adynaton largely because of their avowed subjectivity (as in *quella che anzi vespro a me fa sera,* 'that she who before vespers gives me evening' [CCXXXVII, 33]). It might be argued that subjectivity also privileges oxymoron:

> Amor mi sprona *in un tempo,* ed affrena,
> assecura e spaventa, arde ed agghiaccia,
> gradisce e sdegna, a sè mi chiama e scaccia. . . .
>
> (CLXXVIII, 1-3)

(Love at the same time spurs me and reins me in, reassures and terrifies me, burns and freezes me, is kind and disdainful to me, calls me to him and drives me away.)

A crucial difference resides in the articulation, within the oxymoron, of a simultaneous privative opposition.

We have seen that the *impossibilities* of the adynaton are not to be taken for granted, that *sub specie aesternitatis* they are possible. The pattern is not one of privative opposition but of syntagmatically conceived *reversal,* therefore comparable to the pattern of apocalyptic prediction. No example of a nonpredictive adynaton is to be discovered in the sestinas. The typical form is given in:

> Ma pria fia 'l verno la stagion de' fiori
> ch'amor fiorisca in quella nobil alma,
> che non curò gia mai rime nè versi.
>
> (CCXXXIX, 10-12)

(But winter will be the season of flowers before love flowers in that noble soul that never cared for rhymes or verses.)

The distinction between *rime* and *versi* appears here as well as in CCCXXXII, again implying an allied distinction between rhymed and unrhymed poetry (also Latin and the vernacular).

There is more to this pairing than synonymic iteration. The poet may well have attempted to characterize the status of identical rhyme, unique as the structural basis of the sestina. Elsewhere it is clear that Petrarch, like Dante and his Provençal predecessors, easily accepts identical rhyme within the canon. One example:

> Di tai quattro faville, e non già sole,
> nasce 'l gran foco di ch'io vivo ed ardo,
> che son fatto un augel notturno al sole.
>
> (CLXV, 14-16)

(From those four sparks, and not those alone, is born the great fire on which I live and burn, for I have become a nocturnal bird in the sun.)

The semantic association between *faville* "sparks" and one aspect of *sole* "sun" heralds the actual appearance of *sole* in that meaning, heightening the phonic redundancy.

The play with sound and sense is no less fundamental to Petrarchan poetic language than redundancy itself. Yet it is this very play that reminds poet and reader of the perfect phonic identity of this kind of rhyme. The inability of his rime and versi to persuade Laura is a recurrent theme in the sestinas (CCXXXVII, CCXXXIX, CCCXXXII), and we have seen it paired with the impermanence of Orphic persuasion. The colligation of rime and versi keeps the secondary meaning before us: rhyme and free verse, Latin and vernacular, all encompassed in poetry. Still the peculiarity of identical rhyme evades such characterization as rhyme pure and simple.

A basic poetic function of the rhyme-word is to delineate the architecture of the strophe and to demarcate thereby a portion of the lyric text as a closed economy, founded on the asymmetrical but bilateral relationship of sound and sense.

Identical rhyme, however, eludes the evocative processes created in rhyme. It can point to increasingly diminutive differences of meaning while retaining a perfect phonetic resemblance of the terms. The role of syntactic difference is accentuated, since within the context of exact rhyme syntactic differences appear more marked. The strophes of a sestina would be called, in the terms of the Provençal coiners, *coblas singulars* — "singular" stanzas with "orphaned" rhymes. They point ever outward toward the rest of the poem, demanding its acceptance as an unbroken entity, capable of exploring the significances attached in context to any number of formal configurations.

In rhyme differences in meaning tend to appear dissimulated in the identity of sound. This condition suggests a possibly spurious resemblance of objects, insistently murmuring likeness of substance. Within the poem, this asymmetry introduces the perceptual possibility of imaginative association of the two objects rhymed. The connection is no less tenuous, perhaps more, than that of punning, which epitomizes one possibility of identical rhyme. The same spurious objectivity hovers over the phonetic association whether or not an etymological relationship actually exists.

In the case of identical rhyme, similarity or dissimilarity of the referents reveals itself as a question of degree. It can be invoked in semantic near-blends or denied in the case of pure homonymy. The same rhyme does not absolutely represent the same object, concept, or relation but more cunningly invokes it. The gift of virtuality is conserved. More than other species of rhyme, it plumbs the semantic possibilities of the words involved. Every instance, then, is a self-renewing context.

In the Petrarchan sestina, repetition, both terminally and inter-linearly, usurps the function normally fulfilled by rhyme. Even as we acknowledge the cardinal importance of cumulative association and of the fusions entered into by words that are components of several descriptive systems, multiple reference is secondary to the phonetic similarity of sound. Petrarchan terms represent far more than opposition and equation, whether or not equality of sound is present. Commentators have been content to analyze Petrarch's lexicon in terms of contrast and equivalence. However, the shifting action of the adjacent semantic context and the seeming effects of equivocation issuing from the simultaneous reception of two or more meanings coalesce; the effect is semantic dilatation (as in the case of *acque,* whose quasi-Biblical vastness engulfs whatever pond or sea we have to understand as the most specific referent of the moment). In the face of this condition, we are compelled to admit phonetic recurrence as primary poetic fact.

In Petrarchan song, the natural world often is transformed into an instrument of echo. The poem's speaker expects the sonority of his words to rebound from mountains, valleys, or streams; the echo-effects would constitute a species of repetition. This auditory image is closely associated with the emphasis on forests, valleys, thickets, and other natural enclosures that can serve as echo chambers (Damon 1961). Nature's reply in such cases would be a replication similar to the repetition of words within the poem. It does not, however, carry the mnemonic value of repetition in the poem.

Within the sestina, the possibility of understanding the polysemous import of a word depends on the acceptance of sameness of sound. The equivocation temporarily created by the intertwining of several meanings is contingent on an identity that is spurious with respect to meaning, and perfect with respect to sound. It would appear that the clash of senses is inevitable, since the syntagm is composed of words in partially positive or negative conformity with the preceding word. The resultant semantic dilatation modifies the sign itself as well as the entire semantic field.

In the case of identical rhyme, additionally, the consideration of the "counterlogical" properties of rhyme (Wimsatt 1954: 106) acquires new force, since the element of pure coincidence of sound is drastically reduced. The perfect phonetic identity acts to limit the possibilities of interpretation, of the linkages among rhyme-words, and between rhyme-words and their neighbors. The identical rhyme-word actually provides an extra measure of information by reducing the number of possible interpretations. Whereas rhyme can cement the meaning of either of its terms by their mutual association, identical rhyme reminds us continually of some lost or omitted resemblance between referents. Every reemergence of phonetic identity is crowned by an aura of separate sense. The sestina provides a maximal reflection on the nature of this fact, as it coerces meditation upon repetition.

The effect of identical rhyme in the sestina is, at the same time, semantically cumulative. There is an overlapping of senses between the various instances of a word. It can be the repetition of near-repetition of *meaning itself* that attracts our attention. In other poetic forms, such as the *triolet,* where the repetition of words is essential, a strict reproduction of a *whole phrase* produces a more static effect on a scale ranging from an imagined reproduction of a whole poem to that of one word. Identical rhyme, then, can be a logical as well as a musical repetition.

Through the signifying material of the poem the correspondences created by sheer repetition of end-words occur in response to a growing and sharpened expectation. In regard to the latter, however, the challenges of the sestina are not to be underestimated. The sestina was after all created by a poet whom Dante praised for his seamless strophic schemes—that is, for the absence of singsong or closely placed or facile rhymes. The sestina defies, as do Arnaut's songs, the abilities of any memory that depends excessively on rhyme. The game of suggestion concentrates on the capacity of the word for multiplication, thus on its perpetual otherness of sense. And yet the memory is constantly brought into play. Any expansion of sense departs from the identity of the phonetic manifestation, on the level of the single lexical unit. As the order changes, so does the relationship of each word to the context.

On the level of lexical units, the resonances with which the key terms of his vocabulary are charged through sheer frequency of usage demonstrate that words alone, deprived of context, do not attain a meaning of value. The recurrent imagery of his living words, working with an entire spectrum of connotation, displays the movement between the whole and its parts; the poem becomes a world of reciprocal relations. No poet shows better than Petrarch how the word changes, dilates, renews itself, and acquires the polyvalence that epitomizes the poetic process. The predominance of memory in Petrarch's poetics entails the choice of the substantive over the verb in key positions and accords "rhyme" status in the sestina only to nouns. This practice adds a further restriction on usable poetic material; simpler variations are based on the use of lexical terms in more than one grammatical class.

Sestina CCCXXXII shows just how deeply Petrarch was able to integrate the possibilities of intensification through repetition within poetic structure. In this his double sestina, the point at which the doubling begins is marked by the replication of the word *morte* (previously privileged as a rhyme-word): "né contra Morte spero altro che morte" VII, 6). The doubling appears internally with respect to chronology. Later, in strophe VIII, the process itself replicated to special effect inasmuch as the eighth position signifies a surpassing not only of the number (seven) of strophes comprising the sestina but of mortal life itself (in the numerical symbolism known to Petrarch): "Morte m'à morto, e sola pò far Morte / ch'i' torni a riveder quel viso lieto" (Death has killed me, and only Death has the power to make me see again that glad face [strophe VIII, 18-19]). The paradoxes of the lines encompass the semantics of Petrarchan eternity. The force that outlives death *may* thereby unite the poet with his beloved.

The replication involved in the double sestina continues throughout; identical rhyme demands constant replication. The tour de force is merely a repetition of the patter, a "doppiare lo stile," (redoubling the style [strophe VII, 3])—the thirty-ninth line, the concluding line of a single sestina. Petrarch enables *doppiare* to maintain the requisite polysemy of both quantitative and qualitative increase.

The retelling of myth is to be viewed in the same terms. Its form and meaning coincide with his techniques of lexical repetition on a far greater scale. Petrarch does not lack precedent outside poetry: Synesius, who speculates on the analogy between the history of his epoch and the myth of Osiris and Typhon, offers the following reflections:

Why so troubling a likeness? It has no cause other than the unit of a wholly perfect world in which a close dependence necessarily unites the part which we inhabit and the heavenly bodies that surround us. When the heavenly bodies conclude their cycle and resume their course . . . the return of their influence restores the conjunctures of former times on this earth.
.(Synesius, "On Providence," PL
LXVI, cit. van der Leeuw [1957: 323])

Accordingly, Petrarch suggests the possibility in his anniversary poems that deal with the present moment and with his mythicized moment of enamorment, of maintaining a shared status of both "times." Therein the historical aspect can be elided in order to confer mythical status on the past. But the continuing life of enamorment is claimed to nurture an eternal possibility of repetition. The linear passage of time is challenged in the memory, "dont le rôle serait de conserver exceptionnellement telles ou telles parties du passé en les emmagasinant dans une espèce de boîte" (whose role it would be to conserve, by way of exception, such-and-such parts of the past, storing them in a kind of box [Bergson 1972: 890]). The revelations of memory are selectively produced and woven into the *bel velo* of poetry. At the same time we are made poignantly aware of memory's incompleteness as a cognition of something absent, of how precariously it is relied on for information about the past, of how incomplete a revelation it affords.

As Contini points out, Petrarch's adjectives and verbs acquire a value similar to that of nouns (Contini 1973: 418). While adjectives become epithets (not predicates), verbs in their turn have a metaphoric import that is quite devoid of active energy (he cites the examples *tolse, colse, diè*). Otherwise they are excluded from any nonlyric context, appearing often in the optative mood or in contrary-to-fact subjunctive clauses or as infinitive. Everywhere existents supplant occurrents, and incisive, stringent raw material is converted into lyrical, fluent discursiveness. The paucity of information that would be simultaneously clear and unforeseeable functions as the means whereby a connotative structure recreates and fosters myth. If "la façon la plus simple pour un poète d'imposer ses connotations est évidemment de créer des contextes qui correspondent aux situations qui sont à leur source" (Martinet 1967: 129), then this is "nonfunctional" language. Indeed, it presents us with a linguistic indeterminacy that resides in the improbability of ascertaining the content of what is signified. The context of an utterance extends to the entirety of the *Canzoniere,* the immanent content of "the poem itself" being succeeded by the transcendental one of other, prior Petrarchan experience. The quantity of potentially identifiable material used is small in proportion to the number of poetic "signals" that the reader can soon identify. The crux of Petrarchan language is to be found in its tonality, in the cumulative effect of key terms and turns of phrase that may conceal a complex field of semantic values. We can distinguish them not only by frequency but by stress. Thus it is possible to disengage Laura-*l'aura* as a complex situation at the core of sestina CCXXXIX, with its subsidiaries *auro, aurora, lauro,* in an unbroken paronomastic series, and simultaneously to perceive these sounds as phonetically symbolic of the beloved "L'aura de' sospir," (line 30). The boundary between allegory and allusion becomes obscured; or we may say that Petrarch understands allegory as allusion, with a resultant depletion of the signified. Prevalent in the dialectic is the sense of irreversibility, however, that characterizes the poetic along with all other human activity and marks it as unrepeatable.

It is just this irreversibility as realized in his poems that provides a crucial qualifier to the notion of Petrarch as a poet of fixity. Perhaps such awareness underlies Petrarch's reminiscences on the lines of another poet of fixity, Arnaut Daniel, in sestina CCXXXIX ("In rete accolgo l'aura," from Arnaut: "Ieu sui Arnautz q'amas l'aura"), and his exclusion of lines from Arnaut's sestina, which takes no self-conscious account of temporality.

The same distinction between fixity and repetition must apply to the well-known and much commented on phenomenon of synonymic (and antithetical) pairs in Petrarch's work. The procedure is extremely common in troubadour poetry from its known inception forward. When Contini takes it to be proof of the prevalence of rhythm over semanticity and, therefore, a part of Petrarch's "rhythmic dominant," it would be appropriate to recall the intimacy of words and melody in Petrarch's predecessors and to consider the musical utility of synonymity. At the same time, we must concede the emphatic quality of such iteration and its power to impart to the poetic line an intensification of sense. Then from the cumulative replication of individual structures matched with their likes at the same and other levels, one can "abstract a more general pattern which is itself not describable in linguistic terms" (Fowler 1971: 235).

Strings of apparent semantic equivalences are typical of Petrarchan procedure. About 15 percent of his sonnets (Alonso 1961) have a bilateral structure in the last line, which is the locus of emphasis; and Petrarch's system has been described as "fundamentally binary." Syntactically and rhythmically, as well as phonetically, immanent dichotomy or correlation suggests that, for example, since rhymes tend to be nouns there is a strong probability of another noun in the same line. This correlation may be termed a miniature parallelism, but only in the superficial sense in which symmetry in poetic language is amenable to discussion. It is not the "sistema equilibrato" of Petrarchan poetry that creates resolution and repose in the poem. Rather, dialectical movement ends at a third term. Syntactic suspension and separation influence the impact of members of binary schemes, as does the habitual articulation of synonymous or antonymous chains in a continuous series without apparent nexus, where images are composed into an organic whole only a posteriori. The retrospective demands of the poetry tend to subvert the equilibrium that it pleases some of Petrarch's most expert readers to discern everywhere in his work.

Equivalence can be said to exist only outside poetry itself. In the awareness of temporal movement we can, therefore, posit the presence of an existential judgment of value in the poems. *Cielo* and *terra* each seem to hold an equal share of the poet's mind, but if cielo did not have the greater part, it is quite likely that this poetry would not exist at all. One must recognize that structures of repetition are structures of intensification, that the same word is never heard twice, and that Petrarch's awareness of this fact lies at the heart of his uncommon success with the quintessential poetic form of repetition, the sestina.

Petrarch's experiments with identical rhyme represent another attempt to transcend duality. It is exemplified in the sestina's "seamless" internal logic. In that logic, nevertheless, is a constant tension between sameness and difference, never to be resolved in the repose of perfect identification. It is important that Petrarch's adynata follow the pattern of the reversal of nature; this too disputes the e ineluctability of duality and stasis. Reversal would end in self-neutralization, and all that had gone forward in time would obliterate itself, leaving identity.

The adynaton, then, in its close relation to Petrarch's sestina, denotes a substantial stoppage and reverse movement of nature, whereas in the poem it furnishes end-stoppage for what would otherwise be a perpetual linear movement of cycles. Time, in substance, is linear—in any poem and in the referential context of the Christian poet. Its movement will, therefore, produce history and novelty. Whether or not it appears in final position, the adynaton predicts an end. In this respect it epitomizes Platonic desire superseded by Christian reality. It would be a trivialization of the problem not to note that the adynata bespeak a conspicuous absence of God.

Petrarchan adynata function most prominently as critical points between the realms of the possible and the impossible. The futurity of adynaton is possessed within the poetic matrix of a magic force that underscores the special status of poetry as speech act even as it evokes a myth-bound context. Petrarch reminds us simultaneously of the psychological distance of his implementation of myth from mythicized history and of the hospitality of fiction to mythical resetting. The Ovidian account already makes us aware that the myth-ridden structure of primitive societies is actually at odds with his retelling. Petrarchan comparison augments that divergence to the next power. It is in keeping with his use of adynata in the sestina that the overwhelming majority of impossibilia in classical poetry produced broad generalities, often reduced, even, to the discursive principle "All things will soon come to pass which I once said were impossible; nothing is incredible," enunciated by Ovid (*Tristia* I, 8, 5-8).

The lack of specificity in Petrarchan adynata is certainly apparent in the examples Petrarch may have drawn directly from Ovid (the most conspicuous of ancient poets in their use). "The land will be studded with stars and the plowman will till the sky" (*Tristia* I, 8, 3). The latter may have given rise to Petrarch's "e'l giorno andrà pien di minute stelle," which substitutes the temporal (day/night) antithesis for Ovid's land/sky. Porphyron says that an adynaton of Horace (*Odes*, I, 29, 11: "quis neget arduis / pronos relabi posse rivos / montibus et Tiberim reverti . . . — "Who can discount stories of streams that mount backwards up mountains to their source, or the Tiber reversing its course") is proverbial. In our own culture the image of rivers flowing backward or "upstream" is variously derived. Petrarch uses the figure to describe movements of reversal from which perpetuity is said to ensue.

What is the logical status of this "always"? It has never been proved possible to devise a consistent logical system embodying the assertion that time will have an end. The "end of time" as foretold in Revelations 10 has mystical truth, to be sure, but no intelligibility.

In the Petrarchan sestina the persistent scheme of invariance encompassing transformation invites the ensuing speculation on the endlessness of time. It is an invitation that some of Petrarch's less inspired imitators willingly accepted.

Unlike many classical adynata, Petrarch's are based on the interdependence of two conditions, both of which he appears to regard as impossible. (Things or conditions assumed to be impossible would prove true sooner than the realization of Laura's love or his own abandonment of her.) Fundamental to Petrarch's poetic schemes, one part of the figure is balanced against and measured in terms of th other; they thus reveal a strong mutual dependency. In this way his lover's condition is rendered universal and exemplary. The persistent speculative question of whether temporality eludes linearity, the nagging consciousness that unlike the poem time has no understandable end, ultimately creates (more than does the absence of a God posited as responsible for reversal) the sense of a cyclicity that poetry or any other human endeavor is incapable of translating into action.

In the light of considerations of probability, the persistent future tense of Petrarchan adynata emerges with a particular poignancy. All the modulations of inference, the provisionality of conjecture, of a dauntless hope through which consciousness maps its future are due to verbal manipulation of the unknown. Millenarian fantasy provides a model of a mythical grammar of futurity, though it is scarcely more nonfactual or counterfactual than more general frameworks of factuality expressed in the future tense. Dante's Hell is a grammar without futures; the extension of causality to consequence does not operate there. But the enunciation of the future by the prophets of the Old Testament makes that future alterable. If man repents and changes his conduct, God can bend the arc of time out of foreseen shape, for there is no immutability except in God's own being. The force and axiomatic certitude of the Old Testament prophet's prediction lies precisely in the possibility that the prediction may go unfulfilled: Behind every prediction of disaster there stands a concealed alternative. Whereas Messianic prophecy came to render the will of God enigmatic and the prophet more fully entered on the function of glossing what God did rather than foretelling what He will do, even then the kind of uncertainty exemplified in prophecy could not be compared with the "lacunae of misunderstanding" left by oracular prophecy to the pagen world. The prophesying poet participates in this blending of open message and hermetic code. He can make use of persuasive powers while stressing the optative, indefinite character of futurity.

In accordance with the renewal implicit in future-tense propositions, Petrarch's exclusive choice of adynata expressed through this tense is inextricably interwoven with historical awareness, anticipation, and forward inference. Futurity confers upon them a crucial aptitude for survival, what Ibsen called the "Life-lie" — the dynamism of consoling illusion. Therein nihilistic temptation, akin in Petrarch to the idea of the last great repose that haunted Freud in *Beyond the Pleasure Principle,* is checked. Petrarch's adynata, even if by incantation alone, function within a futurity that must be conceded to the realm of the nonfactual utterance. As such they illustrate the freedom of the poetic word to go beyond and against "that which is the case":

> A qualunque animal che alberga in terra
> Tempo è da travagliare quanto è il sole . . .
>
> (XXII, 1-2)

(For whatever animals dwell on earth, except the few that hate the sun . . .)

The self-perpetuation and life of animals takes place within a constant present. The opening lines of Petrarch's sestina XXII (which first engages the round of terminal words) initiate a contrast of animal with human life that will culminate in the adynaton. There the presence and presentness of the poet's own certain death provide the poetic occasion to make free of time and to reverse its course.

Chapter 4

Dante; Five Sestinas by Petrarch

1. "Al poco giorno e al gran cerchio d'ombra"

No single phenomenon accounts for Dante's curiously static realization of temporal succession in his sestina. The *stantia* exactly defines the perimeter of the lover's consciousness and the psychological barrier that separates his submission to Love from the deeper influence of more fundamentally natural forces. Temporal notations are superimposed on each other in an achronic segmentation that displays virtually no organic principle of succession. The imagery of spatial restriction is omnipresent. Bypassing the process in the corse of which significance is fixed, it invites the establishment of a set inventory of significance within spaces marked out by sacred confines. Time arranged entirely within the coordinates "before" and "after" is eschatological time's obverse, motionless and waiting. Throughout his four poems addressed to a "stony" lady, with the *senhal* (or pseudonym) *Petra*, Dante experiments with the removal of poems from temporal flux, and both constriction and iteration work toward that end.

As in the misnamed "double sestina" (hence not discussed here; see Jeanroy 1913), the poem explores certain near-emblematic metaphors of time without plumbing the word or word-order for multiple senses. Cosmic rhythm is described in terms of the conventions of winter and spring, which counter one another in alternation. Four of six full strophes display maximal mobility: they could be exchanged, as to sense, with any other of them that produce a satisfactory closure of the series (II-V). As in the kind of Provençal lyric against which Arnaut aimed his seamless poems, conquest of organic form takes a backward step. But for the rhyme-word order we would be at pains to determine what comes first. (Durling's excellent translation follows:)

Al poco giorno e al gran cerchio d'ombra
son giunto, lasso — ed al bianchir de' colli
quando si perde lo color ne l'erba;
e 'l mio disio però non canglia il verde,
5 sì è barbato ne la dura petra
che parla e sente come fosse donna.

Similemente questa nova donna
si sta gelata come neve a l'ombra;
che non la move, se non come petra,
10 il dolce tempo che riscalda i colli
e che li fa tornar di bianco in verde,
perche li copre di fioretti e d'erba.

Quand'ella ha in testa una ghirlanda d'erba,
trae de la mente nostra ogn'altra donna;
15 perche si mischia il crespo giallo e 'l verde
sì bel, ch'Amor li viene a stare a l'ombra,
che m'ha serrato intra piccioli colli
più forte assai che la calcina petra.

La sua bellezza ha più vertù che petra,
20 e 'l colpo suo non può sanar per erba;
ch'io son fuggito per piani e per colli,
per potere scampar da cotal donna;
e dal suo lume non si può far ombra
poggio ne muro mai nè fronda verde.

25 Io l'ho veduta già vestita a verde,
sì fatta, ch'ella avrebbe messo in petra
l'amor ch'io porto pur a la sua ombra;
ond'io l'ho chesta in un bel prato d'erba
innamorata com'anco fu donna,
30 e chiuso intorno d'altissimi colli.

Ma ben ritorneranno i fiumi a' colli,
prima che questo legno molle e verde
s'infiammi, come suol far bella donna,
di me; che mi torrei dormire in petra
35 tutto il mio tempo e gir pascendo l'erba,
sol per veder do' suoi panni fanno ombra.

Quantunque i colli fanno più nera ombra,
sotto un bel verde la giovene donna
la fa sparer, com'uom petra sott'erba.

(ed. Contini 1965: 217)

To the shortened day and to the great circle of shade
I have come, alas! and to the whitening of the hills,
when the color is lost from the grass:
and my desire still does not change its green,
it is so rooted in the hard stone
that speaks and has sensation as if it were a lady.

So too this strange lady
stands there frozen, like snow in the shade:
for she is not moved except as a stone is
by the sweet season that warms the hills
and turns them from white to green
and clothes them with flowers and grass.

When she has on her head a garland of leaves
she drives from my mind every other lady:
because the curling yellow mingles with the green
so beautifully that Love comes to stay in the shade there,
Love who has locked me among little hills
more firmly than mortar locks a stone.

Her beauty has more power than a precious stone,
and the wound it gives cannot be healed by herbs:
for I have fled over plains and over hills
to learn to escape from such a lady;
and yet from her face there is no shade,
not of a hill, or a wall ever, or a green branch.

I saw her once dressed in green
such that she would have begotten in a stone
the love that I feel for her very shadow:
and so I have wished to have her in a fine meadow of grass,
as much in love as ever lady was,
a meadow closed in all around with high hills.

But well may the rivers climb the hills
before this moist green wood
will ever take fire (as ladies do)
for me, though I would endure to sleep on stone
all my season, and go eating grass,
so I might only see where her skirts make a shade.

Whenever the hills make blackest shade,
under a lovely green the youthful lady
makes them disappear, like a stone under the grass.

93

Resisting the impulse to forecast, *post hoc propter hoc,* which elements of this poem will be utilized by Petrarch in his magisterial sestinas, the reader decries its very strong tendency toward small units of closure, culminating in the actual poetic enclosure of the lady, or of the line of strophe V depicting her as enamored and captive in a meadow. Here the syntax collaborates most openly with pressure of the lover's and the poet's search for the center, as *un bel prato d'erba* (a fine meadow of grass) is further modified two lines away: *chiuso intorno d'altissimi colli* (a meadow closed in all around with high hills).

Dante modified the form inherited from Arnaut toward the completion of blocks of verse by lengthening the initial line of each strophe to a hendecasyllable. So does the strophe become, like the imagined setting for the lady, a privileged place of central value. Plucked from the flow of experience, the poetic situation harks back to the dream of the center in Provençal lyric, rendered often as a scene of love in a *jardi* (garden) or, as in Arnaut's sestina, a *cambra* (chamber). Such a place would witness the fusion of the dualities of lover and beloved heralded by the poetic structure. How radical a contrast is Petrarch's spatially unlimited outdoors (sestina XXII) supervised by the stars alone!

I have allowed myself this premature glimpse of Petrarch in order to concede that Dante's referral of all life to the amorous myth, and the recitation of his version of the myth, constitute a retelling of "primordial" events in a space entirely new to Italian poetry. Any sestina, with its distantly placed identical rhymes, will challenge the reader's memory and warn away that *vulgus* that Dante attacked in his treatise on poetic composition, *De vulgari eloquentia.* It was the superiority of Arnaut Daniel as creator of poems *sub oda continua,* whose sense could be suspended through complex motions during several strophes, that Dante singles out as his outstanding ability to love poetry (*De vulgari eloquentia* II, x, 2). Moreover, the linkage of immovable will with the sestina form is a principle of internal direction. The spatiotemporal correlative of will in Dante's stony poems is immobility, which recurs in images. The old themes of Provençal love-lyric pervade the sestina: It is winter but the spring of love abides in the lover's heart; the lady is both idol and metaphor for the poet's craft. The near-polarity of *verde/ombra,* when *ombra* is taken in its secondary specific meaning of death and *verde* as the color of hope, is an example of Dante's transcendence of material by will. Rhyme-words contract semantic relationships that come to dominate the phonic relations of alliteration and assonance.

Still compensating for the lack of dual rhyme, these machina-

94

tions of sound betray a reluctance of verse to detach itself from song as Dante's theoretical work would have it do. The *stantia sine rithimo,* or rhymeless strophe, that he mentions in the *De vulgari eloquentia* (II, xiii, 2) and the notion of an indivisible melody point to a conception of the sestinas as identity.

Elsewhere in the treatise Dante gives voice to a certain discomfort with identical and equivocal rhyme: *equivocatio . . . sempre sententiae quicquam derogare videtur* "equivocation always substracts something from thought" (II, xiii, 12). Hearing the punlike phonic resemblance that couples unlike senses, he nevertheless accords his rhyme-words further prominence by making them all substantives, a practice that was to survive into the ideation of sestinas in our time. The ascendancy of the rhyme-word in troubadour song is perhaps its most persistent legacy to Western poetic practice. Perceiving this dominance of the rhyme-word was an inescapable phase in the re-creation of the sestina for Italian poetry: the former displaying a cognizance of change of sense within unity of sound, the latter of change of sound within communality of sense. For Dante, a language is in itself a "nature" (*De vulgari eloquentia* I, 1, 14). And that nature aspires to realization through ordering power, which among its different branches reflects the will to recovery of the universality of speech as it was with primal Man. Identity, then, in and out of poetry, is connected fundamentally with will; hence, so is love.

The pattern of superficial variation underlain by systematic recurrence allows of no center. Having no center, the poem executes a maneuver commonly found in Petrarchan sestinas: It resorts to emphasis by correlation (as in lines 1, 6, 12, 15, 21, 24, 32). Dante selected his rhyme-words from a semantic field far more unified than that of Arnaut, then proceeded to dislocate them, despite his rigid alignment of meter and syntax, from their *semantic* matrices of temporal succession. Now scrambled into the "other" of time that is eternity, the words evade linear progress and transference of energy, often preferring balanced structures (al poco giorno . . . al gran cerchio d'ombra . . . al bianchir de' colli; per piani e per colli; molle e verde) that support hyperstaticity.

Taken together, the predominantly nominal lexicon and end-stoppage of each line certainly do not describe a cyclical order. Nor do recurrences of rhyme-words within strophes, since they are not the same from strophe to strophe and it is rather their order that emerges as identical when the poem constantly remakes itself. The cyclical structure of time is, therefore, not truly regenerated at each new strophic "birth," and to be made present has to be excavated from the *retrogradatio.* This Dante does not do. Furthermore, the single overt reference to *tempo* as structural principle displays its secondary meaning of "season" (*il dolce tempo che riscalda i colli*), which initiates a new measure of time. Not until the *prima che* of the sixth strophe and the final reference to tempo as equivalent to the lover's own life, the favored time between the margins of eternity, does the lover betray his consciousness of time as motion. As for the poet, Dante understood rhythm as "tutto quel parlare ch'en numeri e tempo regolato in rimate consonanze cade" ("all that speech which through number and measured time falls into rhymed consonances") (*Convivio* IV, ii, 12). Lacking this rhymed consonance, how do we understand his conception of time for the sestina?

The Aristotelian and Thomistic idea of time is *quantitas continua*, that is, the measure of successive motion, can apply to the succession of syllables that constitutes a poetic line. Although syllables are themselves discrete quantities, they form a *tempus continuum* through their succession within a complex unity, with a before and and after that is so perceived by the reader (Pazzaglia 1967: 164-166).

If we understand poetic rhythm as a characterization of the strategies through which Dante arrives at stanzaic units of meaning the relationships among stanzas, and the function of these units in the poetic whole, the most fruitful approach to Dante's sestinas is through what is most obviously innovative: the tropes. The presence of Amore, albeit in a form somewhere between personification and generalized hypostasis, haunts the third strophe, enclosing the lover "between small hills"—or in other words, allowing the physical power of escape without the requisite will. This figure is not developed, but it fulfills the function of summarizing imagery from older lyric: the green garland the lady wears, the magical virtue of precious stones, the servitude of the courtly lover, the "newness" in both qualitative and quantitative senses, of the lady, and an adumbrated "pastoral" encounter with her. These are refined and reduced to essentials, the half-repressed reminiscences subverting the blocks of verse. The entire poem can be viewed as a contention of metaphor with a hard matter manipulated by the will's obsession. We may see here the incidence of a guiding principle far from the ascent of the will in the *Commedia* but long detached from the amorous phenomenology of Dante's more youthful "style." What I propose to do further is to explore the relation between the "stony" image and a new kind of song.

The old trope of the cruel lady with heart of stone had become entirely conventionalized by the time of the composition of the *rime petrose* (c. 1296; Contini 1965: 157). Detached from her courtly origin and lacking in its formerly prismatic figural status, the hard lady was fair game for equivocation and for bourgeois assimilation into contexts of marriage and childbirth; and on the other hand, could be abstracted into the figure of the Virgin herself, abstracting her from poetic ambiguity. As the apex of value, the lady's figural status and concomitant poetic value had once dominated her literal status as female. In reestablishing a fusion of the lady and her unyielding character, Dante found a way to the violence of metaphor by replacement. In one sense this procedure built upon the Provençal *senhal* (or sign-name, pseudonym) formerly used to veil the lady's identity and, more important, to provide her with a new, poetic status. In another sense, it reestablished the dominance of the figural over the literal signatum. The lady is a stone, meaning that she is as resistant, as magic, and as heavy a weight on her lover's thoughts. The literal signatum *petra* and the figural signatum *donna* coalesce in the first enunciation of *petra*. At the same time, by making *donna* itself a rhyme-word Dante focuses on the relations contracted by different signata amongst each other. In the first strophe, he establishes the paramount status of the stony image, reversing the rank relation between the preexisting meaning of "stone" and the new, transferred meaning when applied to a human being. This relation makes the first enunciation of *donna* into a weak adjectival modifier for *petra*, in turn voided of its own figural meaning. In the third strophe where Amore imposes closure upon the lover, it is in the shadow of the lady, to whom Amore is connected by entailment as soon as her referent is *donna*, not *petra*. The transfer of dominance from "lady" to "stone" deeply affects the temporality of the poem as well. Five of the seven occurrences of *donna* are referred to women generically or to a hypothetical one (in strophes I, II, IV, V, VI), producing a recurrent alienation of the term from the poem's chief referent. As *donna* detaches itself from *petra*, vestigially remaining in the background, we repeatedly recognize the the "new lady" is like stone, and each instance is a synecdoche for the now familiar. Yet the images also prompt rediscovery, hence their effect of defamiliarization ("a lady," after all, "is not a stone"). From a purely synchronic viewpoint, this semantic complex could seem only unfamiliar, from a purely diachronic viewpoint only familiar.

The poem stresses the segregation of its images from the cyclical recurrences of seasons, to the point at which the lover experiences his own death in life—the extreme degree of closure. In the third strophe, the *ombra* of the lady, however menacing, becomes a kind of refuge. From then on the lover initiates a frantic internal journey (ch'io son fuggito per piani e per colli) to escape her blinding light. This sort of running in place cannot resist comparison to Petrarch's future troping of time. The shadow of his green frond is present.

Escape is offered only through adynaton, which appears in two guises in the sixth strophe: turning the stony lady into wood that can burst into flame, or recourse to the wider and more insistent framework of impossibilia ("Ma ben ritorneranno i fiumi a' colli . . .). The lack of consistent allegorical discourse allows for a ferment of metaphor. Here we also have the striking and puzzling *mi torrei dormire in petra* that suggests the lover as a half-savage, wandering in the wilds (*e gir pascendo l'erba*) as well as a secondary, punlike sense in which he is united with the stone-lady. What fascinates us is the persistent doubling of images first prompted by the co-presence of *donna* and *petra*, which encompasses other rhyme-word relations as well, that with *ombra*, for example.

The interplay of *petra* and *ombra* is of fundamental importance for the understanding of the stone-lady as both death-dealing and life-giving. Clearly the poem has imaged forth the destructive, hypnotic effect of the motionless figure on the lover as emanating from concrete substance. Ombra, on the other hand, while possessing certain negative traits, is also a refuge and not a concrete substance. Their respective effects are often complementary. Ombra both as the lady's shadow and (less distinctly) as her shade provides the figure of the stony lady with a quotient of life, and in order for her stony traits to emerge as paramount, ombra (her own, or that of the hills) has to detach itself from the function of mere delineation and circumscription (as in strophe I) or of agreement with natural elements (strophe II). The lady's concrete substance, stone, has life for the poem as long as ombra (or non-substance) emanates from it. However, the relatively beneficent effect of ombra is a matter subordinate to the lover's strain against his own imprisonment and the concomitant violence of his desire to imprison the lady. As the tornada tells us, though, her "stony" power surpasses and subdues the shadow.

The final line is enigmatic, and much depends on our reading of it. Since the direction of the poem moves toward the lover's death, by way of his hypnotism at the hands of the stone-lady, and since another *petroso* poem speaks of a marble man (uom di marmo), we should accept the reading of Pellegrini (1953: 29-30), who perceives here the ad hoc creation of a syntactic person, *uom-petra* or man of stone. The more frequent reading, according to which *uom* is subject and *petra* object of a pair connected zeugmatically to *donna* and *ombra*, would yield the image of a man making a stone disappear in the grass. If Pellegrini's reading is correct, the gravitation toward death would be complete: Whenever the hills produce darkest shadow beneath their foliage (in spring, when love's power is at its height), the lady can make that shadow vanish and similarly cause the man

98

turned to stone by her beauty to vanish beneath the grass, his burial place. The tornada would then complete the pattern of alternating seasons initiated within the body of the poem, and finally reveal the principle of will to be diffused throughout it as the fatal response to closure and the source of poetic energy. The transference of the "stony" attribute to the lover then displays his own petrification, as well as the correspondent danger inherent for the poet in further pursuit of the stone.

2. XXII: "A qualunque animale alberga in terra"

Ernest Wilkins' chronology of the *Canzoniere* (Wilkins 1951: 97) shows us that the nine sestinas fall into rather close groups of poems: The first four are within the first fifty-eight poems of the collection, the next three within a span of twenty-five poems. Among those *in morte di madonna Laura* there is only one, the double sestina, that strives past the known limits of the sestina's scope and persuasive power. With regard to the autograph of the poems, Wilkins notes that Petrarch probably regarded his canzoni and sestine as poems of a type other and higher than the sonnet, adducing in Petrarch's transcription a tendency toward the rewriting of canzoni and sestine with special care (Wilkins 1951: 111).

The myth of Apollo and Daphne in these poems functions as the conceptual equivalent of a nonverifiable, nonfalsifiable, yet valid hypothesis. Poems are metaphors of life (the world is the tenor, the text the vehicle), and the metaphorical qualities of Petrarch's sestinas actually represent series that are apparent in his shaping and making of poems but also point to a world that is his alone, inaccessible to the consciousness of others. The action of memory, which is the prime moving force behind poetic recurrences, is a linking of experience on the basis of similarity. The expansion and exploration of that memory are essentially metonymic, dependent on contiguity for poetic existence. Yet they all amount to metaphor of a "life, a reality, an object thus put into the flow of the work defined . . . by the break of its ending" (Rosolato, in Macksey and Donato 1972: 202) Our best critical response would be the attempt to put the texts back into their total context.

XXII

A qualunque animale alberga in terra
se non se alquanti ch'ànno in odio il sole,
tempo da travagliare è quanto è 'l giorno;
ma poi che 'l ciel accende le sue stelle,

qual torna a casa e qual s'anida in selva
per aver posa almeno infin a l'alba.

Ed io, da che comincia la bella alba
a scuoter l'ombra intorno de la terra,
svegliando gli animali in ogni selva,
non ò mai triegua di sospir' col sole;
poi quand'io veggio fiammeggiar le stelle,
vo lagrimando, e disiando il giorno.

Quando la sera scaccia il chiaro giorno
e le tenebre nostre altrui fanno alba,
miro pensoso le crudeli stelle
che m'ànno fatto di sensibil terra,
e maledico il dì ch' i' vidi 'l sole,
che mi fan in vista un uom nudrito in selva.

Non credo che pascesse mai per selva
si aspra fera, o di notte di giorno,
come costei ch'i' piango a l'ombra e al sole;
e non mi stanca primo sonno od alba:
chè, ben ch'i' sia mortal corpo di terra,
lo mio fermo desir vien da le stelle.

Prima ch'i' torni a voi, lucenti stelle
o tomi giù ne l'amorosa selva,
lassando il corpo che fia trita terra,
vedess'io in lei pietà, che 'n un sol giorno
può ristorar molt'anni, e 'nanzi l'alba
per uscirmi di braccia, come il giorno
ch'Apollo la sequia qua giù per terra.

Ma io sarò sotterra in secca selva,
e 'l giorno andrà pien di minute stelle
prima ch' a si dolce alba arrivi il sole.

(ed. Ponte 1968: 16)

For whatever animals dwell on earth,
except the few that hate the sun,
the time to labor is while it is day;
but when the sky lights up its stars
some return home and some make a nest in the wood
to have rest at least until the dawn.

And I—from when the lovely dawn begins
to scatter the shadows from about the earth,
awakening the animals in every wood—
I never have any truce from sighs with the sun;
and then when I see the stars flaming
I go weeping and longing for the day.

When the evening drives away the bright day,
and our darkness makes elsewhere a dawn,
I gaze full of care at the cruel stars
that have made me out of sensitive earth;
and I curse the day on which I saw the sun,
for it makes me seem a man raised in the woods.

I do not believe that there ever grazed in any wood
so cruel a beast, either by night or by day,
as she whom I weep for in the shadow and in the sun,
and I am not slowed by the first sleep or the dawn,
for although I am a mortal body of earth
my firm desire comes from the stars.

Before I return to you, bright stars,
or fall down into the amorous wood
leaving my body which will be powdered earth,
might I see pity in her, for in but one day
it could restore many years, and before the dawn
enrich me from the setting of the sun.

Might I be with her from when the sun departs
and no other see us but the stars,
just one night, and let the dawn never come!
and let her not be transformed into a green wood
to escape from my arms, as the day
when Apollo pursued her down here on earth!

But I will be under the earth in dried wood,
and the day will be lit by the tiny stars,
before the sun arrives at so sweet a dawn.)

The central paradox of the structure of Petrarch's amorous fiction is embedded in the intersection of cyclical and linear time. Although the love story is self-contained, its particulars refer to the natural cycle of life and death, and most of the rhyme-words deal with time, for the metamorphoses of lover, lady, and *selva* express the lover's subjection to a chronologically sequential variety of psychological states. Existents supplant occurrents, however, sustaining the system of potentially infinite variations balanced by thematic scarcity.

Verbs excluded from the nonepic present tense appear in contrary-to-fact subjective or infinitive modes, markers of a time "in which nothing is happening" (Durling 1965: 69). Rhyme-words are generally governed by epithets. The pronominal subject of every strophe is *io*, a fact not to be taken for granted even in this most autoreferential of poets. However at odds with his surroundings, the lover is not sufficiently alienated to abandon the connection of human emotions and their intimacy with nature, and his standardization of natural elements actually facilitates their merging with symbolic fantasies, two of which (in strophes III and VII) have momentous things to say about the poem. Both define the persona of the lover (of society but not from it, in nature but not of it) across a network of converging and diverging rhyme-words (terra/selva, giorno/alba, stelle/sole; terra/ sole). It is not series of sharp polarities that create the degradation of matter but an interstrophic progression that is a descent in value (alberga in terra/intorno de la terra/ sensibil terra/mortal corpo di terra/trita terra/qua giù per terra/ sotterra). The most flexible rhyme-word, *selva*, measures the current value of the others and defines the dynamic relationship between them. It is the point of convergence of the alternations of vigil and sleep, activity and rest, possibility (openness) and impossibility (closure).

It should be profitable to dwell on the question of what *selva*, a participant in the classical chart of polysemy by Hjelmslev (1961: 13) might be for Petrarch, whom Boccaccio named Silvanus (*De genealogie Deorum Gentilium*—'On the Geneology of the Gentile Gods,' III). As expected, we find two governing images of the sylvan environment, each of which has merited vast study (see the bibliography in Bernheimer 1952). On the positive side, the wilderness was interpreted in Judeo-Christian theology variously as a place of refuge, protection, and contemplative retreat, correspondent to one's inner nature or the precinct of the divinity. In its negative sense we know it as the wasteland, the world of the unredeemed, or as the realm of purgation, at the kindest, of self-discovery. It is either a place of testing or of punishment, implying the advent of renewal. Virgil speaks of the *densa ferarum tecta* (the tangled dens of beasts [*Aeneid* VI, 7-8]) surrounding the entrance to Avernus with gloom, yet he also declares, in the context of pastoral, *placeant ante omnia silvae* (before all else the woods are pleasing [*Ecl.* II, 62]). Dante has both kinds of woods—the terrestrial Paradise, the *selva oscura*, the fierce woods of Cecina and Corneto and of the suicides, to say nothing of Florence itself, a *trista selva* (wicked wood [*Purg.* XIV, 64]) of confusion and exile. The forest—surrogate Paradise or untamed wilderness—is fraught with paradox and "otherness." Even the blessedness of life for Dante was to see as only *poco tempo silvano*.

In the first strophe, the pattern is set for the grammatically contextual circumstances of *selva* throughout the poem: Each time it recurs introduced by a preposition or prepositional phrase, emphasizing contextual dependency. At the moment of its initial occurrence, however, it has acquired a coloration as a member of the pair *casa/ selva*, with the function of shelter and refuge from labor. At the same time, their opposition divides the domestic from the wild. This property of providing ambiguously valued shelter is stressed at the expense of all the rest, mirroring the landscape of a soul caught betwixt and between.

The strophe evokes post-Paradisiacal conditions, from which the emotions of the lover will detach themselves. Overriding the dialectic between positive and negative meanings of the formative "wilderness state" is a sensation of flow. Flow produces change, unchecked by qualifying modifiers while quantifiers abound: *qualunque, alquanti, qual.* The generality of the scene prefigures the exceptionality of the lover himself. The nocturnal, concealing selva offers satisfaction to creatures in nature. But Petrarch undermines this attraction, with the incision *Se non se alquanti . . .* that leaves doubt as to the proper habitat of the lover. These unstable conditions and temporal lack of fit convey the uncertainty and mutability of desire, a theme whose full psychological exploration is at its roots both amatory and Christian (Spitzer 1944: 73).

At first, in strophe II, the lover identifies himself with the wild life of the forest. But as he transforms himself from speaker to participant, the move occurring through expansive postponement ("da che comincia . . . ") undermines its own urgency. By day the wood has lost its protective function and the lover rests no more than the animals from his travail, suffering because of his tangential relationship to creation. He evades the purely animal world that divides work from rest. Beyond the protection of solar and lunar alternations he is simultaneously beyond the behavioral confines they seem to dictate. The contraries that move him have their own laws, with their correspondents in the laws of the sestina itself. Unlike an animal, he can accomplish a distinctive, personal thing, once he has singled out the animal aspect of his nature. Like the remainder of creation, he has lost Paradise, but he desires it only because consciousness in desire is given to man.

The lover's variance from the refreshment of nature was an old topic, but unlike the Provençal troubadours who generally rendered this contrast in terms of the recurrence of spring, Petrarch here places renewal not in emergence but in retreat, with the attendant ambiguities of sleep (most dangerous and illusory precisely in the area of greatest appeal). The antonymy built of contraries gradually intensifies through repetition, crystallizing into an image of a wild man: *un 'uom nudrito in selva.* Perhaps by analogy with the *abitador d'ombroso bosco* (CCXIV) and *cittadin de' boschi* (CCXXXVII) of other sestinas, or the *uom selvaggio* of sonnet CCXLV, commentators have generally been content to see in this figure an intermediate, composite phase between animal and man (Zingarelli 1963: 342; Bellorini 1929: 23; Antona-Traversi and Zannoni 1889: 38), with little regard for the sestina's structure of warring contradictions.

In support of my notion that the *uom nudrito in selva* is a figuration of a mythical type known to Petrarch, I cite from sonnet CLXXVI:

> Per mezz'i boschi inospiti e selvaggi,
> onde vanno a gran rischio uomini et arme,
> vo securo io; che non po spaventarme
> altri che'l sol c'ha d'Amor vivo i raggi.
>
> E vo cantando (o penser miei non saggi!)
> lei che'l ciel non poria lontana farme;
> ch'i' l'ho ne gli occhi; e veder seco parme
> donne e donzelle, e sono abeti e faggi.
>
> Parme d'udirla udendo i rami e l'ore,
> e le frondi e gli augei lagnarsi, e l'acque
> mormorando fuggir per l'erba verde.

(Through the midst of the inhospitable savage woods, where even armed men go at great risk, I go without fear, nor can anything terrify me except the sun that has Love's living rays.

And I go singing (oh my unwise thoughts!) of her whom the heavens could not make far from me, for she is before my eyes and with her I seem to see ladies and damsels, but they are firs and beeches.

I seem to hear her, when I hear the branches and the breeze and the leaves, and birds lamenting, and the waters fleeing with a murmur across the green grass.)

The ecstatic tone of these lines distinguishes their import from that of the sestina, yet the similarities speak eloquently: The sun he fears yet guides and illuminates the lover, Laura as sun representing the limitless course of time in the cosmos. Love then makes the singer intrepid and confers on him his emotions, at variance with his surroundings. Although the negative aspect of the forest prevails more than in the sestina, its rigors impose no real obstacle, for the figure of the woodland dweller and that of the traveler are both extremes of contradiction, embedded in a medieval literary type.

A number of attestations to the *selvaggio* tradition occur in the late Middle Ages in Italy. Its immediate antecedent is a form of disguise that often ornamented masques and festivals: the *omo silvatico,* (man of the woods) fearsome in appearance, often covered in fur and feathers and carrying a powerful stick (Neri 1951: 158-178; Bertoni 1927: 93-101). A well-known instance occurs in Boccaccio's

Decameron (IV, 2), where we find the fraudulent Frate Alberto gotten up defensively as a savage. In Duecento lyric, the selvaggio is noted for his counterrealistic optimism in adversity and is later recalled by the early fourteenth-century *poète maudit,* Cecco Angiolieri (sonnet XCIII). All references in poets preceding and following Petrarch emphasize the selvaggio's contrariness.

To return to the sestina, heretofore the selva has functioned as the domain for contending elements in the poet's soul. Now it is subordinated entirely to what it tells about the man. The figure of the *uom nudrito in selva* occurs near a crossroads in the sestina, where it marks a further intensification of desire and nonpossession. It would seem to signal a transformation of the lover, but the distancing factor of *in vista* must not escape notice. The idea of a human being nourished in the wild delineates one level of paradox, his literary embellishment another. Its nature describes a certain pair of contradictions, but a second set confronts us with the possibility that the mass of clashing opposites exists in the eye of the beholder. The image confirms the oxymoric situation of the lover, but it does not remain static. In accordance with Petrarchan flow, nonpossession will shade into another state of possession, the object now showing its aspect of poetic conquest. In the following strophe, the image of the *uom nudrito in selva* gives rise to the first transformation of Laura.

The selva sustains its metaphorical status, even more menacing as a lair of beasts. Transference to the *fera Laura* springs form the third strophe, actuated by the semantic connection of *nudrito-pascesse.* Throughout the rest of the poem it is the beloved, not the lover, who will be subject to transformation.

A renewed statement of "firmness" inaugurates the turning point: *E non mi stanca primo sonno od alba,* furrowing the ground of disjunction between nonpossession, or death-in-life, and possession, or life-in-death. Literary allusion is but one means whereby Petrarch effects this dramatic shift. In the fifth strophe the selva is a literary metaphor, the Virgilian wood of the shades who died for love (*Aeneid* VI, 442). From here on it will be joined with epithets endowing it with the specificity of a proper noun. Phonetic and syntactic linkages cooperate. The paronomastic and grammatical affinities of *torni/tomi* entwine things that are in turn related grammatically and semantically: *lucenti stelle/amorosa selva.* Both of these content-forms have their origin in classical culture, strengthened by reference to the doctrine of Plato's *Timaeus,* that the soul returns to the star whence it descended. As epithets, both reveal the ambiguity that defines a phase in the lover's progress toward a new kind of possession.

Since immortality must be clearly conceived in terms of death, the

105

lover averts them both when he projects reunion with the beloved into a future, compressed time ("'n un sol giorno"). He foreshadows the fulfillment of his wish, thereby enlarging on the firmness of will capable of controlling both conjugate and opposed things—lucenti stelle and amoroso selva. But of this pair, the mythical myrtle-grown forest undergoes the permutation that is decisive for the poem. Now Petrarch, directing his discourse to the stars, draws Laura into the enchantment of poetry's magic, incantatory aspect, and she is indirectly converted into a secondary addressee. The lover veers from imprisonment within his desire toward enlargement by repetition and analogy, an extension of his grief that roams the paths of literature.

Petrarch's astonishingly immediate evocation of a night of love has a superseding dynamics as a game with time. The mythical context is established at the outset: the lover wishes only one night, but may it never be dawn! The copulative "and" invalidates the lurking contradictions (one night versus eternity), and aids in nullifying sequential time. Set in motion immediately, the lovers' transformation into myth occurs in a fabled present, constituted by parentheses between anticipation and retroaction.

It is the pattern of syntagmatic arrangement that propels the myth of this sestina forward into the realm of the imminent: The transformational sequence is not Laura/Daphne/laurel, but Laura/laurel/Daphne, so that in the wake of the image is the notion of a metamorphosis perpetually about to occur. Laura represents not only the laurel but Daphne herself, this change occurring at a dizzily accelerated pace. Energetic syntax is achieved by the dominantly paratactic construction of the first, and hypotactic construction of the second half of the strophe, miming the chase it describes. This strophe contains the only instance in which a secondary meaning of selva (plant) overshadows the basic "forest." Laura's myth is endowed with the synchronic totality of amorous paradox itself. Diachronically, the image of the Virgilian amorosa selva has given way to the Ovidian evergreen (*Metamorphoses* I, 525-550) so that the literary content of selva comes to dominate the strophe, in tandem with the urgency and implacability of desire, one and the same where the poem is concerned.

A series of impassioned negatives (*et non ci vedesse . . . et mai non fosse . . . et non se transformasse*) delineate the lover's continually agonistic stance, contending in vain with immortal myth. Petrarch's erotic instrumentation of the Ovidian tale is characteristic. It is no wonder that the insistently emergent secondary features of selva have conferred on it an increasingly metaphorical and literary signification. Herein lie unlimited areas of possession that will determine the poem's final direction.

Although the literary content of this sestina seems so far to have been allotted to secular poetry (Arnaut Daniel, Virgil, Ovid), we recall that the first strophe declares a background that is profoundly Christian, not only in the divergence of the lover from animal and vegetal life, but in the distance of nature as it is now from original justice, suffused with the loss of Paradise. The gift of relief through sleep is but the obverse of sleep's deprivation of reason and control. Then, where the center of the poem would be, there occurs a developmental shift from the premise of nonpossession to possession in language. Clearly the love so documented does not transcend earthly bounds; even its mythological corollary is situated firmly *giù per terra*. The process of linguistic intensification is the means that confers heroic possibilities on the love story.

Examining the tornada, we note that the adynaton of the second (and central) line stands syntactically and morphologically in parallel relation to the first line, equivalent entities confronting one another in a pairing that constitutes a summation of the poem's paradox. We have had to depart from the language of the poem itself to recognize Petrarch's retelling of Daphne and Apollo, the screen-story that does not quite achieve metaphor-by-replacement. We have had to ask, however, why and how the myth returned in the new context, checked and redirected by dreams of fulfillment. Now is the moment to review the contexts of selva. In the fifth strophe, the near-contiguity of *secca* and *verde* exploits both their basic antonymy and their ambiguous convergence. *Verde selva* evinces both the aspect of death-as-woman and of immortality-as-laurel while *secca,* in the tornada, invites a concentration on death. Confirmed by the preceding *sotterra* and the following adynaton, the death meaning of the lines is unmistakable. Yet the juxtaposed images in the first two lines and their association with the third ("before the sun arrives at so sweet a dawn"), as well as the complementarity of the first and final strophes raise the problem: Whose death? "Possible" or impossible"?

By its nature the adynaton threatens to collapse the dichotomous structure with the advent of a chaos suggesting the end of the world, "quando non ci saranno più selve" (Contini 1951: 21). And yet there is little in Petrarch that would confirm this hypothesis or make it hermeneutically useful, only passages perfectly analogous to this one and equally in need of reinterpretation (such as CCXXXVII 37-39). For in any case the unification of opposites is an impossibility within the Petrarchan scheme. Since the two events of the tornada are linked, the first could not occur more probably than the second.

Dispersed throughout the poems we find a number of explicit allusions to the lover's thoughts of suicide. Repeatedly, piety constrains him to abandon the notion or at least to exclude it as a plan, however intolerable his life may seem. Thereupon hangs the weight of his suffering. Returning to the confrontations of selva in strophes V and VI, we see them as crowning the absolute fixity of desire. But an eternal night of love, even outside temporarl limits, would interrupt desire and destroy the basis of the lover's implacable stance. The reading of the line that I propose takes this into account and accords with the complementarity of strophes VI and VII. As the former strophe realizes dream-fulfillment, the latter denies it; as the former evokes a mythical and pagan world of luxury and classical culture, the latter strives toward Christian imagery. I take the *secca selva* to be the Dantean wood of the suicides (*Inf.* XIII), bound up with misuses of love and, like them, physically denatured. Recalling the perpetual "second death" of Dante's suicides, it recapitulates both the Dantean experience included within this sestina and its opening summary of post-Edenic conditions. The final transformation and the rejection of the selva summarizes the rejection of closure. Even as the lover strains at his bond and is remitted to the sphere of bondage, Petrarchan "evasiveness" eludes both the extremes of the animal world of work and the world of "second death." Finally, if suicide is not a possibility for the lover, any more than the appearance of myriad stars by day, then on the same level we are invited to enter a realm of "immortal" possibility.

3. LXVI: "L'aere gravato, e l'importuna nebbia"

If ever the history of poetry is to be revealed all at once, in its entirety as human creation, then the declarations poets make about their filiation with other poets will indicate only the presence of a link, not its direction. Our reading of precursors is already pervaded by our previous reading of their descendants. This poem provides an example of Petrarch's internalization of Dante's sestina, but also illuminates our understanding of it. Petrarch's conversion of the known lyric world into terms for inner experience is encapsulated within the constancy of change embodied in the sestina form.

Whereas in Dante's winter, light and darkness alternate, in Petrarch's shades are important. It is not a poem about fluctuation and static opposition, not even about alternation, but about change. Terms for change propel it; the internal referent is a portent of unearthly, meteorological change and the lover's plight is dramatized against a background of perpetual motion.

> I. L'aere gravato, e l'importuna nebbia
> compressa intorno da rabbiosi venti

108

tosto conven che si converta in pioggia;
e già son quasi di cristallo i fiumi,
5   e 'n vece de l'erbetta per le valli
non se ved'altro che pruine e ghiaccio.

II. Et io nel cor via più freddo che ghiaccio
ho di gravi pensier tal una nebbia,
qual si leva talor di queste valli,
10   serrate incontra a gli amorosi venti,
e circundate di stagnanti fiumi
quando cade dal ciel più lenta pioggia.

III. In picciol tempo passa ogni gran pioggia,
e 'l caldo fa sparir le nevi e 'l ghiaccio,
15   di che vanno superbi in vista i fiumi;
ne' mai nascose il ciel sì folta nebbia
che sopragiunta dal furor di venti
non fugisse da i poggi e da le valli.

IV. Ma, lasso! a me non val fiorir de valli;
20   anzi piango al sereno et a la pioggia,
e a' gelati e a' soavi venti:
ch'allor fia un di madonna senza 'l ghiaccio
dentro, e di for senza l'usata nebbia,
ch'i' vedro secco il mare, e' laghi, e i fiumi.

25   V. Mentre ch'al mar descenderanno i fiumi
e le fiere ameranno ombrose valli,
fia dinanzi a'begli occhi quella nebbia
che fa nascer di' miei continua pioggia,
e nel bel petto l'indurato ghiaccio
30   che tra' del mio sì dolorosi venti.

VI. Ben debbo io perdonare a tutt'i venti,
per amor d'un che 'n mezzo di duo fiumi
mi chiuse tra 'l bel verde e 'l dolce ghiaccio,
tal ch'i' depinsi poi per mille valli
35   l'ombra, ov'io fui; che nè calor, nè pioggia,
ne suon curava di spezzata nebbia.

VII. Ma non fuggio gia mai nebbia per venti,
come quel dì, nè mai fiumi per pioggia,
ne ghiaccio, quando 'l sole apre le valli.

(ed. Ponte 1968: 54)

(The burdened air and the importunate cloud
compressed from without by the furious winds
must soon convert themselves to rain;
and already almost crystal are the rivers,
and instead of the grass through the valleys
one sees nothing but frost and ice.

And I have in my heart, much colder than ice,
heavy thoughts in such a cloud
as rises sometimes from these valleys,
closed around about against the loving winds
and surrounded by stagnating rivers,
when there falls from the sky the gentlest rain.

In a short time passes every great rain;
and the warmth makes disappear the snows and ice
that make the rivers look so proud;
nor was the sky ever covered by so thick a cloud
that, meeting the fury of the winds,
it did not flee from the hills and the valleys.

But, alas! I am not helped by the flowering of the valleys;
rather I weep in clear weather and in rain,
and in freezing and in warming winds;
for one day my lady will be without her inner ice
and without her outer customary cloud —
when I shall see the sea dry, and the lakes and the rivers.

As long as the sea receives the rivers
and the beasts love shady valleys,
before her eyes will remain the cloud
that makes my eyes give birth to constant rain,
and in her lovely breast the hardened ice
that draws forth from mine such sorrowing winds.

Well may I pardon all the winds
for love of one who between two rivers
closed me in lovely green and sweet ice,
so that I depicted then through a thousand valleys
the shade where I had been; for neither heat nor rain
I feared, nor the sound of shattered cloud.

But never did cloud flee before winds
as on that day, nor river because of rain,
nor ice when the sun opens the valleys.)

At first it appears that the *frej'aura* (cold breeze) of the Provençal troubadour blows over this winter to arouse the lover's opposition, like the concreteness and substantiality of so many of its terms that are nouns. For nouns refer stubbornly to things, predicates to "anything." The poem seems ambushed by things, rendered in what Petrarch elsewhere calls "raucous rhymes"; and it is a work about closure. But the gravid air, compressed fog, and raging winds are about to be "converted" to rain that will fill rivers in turn and become ice again, the entire cycle of water made present and completed. If the sestina replicates the sun's annual course around the ecliptic, recording the intimate and binding analogies of that movement to seasonal change, this poem also effectuates a fragmenting of that alternation, showing a world enveloped in a simultaneous present; dry land and water presenting the vulnerable, brittle face of ice. The pincer-movement of rhyme-words closes in to no material solidity.

Semantic relationships among the rhyme-words are supported by a more surreptitious phonetic network, assonance both tonic (nebbia/venti; valli/ghiaccio) and posttonic (nebbia/pioggia; venti/fiumi/valli), which makes them contract spurious semantic associations, as well as other common phonetic features, such as the diphthons of the initial syllables of three words (pioggia, fiumi, ghiaccio) or affinities of consonantal grouping (pioggia/ghiaccio and the sonorants fiumi/valli). All refer to elements in nature but range themselves within fluid associations by changing affinities: *Nebbia/pioggia/ghiaccio* denote a progression of the water cycle, *valli/fiumi* an opposition of land and water, *venti* the agent of conversion, transforming the Provençal conceit of winds breathing the presence of the distant beloved.

The expository first strophe is answered by the inner landscape of the second. Dante's claustrophobic situation is the prior content, the immovable given of the poem. The lover finds himself pressed by his own materiality, the Old Adam in turn surrounded by enclosed valleys offering the illusion of spaciousness. These in turn are circumscribed by stagnant rivers, the pattern of roughly concentric circles, describing a kind of Ptolemaic order in which the lover finds no spiritual residence. Nature has become the walls of a menacing city, not perceivable as a place of refuge. *Valli serrate* are a play on Petrarch's beloved but tormenting *Vau/cluse* ("closed valley"), but the punlike dance of words stops short against the assault of "amorous winds." We realize that Vaucluse is within him, the leap of the poet's mind now transforming himself into the place where his beloved is, each attacked from without. At best, she would be the center, the metaphor of the enclosed valley. But the mist of heavy thoughts rising from his "frozen heart" crystallizes, and is compared with the stopped flow of waters forming a lake (Dante's *lago del cor* ["lake of the heart] must be recollected here—the habitat of vital spirits and receptacle of the passions, *Inf.* I, 19). Petrarch's Valley of the Shadows has no well-defined boundaries. By repressing the physicality of mountains bearing in upon his desired center of value, he locates the country of doubt within himself, making the barrier between that self and the land of the beloved invisible. Petrarchan enclosure allows for an open door.

Accordingly Dante's firm boundaries (*colli* "hills or mountains") are demoted from rhyme-word position, and in the third strophe the word is conflated with *valli* as its coordinate, like *nevi* and *ghiaccio*. As in many cases of adynaton, Petrarch draws together unlike things into syntactic relations otherwise perfectly resembling those of like things. Coordination thus substitutes at times for adjectival modification, always pointing to paths leading away from closure. Whereas the lover in Dante's sestina can conceive of his end as lover only in the prison of the tomb, the speaker in Petrarch's poem, even as he substitutes repetition and coordination for progress makes his way out.

The experience of transitivity resumes in the third strophe. The lover's heart receives all the varied actions of the winds breaking into it from without, alternately savage and benign (I *rabbiosi;* II *amorosi;* III *furor;* IV *soavi*); all of these ultimately contribute to the flow as passage through space in time and as poetic expression. Ruptures in rigidity abound, for example, in the enjambment that announces the adynaton of the fourth strophe. Here the opposition of syntactic and metrical units reflects the lover's irrepressible hope of openness and reunion against natural odds. This opening out near the fictional center of the poem marks both the poet's search for centrality and his negation of simple or formulaic solutions.

In the starkness of cold, love hibernates within a besieged enclosure. But this subject as adapted by Petrarch becomes ultimately subordinate to his meditation upon temporality, his triumphant comprehension of iconic potential. Marks of time (*tosto, talor, quando, in picciol tempo, mai*) punctuate a flow whose measure is determined only by the internal clock of amorous subjectivity. Opposition and coordination enhance the cyclical aspect of the sestina, but the rush of linearity is also understood as a mysterious cosmic rhythm—hence the successful interpenetration of internal and external landscapes. Petrarch's binary division of the rhyme-words into terms for earth and terms for sky invites our perception of identity and difference, but the networks of secondary relations overrun this boundary; for example, strophe IV abandons hypotaxis for enumerative series. Gradually, Laura becomes the sign for nature, an exchange that occurs supported by an apparent rhetorical symmetry that provides the illusion of freedom from reference, seeming not to tend anywhere. But like the adynaton's formal resemblance, quasi-proverbial even, to the fact of impossibility, this poem proclaims a dominance of form over minute contrasts-and-comparisons.

At the same time this reconciliation of unlike things does not provide the lover with identity (or union with Laura). What triumphs is his resoluteness in interiority, the inner life accommodated to the myth of Orphic power. The poem is dominated by the virtual presence of a hero true to his nature who, like Orpheus, never quite dies. Continuities in external reality are perceived in consequence of this stance. In the fifth strophe *mar* grows out of *fiumi* as the emanations of Laura/nature become the cyclical perpetuity of a world. In the sixth strophe, she (*l'aura*) is herself transformed into one of the winds, masked for an instant by a masculine pronoun (*per amor d'un*). The ductility of Petrarchan idiom conceals sources. Whereas adjectives are little more than white spaces through which objects are glimpsed as through mist, the complexity of rhythmic units and sustained articulation distend the syntax. Petrarchan idolect welcomes near-oppositions like *dolce ghiaccio* that suggest asymmetry, an early example of the *sprezzatura* to be idealized by his sixteenth-century followers. Since expressions like this are not pure oxymorons, they preclude even a formal resolution of tension. In this case, the spaces and shadows between opposites appear just before an evocation of painting (*tal ch'i' dipinsi*).

The comparison of meditation upon the beloved with painting is a very old one, known to Petrarch as well through medieval and ancient poets. Now its figural power is attenuated, as the codified idea of the inner image subserves aggrandizement: *Mille* evokes Virgil's narrative hyperboles. Not if I had a thousand tongues, we are told, could I exhaust the topic of Laura, so that *mille* approaches "every" or "all possible." Laura's image is enclosed now, twined into the syntactic flow. Not to articulate the terms more closely or subtly, but to provide links in an elaborated, sustained rhythm, the period unfolds. Dante's imprisoned lover had conjured up the amorous imprisonment of the beloved within the neat green setting of the Provençal *pastorela,* which would be filled with her love. Here the lover entrapped by the will of his fantasy also has plenty of room to stray in, and even forced retreat holds comfort and renewal. If the ice belongs to one of Laura's rivers, it is sweet, not essentially opposite to *bel verde* any more than its own terms between themselves.

This kind of "painterly" shading was noted by the Renaissance commentator and poet Alessandro Tassoni, who attributed to *ombra* the technical sense of *ombreggiare,* paraphrasing these lines: "Talchè per mille valli, ov'io fui, dipinsi poi l'ombra sua, cioè ombreggiai la sua immagine, come fanno i pittori" ("such that throughout a thousand valleys where I was I painted her shadow, that is, I shaded in her image, as painters do" [cit. Carrara 1953: 98]). It is another way of obliterating boundaries, but not the only one. The lover's firmness of will is also protected by the "shade" of the laurel tree from sun, rain, and thunder. Laura's supernatural powers provide independence from weather, hence from time. The poem establishes its privileged duration, to be broken in the new *tempore* by the correspondingly supernatural force of adynaton. Under Apollo's protection, the laurel submits to its own kind of hierarchy, comprehending the poet, who is now able to fragment thunder itself into its harmless components (*spezzata nebbia*).

Petrarch's deft syntax manages to unite the lover and beloved in a poetic union by making it possible to read the final lines of the sixth strophe with either as subject. If meteorological phenomena are read in their external meaning, then it is the lover who confronts them without fear. If they are read as manifestations of the inner landscape (his fire opposed to her ice; the rain of his tears; the broken thunder of his complaint), then the subject is the immutable laurel or better, her image or shade. However, there is as always a final determination: Both punctuation and textual comparison up to this point accord reference to the poet-lover himself. We only glimpse the possibility of atomizing verbal leaps; the inner landscape never compels re-arrangements of the external one, which remains transparent.

Stanzas proceed as a dialogue between the two. From such dialogue, the pattern of anaphora and parison that marks Renaissance sestinas in dialogue derived its particular form. A seeming parallelism of lexical and syntactic echo, of assonance and alliteration, confers a superficial resemblance that facilitates communication. But Petrarch exploits to the fullest the features of the sestina that demonstrate the impossibility of perfect recurrence. It is in the area of difference that we see his legacy most clearly.

Possibility, like Laura herself, is perennial in the spaces between retrospection and transformation. Change is integral to all other things in nature, even to the fact of "enclosure," as the tornada reveals. "That day" (of the lover's imprisonment) has its definition in Laura. But no remembrance is perfectly accurate, no sketch quick enough. Each term represents the obliteration of a phenomenon (fog, rivers, ice) by a supervening *force majeure;* only Laura is endowed with a changeless presence, overcoming all natural strife. The conqueror is *sole*, for Petrarch a term for Laura, more generally a term for God.

Dante's stone-lady also casts a shadow. It too formed the perceptions of her lover, led him through the tortuous paths of previously repressed signification and offered the lady an idol's perpetual life. But where Dante defined, sealed the semantic import of each word, the experience of idolatry released a flow in Petrarch, a rain that increases rivers even as it causes overreaching and loss. So did Laura's *sole* open the "valleys" as in the conclusion of this sestina. The precious way out of imprisonment leads into the endless space of a laterally conceived world.

4. CXLII: "A la dolce ombra delle belle frondi"

I. A la dolce ombra de le belle frondi
corsi fuggendo un dispietato lume,
che 'n fin qua giù m' ardea dal terzo cielo;
e disgombrava già di neve i poggi
5 l' aura amorosa che rinova il tempo
e viorian per le piagge l' erbe e i rami.

II. Non vide il mondo si leggiadri rami
nè mosse il vento mai si verdi frondi
come a me si mostrar quel primo tempo;
10 tal che temendo de l' ardente lume
non volsi al mio refugio ombra di poggi,
ma de la pianta più gradita in cielo.

III. Un lauro mi difese allor dal cielo,
onde piu volte vago de' bei rami
15 da po' son gito per selve e per poggi;
ne già mai ritrovai tronco ne frondi
tanto onorate dal superno lume,
che non mutasser qualitate a tempo.

IV. Però più fermo ognor di tempo in tempo
20 seguendo ove chiamar m' udia dal cielo
e scorto d' un soave e chiaro lume,
tornai sempre devoto a i primi rami,
e quando a terra son sparte le frondi
e quando il sol la verdeggiar i poggi.

25 V. Selve sassi campagne fiumi e poggi,
quanto è creato, vince e cangia il tempo;
one' io cheggio perdono a queste frondi,
se rivolgendo poi molt' anni il cielo,
fuggir disposi gl'invescati rami
30 tosto ch'i' 'ncominciai di veder lume.

VI. Tanto mi piacque prima il dolce lume
ch'i' passai con diletto assai gran poggi
per poter appressar gli amati rami;
ora la vita breve e 'l loco e 'l tempo
35 mostranmi altro sentier di gire al cielo
e di far frutto, non pur fior' e frondi.

115

VII. Altr' amor, altre frondi ed altro lume,
altro salir al ciel per altri poggi
cerco, che n'è ben tempo, ed altri rami.

(ed. Ponte 1968: 120)

(To the sweet shade of those beautiful leaves
I ran, fleeing a pitiless light
that was burning down upon me from the third heaven;
and already the snow was disappearing from the hills
thanks to the loving breeze that renews the season,
and through the meadows the grass bloomed and the branches.

The world never saw such graceful branches
nor did the wind ever move such green leaves
as showed themselves to me in that first season;
so that, fearing the burning light,
I chose for my refuge no shade of hills
but that of the tree most favored in Heaven.

A laurel defended me then from the heavens;
wherefore often, desirous of its lovely branches,
since then I have gone through woods and across hills:
nor have I ever again found trunk or leaves
so honored by the supernal light
that they did not change their quality according to the season.

Therefore, more and more firm from season to season,
following where I heard myself called from Heaven
and guided by a mild and clear light,
I have come back always devoted to the first branches,
both when on earth are scattered their leaves
and when the sun turns green the hills.

Woods, rocks, fields, rivers, and hills—
all that is made—are vanquished and changed by time;
wherefore I ask pardon of these leaves
if, the heavens turning many years,
I have made ready to flee the enlimed branches
as soon as I began to see the light.

So pleasing to me at first was that sweet light
that joyfully I traversed great hills
in order to approach the beloved branches.
Now the shortness of life and the place and the season
show me another pathway to go to Heaven
and bear fruit, not merely flowers and leaves.

Another love, other leaves, and another light,
another climbing to Heaven by other hills
I seek (for it is indeed time), and other branches.

116

Informed that this poem closed the first version of Petrarch's collected poems (Wilkins 1951: 97), we are moved to seek in it an ending. And the direction of its spatial and temporal relationships is from the general to the particular, extending as far as Petrarch's "vanishing point." The lover recalls how as being in love with love, he sought shelter in the very place of his future imprisonment, the shade of the laurel tree. From the love of women he narrowed to that of Laura alone. Now straining away from her enclosure, he looks to the time of his liberation from all earthly love. To achieve a reading thus far, the reader has had to fill the semantic voids placed for his steps, to become the poet's accomplice. Not the light of defining reason but the half-light of suggestion guides us. The most changeable term is *lume,* which functions variously to stand for the light of Venus (or sexual desire), of God, of Laura's eyes, of reason and divine truth—in other words, as a thing existing in virtue of its possessor. The meanings denoting sexual love and devotion alternate, so that the notion of a progress emerges as only one aspect of the lover's fate, the other represented in a perpetual imperfection, striving, and entrapment. It is a poem about closure and its relationship to change.

All of nature, the lover laments, is subject to change, but the agent of change is in nature, *l'aura amorosa* that is the breath of spring, renewing time. Laura's protean quality is, of course, another avenue of the relation to poetry as such, and the poet's ironic relation to nature a major difference between himself and the beloved. No impulse in nature it is that leads him to seek his liberty, not the passage of his life but a break in its continuity that educes a different aspect of his consciousness. We look in vain for external incident in this confession. We cannot know how he moves from one state to another. Irreconcilable, these states are juxtaposed and intertwined so that asymmetry is constant but not final.

Changes in the lover are not reflections of natural states, so nature is revealed as less powerful in him, or neutralized. He is in all states a desirer and a seeker. The fable of Apollo and Daphne woven into the sestina clarifies Laura as an object gradually gaining ascendancy, one over many. But the pursuer is subdivided into pursuer and pursued: The internal narrative bisects its hero into one driven by opposing sides of his personality in conflicting directions, ending in stasis. Despite her ability to assume different guises, Laura in nature never changes. A disappearing object always one step ahead of her pursuer, she confers upon her poet the prize of his dedication—earthly immortality or fame. She is, as beloved and as poetic object, the one element that can disturb the cycle of seasons (tempo) in its secondary sense) and the linear trajectory of life. The relation between the sun's daily orbit around the earth, the movements of years and of hours, are perceivable through the action of Venus.

The term *frondi* retains its metaphorical sense of "Laura" up to the sixth strophe, where it takes on the additional figurality of religious metaphor as the fruitful tree of the love of God. The laurel transcends the limits of time and change, forever producing flowers and leaves, but since it bears no fruit, her transcendence is incomplete. The poem has turned around substitution in time of a constant object for a false one, rendered by modulations of the focal image. As the laurel is now understood through the theological image of the dry tree, the spatial and temporal coordinates of his life in time ("la vita breve, e 'l loco, e 'l tempo" [now the shortness of life and the place and the season]) turn the lover away from the continuum of pursuit. He sees himself, for a moment, as the tree, participating in the great medieval commonplace of spiritual fruitfulness or dryness, knowing himself, after all, as the flawed protean creator. The connotations of biblical places abound: "Quia si in viridi ligno haec faciunt, in arido quid fiet?" (For if they do these things in a green tree, what shall be done in the dry? [Luke 23: 31]). The things done in the green tree would be the persecution of desire in love and in writing. The very immobility of the laurel accomplishes great feats of cruelty toward her lover that stimulate him to compose. It is the wished-for center to which he returns with an ever-renewed "firmness of will," recapitulating his poetic and amorous experience of her. Again as near as possible to the missing center of the poem, he declares himself "più fermo ogni or" (more and more firm), obedient to the light of Laura's eyes, independently of the seasons' natural cycle. This cycle we know, and it is the same for all under nature. It is the linear quotient in time that continues mysterious. When in the number of seasonal revolutions was the lover first moved to seek an ending? That wish for new beginnings occurring somewhere between the fourth and fifth strophes of the poem and in an unknown place in the poet's life has, as it were, no place of origin. In contrast to the marked presence of the anniversaries and landmark days that convulse the lover's narrative existence, the desire to stop desiring can only be expressed as "altro," as virtually absent. Centuries later, when the elegiac smile of Ariosto alights upon Astolfo in the Moon, he will express the obverse and converse of earthly desires only as "other," then clearly reveal as present the detritus of trial and loss (*Orlando Furioso* XXXIV, 72). Here the reversal is expressed as an opening out that even covertly takes account of love for Laura as a "salir al ciel," albeit of the wrong kind. Already the poet takes cognizance of a relativity bearing little reference other than to itself. Of course there is no question of characterizing the love of God as other than simply beyond reach, as the defining terms remain beyond reach ("altro"). But the sexual and poetic desire that are intertwined and entrap the lover (*invescati rami,* as he has it, both bound and binding) are known. They are both in nature, which alters all things, and outside of nature, pertaining only to the uniqueness of one man.

Laura's eyes rest on her poet in a fixity underscoring his movement (*scorto,* escorted), but he can project onto her all the permutations of poetic language—from watchful eye to entwined laurel. The final enjambment ("altro salir al ciel per altri poggi/cerco") is the lover's stake in the claim of openness, of possibility. The natural cycle, however, is the only place he has ever been before. The metaphor for poetry, Laura who renews the seasons, always reopens the possibility that eventually the fall into Venus' lures, and even their intensification by her, will be revealed as a *felix culpa,* and the seeming parallelism of laurel and "dry tree" is dispelled. But searching for the call of a more permanent love than hers, the poet discovers the firmness of his will only under the eyes of the beloved.

5. CCXIV: "Anzi tre dì creata era alma in parte"

I. Anzi tre dì creata era alma in parte
da por sua cura in cose altere e nove,
e dispregiar di quel ch'a molti e 'n pregio;
quest'ancor dubbia del fatal suo corso,
5   sola, pensando, pargoletta e sciolta,
intrò di primavera in un bel bosco.

II. Era un tenero fior nato in quel bosco
il giorno avanti, e la radice in parte
ch'appressar nol poteva anima sciolta,
10   chè v'eran di lacciuo' forme si nove,
a tal piacer precipitava al corso
che perder libertate ivi era in pregio.

III. Caro, dolce, alto e faticoso pregio
che ratto mi volgesti al verde bosco,
15   usato di sviarne a mezzo 'l corso!
Ed ò cerco poi 'l mondo a parte a parte,
se versi o petre o suco d'erbe nove
mi rendesser un dì la mente sciolta.

IV. Ma lasso! or veggio che la carne sciolta
20   fia di quel nodo, ond'è 'l suo maggior pregio
prima che medicine antiche o nove

saldin le piaghe ch'i' presi in quel bosco
folto di spine, ond'i ò ben tal parte,
che zoppo n'esco, e 'ntravi a si gran corso.

25 V. Pien di lacci e di stecchi un duro corso
aggio a fornire, ove leggera e sciolta
pianta avrebbe uopo e sana d'ogni parte.
Ma tu, Signor, ch'ai di pietate il pregio,
porgimi la man destra in questo bosco;
30 vinca 'l tuo sol le mie tenebre nove.

VI. Guarda 'l mio stato, a le vaghezze nove,
che 'nterrompendo di mia vita il corso
m'an fatto abitador d'ombroso bosco;
rendimi, s'esser pò, libera e sciolta
35 l'errante mia consorte, e fia tuo 'l pregio
s'ancor teco la trovo in miglior parte.

VII. Or ecco in parte le question mie nove:
s'alcun pregio in me vive o'n tutto è corso,
o l'alma sciolta, o ritenuta al bosco.

(ed. Ponte 1968: 161)

(Three days before, a soul had been created in a place
where it might put its care in things high and new
and despise what the many prize.
She, still uncertain of her fated course,
alone, thoughtful, young, and free,
in springtime entered a lovely wood.

A tender flower had been born in that wood
the day before, with its root in a place
that could not be approached by a soul still free;
for there were snares there of form so new
and such pleasure hastened one's course
that to lose liberty was there a prize.

Dear, sweet, high, laborious prize,
which quickly turned me to the green wood,
accustomed to making us stray in the midst of our course!
And I have later sought through the world from place to place
if verses or precious stones or juice of strange herbs
could one day make my mind free.

But now, alas, I see that my flesh shall be free
from that knot for which it is most greatly prized,
before medicines old or new
can heal the wounds I received in that wood
thick with thorns; on account of them it is my lot
to come out lame, and I entered with so swift a course!

Full of snares and thorns is the course
that I must complete, where a light, free
foot would be in need, one whole in every place.
But you, Lord, who have all pity's praise,
reach me your right hand in this wood:
let your sun vanquish this my strange shadow.

Guard my state from those new beauties
which, breaking off my life's course,
have made me a dweller in the shady wood:
Make again, if it can be, unbound and free
my wandering consort; and let yours be the praise
if I find her again with You in a better place.

Now behold in part my strange doubts:
if any worth is alive in me or all run out,
if my soul is free or captive in the wood.)

Few relationships are defined by Petrarch's poems, but they are enlarged into principles the more nearly universal as their number decreases. Two dominate this sestina: that of the poet to Dante and of the lover to his soul. Petrarch evokes Dante's exposition of the development of the human soul:

Esce di mano a lui che la vagheggia
prima che sia, a guisa di fanciulla
che piangendo e ridendo pargoleggia,
l'anima semplicetta che sa nulla . . .

(*Purg.* XVI, 85-88)

(From his hand who regards it fondly before it is comes forth like a child that sports, tearful and smiling, the little simple soul that knows nothing . . .)

In "her" newborn state, the soul knows and seeks only what is pleasurable, then avidly follows it, requiring the "freno" (rein) of will. From this point Dante leads into the center of his second canticle, to a full analysis of love as potential attraction to the beloved object, then a delight, and finally a desire that can be stilled only by fruition. The nature of love as a relation is recognized by Dante, as by Scholastic philosphers and poets generally: The loved thing is the appearance of it as apprehended by the lover. The need to measure or evaluate follows, but any good less than God (to whom the soul willingly returns) is merely a term for value, or more properly, evaluation.

In Petrarch's reading, the soul appears as part of a knot or conglomeration of soul and body, albeit the better "part":

121

IV. Ma lasso! or veggio che la carne sciolta
fia di quel nodo, ond'è 'l suo maggior pregio . . .

His cure, the lover states, is impossible since it will come only upon his death. We have here another instance of the curiously reversible adynaton to which Petrarch's sestinas constantly recur. Petrarch deals with the contradiction by means of another borrowing from Dante. Readers of the *Commedia* would easily recall the passage in which the pilgrim sets forth upon his journey, "sì che 'l piè fermo sempre era 'l più basso" (so that the firm foot was always the lower [or left] [*Inf.* I, 20]). It has been shown (Freccero 1959) that the line is to be understood in terms of the Christian allegory of the interior feet of the soul, and that the dragging left foot signifies the lame will of the pilgrim limping in his efforts ultimately to reach God. The last line of Petrarch's fourth strophe represents this lameness and signals the discontinuity of Petrarch's treatment of it. Unequipped with enabling grace, the lover knows, even a "leggera e sciolta / pianta" will not be liberated from its peregrinations in the wood. In escape would lie the resolution of the crushing conflict of human time and eternity, of history (personal or collective) and eschatology, the wherefore of self-denial. Petrarch might well have had Dante's "sun" in mind when he invoked God from the dark wood "dove 'l sol tace" (*Inf.* I, 60). But speaking from within experience, his view is ineluctably tentative, for God is given the term of relativity, *pregio.* We cannot be certain that this appearance of "value" is not tainted with the uncertainty of "reputation." This is a God approaching the courtly Lord of Francesca, whom she envisioned as a traitor to love's cause. Only the poet fills silence. To know this makes error and passion "new."

All the shades of meaning of *nove* denote the unprecedented in kind or degree. Coupled with *altere* it sketches the unforeseen achievement of great undertakings such as those of a knight or warrior, opposed at any rate to feminine elements. In the second strophe it applies to the extreme degree of Laura's allure. The alternations continue. In the third, it refers to the desired miracle of cures for sickness of will, but here the term *erbe,* so often a metaphor for Laura, attaches *nove* back to the disease itself.

Corso alternately denotes the course of human life and the movement of running that can mimic time's flow or man's pursuit of some goal. Within this "course" of behavior, man is bound. Countering this imprisonment in time is the term *sciolta,* feminine and "unbound." These two terms linking time and movement encounter a term for space: *bosco,* which is a partial representation of the

122

Petrarchan *selva,* now defiguralized as the single narrow meaning of "forest." *Parte* is the synecdochic ground for representations of place, designating in turn the lover's body, Laura's body, sections of a fragmented world, the lover's share of thorns, part of the human foot, "a better place," or heaven, at last serving to confess the incompleteness of the lover's self-questioning and accounting, particularly as a setting for the *disjecta membra* of a moribund epistemology.

The lover knows himself bound, and the sestina explores his prison walls, imaging freedom as a fait accompli (the past participle, *sciolta*). Again the feminine term bridges a fundamental duality, attaching itself to *anima, mente, carne, pianta* — the things that signal closure. The concerns designated by the rhyme-words denote within the poem and connote outside of it the tension between openness and closure, linear and cyclical time.

Any meaning must "fit," retaining a plausibility apart from private significance. The ultimate constraint on subjective reading is the subtextual presence of Dante. Near the center of the poem Petrarch (as in the opening strophe) embeds references that go back to key passages of *Inferno* and *Purgatorio.* First there is the echo of Dante on the subject of birth and death in an explication given by the Christianized poet Statius:

> Quando Lachesis non ha più del lino,
> solvesi dalla carne, ed in virtute
> ne porta seco e l'umano e l'divino.
>
> (*Purg.* XXV, 79-81)

(When Lachesis [the fate] has no more flax, it is dissolved from the flesh, and carries with her, in potential, both the human and the divine faculties.)

This Dantean passage is one of many subtending the movement of Petrarch's poem. From the architectonic solidity of Dante's three realms, Petrarch conserves images of discontinuity. The youthful soul, only past two of the ages of man, if not entirely innocent, appears only to fall within parentheses. No sooner does she make her entrance than she comes upon a tempting pastoral scene. This *locus amoenus* is the place where the lover awaits the touch of God's hand. The rhetorical reminder of the Dantean world serves as the ground from which to judge Petrarch's, its opening allegory little more than a mnemonic device. While much of this poem's lexicon derives from the descriptive system of medieval morality, it is there to help us ask how much that system still retains its cognitive power.

Even the femininity of the soul, determined simply by language itself, is examined together with its concomitant topoi of marriage (*l'errante mia consorte*) and with the triumphant allure of Laura, as if to ask, who is the real lady of the poem? The use of typology as a means of transcending contingency, and the use of terza rima as an icon of ascending enchainment, both submit to sporadic allegorical discourse and a strophic construction that underscores discontinuity. Mechanisms of entrapment and closure show within the poem against visions of certainty vouchsafed by Dantean subtexts. What begins as a discourse on the life of a human soul becomes a process of internal questioning without cosmological ratification.

It is during the third of the oddly belated ages of man computed as five in all that Petrarch's enamorment takes place, the concomitant of his poetic beginnings (Ponte 1968: 981). But the allusion to the span of human life acquires a greater measure of force through the association of "three days" with Christ's resurrection and Petrarch's extension of that association throughout his poems. The love story is the poem's actual presence, seeming to repress its Christian obverse. This pairing could offer itself to representations on any level of medieval discourse. It raises questions Dante dealt with early in his work, in the *Vita Nuova*, and later in his *Commedia*, but would be easily adapted to the premises of a fabliau. In such a case the poet might delight in the interchange between metaphors of love and of religious devotion. Petrarch as in all of his other work rejects the possibility of humorous intrusions far more than did Dante, for whom the love of women eventually found its hierarchical place, where it could be contemplated almost with the detachment of an anthropologist. As if to establish that this is no laughing matter, Petrarch recurs to the worth of the human body, his body, as a fit dwelling and later as mate for the soul, but does so metonymically (*parte* has its first reference in the body). Together with *alma*, *parte* has to complete the man. To counterbalance this quotient of concrete reference, there is an overwhelming presence of transparent terms denoting relationship, ways of classifying, measuring, or evaluating (*por sua cura, cose, quei, molti, pregio*). Before her entry into the alliterative wood of art and love, the soul is already weighted with thought, *dubbia* carrying the secondary sense of "questioning" together with the primary sense of ignorance. The soul is now conceived of as previously endowed with a kind of mid-life crisis.

Where "things" are categorized according to the oppositions common/rare and old/new, much is left o judgment as long as familiar features of secular aristocracy are the points of comparison. Yet *nove* as a term for the young, the wondrous, the previously unknown or unsung, transcends these as the determinant of value, calling attention to "newness" alone. The Dante/Petrarch tension cannot be leveled to the status of an academic controversy, nor can this poetry be considered to be "about" aesthetic values taken out of context. What is at stake is the dehierarchization of scholastic epistemology and a witness that poetry does not reflect but creates the context in which its meanings are located. Petrarch's reader has to cooperate in the progressive discovery of signs and objects becoming signs in their turn. To perform this task, he has to reconstruct the context of situation and motive, to draw upon his other literary and extra-literary experience, moving outward in a continuous extension of meaning. The status of *pregio,* a rhyme-word whose primary meaning is value or positive relatability, affects everything else that is said, drawing all other material into contingency. Its changes, from the idea of value, to the past of that idea, to a prize, a valued quality, reputation (even of God), triumph, and back to generalized "value" follow a curve describing fortune's rise and fall. Most of all the term bespeaks the mutability of man in the world, offsetting *nove,* which is always feminine. Petrarch states that he has asked only in part the questions he harbors about his destiny. It is not, this *bosco,* the universe of human existence, but specifically a piece of it enlarged to a whole—the experience of fatal love. And this is only one part cut from Dante's plan. Petrarch acknowledges these parts to be in turn a part of his store of content-forms. The full extent of his questions has not been discovered before. It concerns the teleology of poetry as much as any other knotty matters in the lover's existence.

Novelty is relatively and sequentially determined. True, Dante had recognized this relentless succession in his discussion of the vagaries of literary fame. It is hinted to the pilgrim that he may "chase from the nest" the precursors of his early work, but he too will be succeeded by other poets, human life being as the wink of an eye compared with eternity. (*Purg.* XI, 103-108). Fame is yet another rite of passage as far as man in concerned, and permanent only for God (line 36). In a later key place of the *Purgatorio,* the pilgrim and the poet effect one of their open meetings, where the versifier Bonagiunta da Lucca is given to understand that poetry "signifies" the dictates of "Love":

> "O frate, issa vegg'io" diss'elli "il nodo
> che 'l Notaro e Guittone e me ritenne
> di qua dal dolce stil novo ch'i'odo."
>
> (*Purg.* XXIV, 55-57)

("O brother, now I see," he said, "the knot that kept the Notary and Guittone short of the sweet new style I hear.")

This key passage is also set into a discussion of literary fame, a retrospective on the novelty of Dante's style. Here the status of fame is revealed to the lesser poet as contingent, a part subordinated to a whole of signification. *Nodo* is not a "Petrarchan" word, and its appearance in our sestina must alert us to the presence of some kind of foreign information. At the same time, Bonagiunta sees himself as having been held back, and the knot that does so consists in his inability to follow inner dictates, to free himself from (plebian) concrete referentiality. Petrarch's overriding concern with the impossibility of "following the dictates of Love" comes from another kind of source, and has to do with temporality. His awareness neither reading nor writing can be performed as a whole, complete in itself, but that each traces developing responses in order of succession, leads to his painful recording of the disjunction between word and impulse, playing the Dantean components off against a new reality. What are the names for these failed cures? Verses, first—certainly a circular process of cure and affliction. Then stones: Must we accept a simple reference to medieval science, or are these *petre* sections of a "stony" poem or "stony" lady? The third name, *erbe* (curative herbs or Laura herself) would complete the progression of the lover's search in the direction of his greatest danger. Even as the negation of sciences of the past plays a propulsive role in the search for the "new," the lover shows that any novelty he could conceive of is probably not new enough. For the fifth appearance of *nove* emphasizes the difference of his affliction from any that had ever preceded it.

That statement goes far beyond the poet's claims of artistic discovery or uniqueness. The oblique and subterranean relationship of Petrarch to Dante calls for Petrarch's rejection of old epistemologies. Note that he does not forget even Dante's "harsh rhymes" for the lady Petra, which contain a sestina. But even if form could be abstracted from content, Petrarch's choice of a sestina as the ground for discussing the great matters of the *Commedia* would be "new." Because the sestina points beyond its representations to an unending relationship among a finite number of words, because it suggests ideas that it could potentially articulate but does not, it continues and enlarges Dante's experimentation with non-closed, cumulative form. Dante's achievement of linear progress within the self-contained whole of the *Commedia* can never be surpassed, but it can be challenged as an epistemological tool and will be challenged in the flow of time. Newness is the property of every successive author simply by virtue of this flow, each new poet superseded in the temporal sense no matter what his *pregio* (worth, value, renommée). In that the vision of God can never be described, the *Commedia* points forever beyond itself, yet this loss of ultimacy and perfect reference is subordinated to the dominance of Dante's self-contained literary system. It is the subordinate status of incompleteness to plenitude, of openness to closure, that determines the imperviousness of the *Commedia* to imitation and to relativism. In the Petrarchan context, and in that of the sestina, things are perceived precisely in their relation to one another.

Our ability, and Petrarch's, to draw this kind of comparison is itself a manifestation of relativity and of the necessity of arbitrary boundaries. The principle of representation has a correlated principle: It concerns the very structure of the poetic sign and of its signifying system. A sign divides the *relation* of representation into two subrelations: That between ideas and signs, and that between signs and things. But a sign allows a substitution to take place between its object and the idea of the object, a substitution that works from the thing to the sign. The idea of the signified object is substituted for the sign. The high degree of this substitution determines the semioticity of Petrarchan language—always a matter of degree. It is heightened by his choice of the sestina as a total representation. That level of self-reference interfacing signifier and signified, signified and referent, constitutes in toto his use of Dante. "Poetic" truth supervenes so that Petrarch's assertive operation has an ontological effect in the world, articulating things in the world. Figures, like the Petrarchan adynaton, make discrete things signify one another and play with expansion and reduction "at will."

The Infernal forest of wandering is reduced to the essential characterization: Enamorment, with its subversive feminine associations. Petrarch loses no time in establishing it as a background of contending values, *altere e nove* against *quel ch'a molti è 'n pregio,* and the image of the beloved as a tender flower (strophe II) recalled the object of chief value in courtly literature before Dante: the rose of the *Roman,* for example. Even as the speaker protests that the soul is that flower's root, the trick of time works its magic. It has put behind the lover his own capture and loss. No "free soul," he laments, could approach such a beautiful flower. That is to say: In the very act of approaching it, the free soul is transformed and bound. Now the wood of Dante becomes a site of nostalgia, its polysemy displaced and neutralized, just as the wood itself according to Petrarch sways us in the midst of our course (line 15). It is no wonder that freedom is not to be found within the idiom of known love-literature, for the *bosco* is itself the generator of the herbs, stones, and poems, the nets and lures that obstruct the speaker's course. Laura's "value" crosses with the idea of her as a "prize" (line 13), exposing the tangle of interests between the end of desire as free will and the end of desire as union with her. Qualification and quantification inform a sea of relationships. Consciousness of sin is the precondition of this poem. Where is it to fit with its persistent relativism? What is Petrarch's place in Dante's wood—or even, in any aspect of it?

When the Dantean pilgrim is almost ready to proceed out of Purgatory, he enters a wood again, this time the *selva antica* that Adam through his fall had turned *oscura:*

> Già m'avean trasportato i lenti passi
> dentro a la selva antica tanto ch'io
> non potea rivedere ond'io entrassi.
>
> (*Purg.* XXVIII, 22-24)

(Already my slow steps had brought me so far within the ancient wood that I could not see the place where I had entered.)

This forest, Beatrice informs him, will be his dwelling for a short time:

> "Qui sarai tu poco tempo silvano
> e sarai meco sanza fine cive
> di quella Roma onde Cristo è Romano."
>
> (*Purg.* XXXII, 100-102)

(Here you will be a little while a forester, and shall be with me forever a citizen of that Rome of which Christ is Roman.)

Petrarch as *abitador* of the shadowed wood obviously recalls this *silvano*. But the opposition between "forest-dweller" and "citizen" is neutralized, a "shaded" region between them, and a creature something like an habitué. The whole is conceived not in terms of a political relation but simply in a neutral state of existence—the passing of time. Nor is the forest an *antica selva* comprising human existence but simply the wood of enamorment, the locus of sin alone. Dante's emergence from Purgatory enables him to continue his ascent into Paradisiacal light and grace with no fear of further impediments, so that the forest serves as connecting link between two of the three realms, hence as a principle of poetic structure. The wood of Petrarch's sestina recurs to the pre-Dantean world of medieval romance, yet unlike the usual wandering lover, this traveler is no passerby but part of the place itself.

Petrarch's is an interrupted journey, a *mezzo 'l corso,* imbued with the weight of choice—unlike Dante's without a guide. At other cross-roads the Petrarch of the Letter on the ascent of Mount Ventoux measured himself against a monastic ideal, the better to discover his own newness. Moments of pause, of beginning and ending, are those that Petrarch extracts from the Dantean text. At the close of the Dante-pilgrim's purgatorial journey, Virgil acknowledges him as master of his own will: You have arrived now, he informs him, in a place (*parte*) where I cannot accompany you:

> . . . disse: "Il temporal foco e l'etterno
> veduto hai, figlio; e se' venuto in parte
> dov'io per me più oltre non discerno.
> Tratto t'ho qui con ingegno e con arte;
> lo tuo piacere ormai prendi per duce;
> fuor se' dell'erte vie, fuor se' dell'arte."
>
> (*Purg.* XXVII, 127-32)

(and he said: "The temporal fire and the eternal you have seen my son, and you have come to a part where I, for my part, discern no futher. I have brought you here with understanding and with skill. From now on take your pleasure for guide. You have come forth from the steep and narrow ways.")

Now the pilgrim will find his choices motivated by desire, the need for choice vitiated by the alignment of his will and God's will, "libero, dritto e sano" (free, upright and whole [*Purg.* XXVII, 140]).

The sestina recalls that moment in his need for a *pianta* that is "sana d'ogni parte," for the return of his body's consort, the soul, to the jurisdiction of will (rendimi . . . libera e sciolta). Glimpsing the potential grace of the sun, Petrarch's speaker recognizes that it is denied him and even if vouchsafed it would have to fight his *tenebre nove* on an equal basis, like two warriors. The soul as *consorte* in this context does not fit easily as "wife" to the whole person, athough it shares his fate as part of him.

Dante's organization of parts and wholes is a model of systemic integration. The uncertainty of metonymic structure, if ever present, had long been worked out in his *Vita Nuova* (Shapiro 1979). In the Dantean text to which Petrarch alludes, cruxes occur literally at crossroads in the pilgrim's existence as man and poet—at the entrance to the wood of sin; at the exit of the wood of endeavor and repose, where he confronts as through the eyes of another a condensed view of his own poetics; where his will is crowned sovereign and he is ready to move on. *By virtue of containing extracts,* the Petrarchan reading of the *Commedia* in this sestina undermines the cohesion of the earlier text, itself a triumph of closure and cohesiveness. Partly accounting for this violence is Petrarch's historical position at the decline of syllogism and the debasement of Christian social and political hierarchies. A newer, more pertinent question concerns the bond between Petrarch's use of Dante and poetic invention.

The rhyme-word *nove* in its final appearance sums up the questions, doubts, and fears in the lover's mind. Like the other key terms, it is revealed as belonging to a system of internal relations dependent on the coincidence of spatial and temporal coordinates. The poet-lover asks whether he has spent his full value in sin, moved by the rival logic of desire. For the intertwining of body and soul is a hard knot, without a discernible center, that motivates the poet to yield to the subversive, the weak, the marginal, and the feminine, propitiating God while straining against closure. There may be a "value" that survives sin.

In the native theology that provides our expression of what God is, the prime attribute is infinity. Poems cannot aspire to it; like men and their fame they are finite, taken as entities. Nevertheless in his sestinas Petrarch came upon new and daring possibilities of openness. Finite in himself, man may be viewed as part of an infinite flow. Whereas Dante ensured that the closure of his poem would never make it rival the relation between man and God, Petrarch by articulating human potentiality subverted that system self-containment, and thus ensured his succession, promising an "unbinding" futurity of memory.

6. CCCXXXII: "Mia benigna fortuna e 'l viver lieto"

I. Mia benigna fortuna e 'l viver lieto,
i chiari giorni e le tranquille notti
e i soavi sospiri, e 'l dolce stile
che solea resonare in versi e 'n rime,
5   volti subitamente in doglia e 'n pianto,
odiar Vita mi fanno e bramar Morte.

II. Crudele, acerba, inesorabil Morte,
cagion mi dai di mai non esser lieto,
ma di menar tutta mia vita in pianto,
10   e i giorni oscuri e le dogliose notti;
i mei gravi sospir' non vanno in rime
e 'l mio duro martir vince ogni stile.

III. Ove è condutto il mio amoroso stile?
a parlar d'ira, a ragionar di morte.
15   U' sono i versi, u' son giunte le rime,
che gentil cor udia pensoso e lieto?

ove 'l favoleggiar d'amor le notti?
Or non parl' io, nè penso, altro che pianto.

V. Già mi fu col desir sì dolce il pianto,
20   che condia di dolcezza ogni agro stile,
e vegghiar mi facea tutte le notti;
or m' è 'l pianger amaro più che morte,
non sperando mai 'l guardo onesto e lieto,
alto soggetto a le mie basse rime.

25   V. Chiaro segno Amor pose a le mie rime
dentro a' belli occhi, ed or l 'à posto in pianto,
con dolor rimembrando il tempo lieto:
ond' io vo col penser cangiando stile
e ripregando te, pallida Morte,
30   che mi sottragghi a sì penose notti.

VI. Fuggito è 'l sonno a le mie crude notti
e 'l suono usato a le mie roche rime,
che non sanno trattar altro che morte;
cosi è 'l mio cantar converso in pianto:
35   non a 'l regno d' Amor sì vario stile,
ch' è tanto or tristo quanto mai fu lieto.

VII. Nessun visse già mai più di me lieto,
nessun vive più tristo e giorni e notti;
e doppiando 'l dolor, doppia lo stile,
40   che trae del cor sì lacrimose rime.
Vissi di speme, or vivo pur di pianto,
nè contra Morte spero altro che morte.

VIII. Morte m'a morto, e sola pò far Morte
ch' i' torni a riveder quel viso lieto
45   che piacer mi facea i sospiri e 'l pianto,
l' aura dolce e la pioggia e le mie notti
quando i penseri eletti tessea in rime,
Amor alzando il mio debile stile.

IX. Or avess' io in sì pietoso stile
50   che Laura mia potesse tôrre a Morte
come Euridice Orfeo sua senza rime,
ch' i' viverei ancor più che mai lieto!
S' esser non po, qualcuna d' este notti
chiuda omai queste due fonti di pianto.

55   X. Amor, i' ò molti e molt' anni pianto
mio grave danno in doloros stile,
nè da te spero mai men fere notti;
e pero mi son mosso a pregar Morte
che mi tolla di qui, per farme lieto,
60   ove è colei che i' canto e piango in rime.

XI. Se sì alto pon gir me stanche rime
ch' aggiungan lei ch' e fuor d' ira e di pianto
e fa 'l ciel or di sue bellezze lieto,
ben riconoscerà 'l mutato stile
65   che già forse le piacque, anzi che Morte
chiaro a lei giorno, a me fesse atre notti.

XII. O voi che sospirate a miglior' notti,
ch' ascoltate d' Amore o dite in rime,
pregate non mi sia più sorda Morte,
70   porto de le miserie e fin del pianto;
muti una volta quel suo antiquo stile
ch' ogni uom attrista, e me pò far sì lieto.

XIII. Far mi pò lieto in una o 'n poche notti:
e 'n aspro stile e ' angosciose rime
75   prego che 'l pianto mio finisca Morte.

(ed. Ponte 1968: 237-238)

(My kind fortune and glad life,
bright days and tranquil nights,
and gentle sighs and a sweet style
that used to resound in verses and rhymes,
suddenly turned to grief and weeping,
make me hate life and yearn for death.

Cruel, untimely, inexorable Death,
you give me cause never to be glad
but to live my life ever weeping,
with dark days and sorrowing nights;
my heavy sighs cannot go into rhymes,
and my harsh torment surpasses every style.

Where has it been led, my amorous style?
to speak of sorrow, to talk about death.
Where are the verses, where are the rhymes
that a noble heart used to hear thoughtful and glad?
Where is that talking of love all the night?
Now I speak and think of nothing but weeping.

Formerly, so sweet with desire was weeping
that it seasoned with sweetness every bitter style
and made me keep watch through all the nights;
now tears are more bitter to me than death,
since I do not hope ever to see that glance, virtuous and glad,
the high subject of my low rhymes.

A clear target did Love set up for my rhymes
within those lovely eyes, and now he has set it up in weeping,

132

sorrowfully reminding me of that glad time,
and I go changing with my cares my style
and begging you often, pale Death,
to rescue me from such painful nights.

Sleep has fled from my cruel nights
and their usual sound from my hoarse rhymes
that cannot treat anything but death;
thus my singing is converted to weeping.
The kingdom of Love does not have so varied a style,
for now it is as sorrowful as ever it was glad.

No one ever lived more glad than I,
no one lives more sorrowful both day and night
or, sorrow doubling, redoubles his style
that draws from his heart such tearful rhymes.
I lived on hope, now I live only on weeping,
nor against Death do I hope for anything but death.

Death has killed me, and only Death
has the power to make me see again that glad face
that made sighs pleasing to me and weeping,
the sweet wind and rain of my nights,
when I wove my noble thoughts into rhymes,
Love raising up my weak style.

Would I had so sorrowful a style
that I could win my Laura back from Death
as Orpheus won his Eurydice without rhymes,
for then I would live more glad than ever!
If it cannot be, let one of these nights
now close my two fountains of weeping.

Love, for many and many years I have been weeping
my heavy loss in grieving style,
nor from you do I ever hope to have less cruel nights;
and therefore I have turned to beg Death
to take me from here, to make me glad
where she is whom I sing and bewail in rhymes.

If they can go so high, my weary rhymes,
as to reach her who is beyond sorrow and weeping
and with her beauties now makes Heaven glad,
she will surely recognize my changed style,
which perhaps used to please her before Death
made for her bright day, for me black nights.

O you who sigh for better nights,
who listen about Love or write in rhymes,
pray that Death be no longer deaf to me,

the port of misery and the end of weeping;
let her for once change her ancient style
that makes everyone sorrowful but can make me so glad.

She can make me glad in one or a few nights,
and in harsh style and anguished rhymes
I pray that my weeping may be ended by Death.)

Petrarch's system is one that invalidates, once and for all, the explanation of a literary fact by a bibliographical one, at the very time when man writing as a "universal" speaker (Spitzer 1946: 414) was extending this self-conception to the meshing of exemplum and anecdote in a fictional whole. Literary fact, he shows, can also be biographical fact, but that does not explain what it is doing in a work of poetry. For when such facts pass from life into literature, their meaning changes. They have been chosen and set into a structure that is never the equivalent of a life. The poet's moving mind generates fictions that derealize reality by a particular use of language and a bold exploitation of literary traditions. In the course of this alchemy content-substance is transmuted into something not its reflection but even, at times, its antithesis.

One of Petrarch's major innovations was to show how the same poem could be reinvented endlessly. The double sestina appropriately comprises his most openly Orphic lament. The presence of Orpheus throughout Petrarchan lyrics is proleptic, urging the advent of adynaton, bringing anticipation out of the future and onto the verge of present delight and fulfillment. It is the rhetorical presence, however, most adapted to the poetic embodiment of an erotic world, opposing poetic truth to the finality of death. Petrarch's accomplishment in this poem and the lover's concurrent striving for unprecedented poetic excellence is a contest against the self. As the eclogue becomes monologue, the power of myth in it is revealed as deriving from the quality of the incantation itself. And in itself the poem constitutes the meaning toward which the several ellipses of its language move: the power of incantation to sway Hades and survive death.

In Plato's account (*Symposion* 179d) Orpheus, derogated singer that he is, lacks the courage to die and is punished for entering the underworld alive with the mere shadow of Eurydice. We recall the uncertainty and flexibility of the *in bono* and *in malo* views of Orpheus. This is not the time of the Renaissance readings of Plato that establish Orpheus as lover and theologian, even to making his myth allegorize the death and new life of the rational soul (Pico della Mirandola in Garin 1952: 554). Petrarch's is the Orpheus that did not give his earthly life for the life of his beloved.

This is, however, the one sestina *in morte di madonna Laura,* and it is a farewell to "rhyming" in the lover's former style. At the same time, as it takes leave of poetry of the *stil novo,* and from the store of Dantean topoi, it begins from the familiar stance of leave-taking that sets the tone of Dante's own song in praise of the moral value of nobility. Dante had said good-by to his *dolci rime d'amor* in the fourth song of the *Convivio,* declaring that his new task would require an utterly different style. This loan-contract glances off Petrarch's double sestina, as do many that emphasize terms for change. Like the farewell to the beloved of Orphic myth, and like the rhymer's parting with his poem in the songs of the earlier Florentines, this seems to be a farewell-song of the immediate type characterized by Paul Zumthor as *congé* (1972: 407).

The materials of craft are exposed: *rime, stile,* counterposed to the inner life of art. The rhyme-words are semantically heterogeneous, more so than in any of the other sestinas, and their meanings fluctuate so little that context affects them maximally. From one six-strophe cycle to the other the poem is semantically cohesive in virtue of contextual, and specifically syntactic, linkages. The musical structure accordingly becomes dominant, to the extent that the reader is affected by the patterns of antithesis and other kinds of twining (*benigna fortuna/viver lieto; versi/rime; doglia/pianto*). Although we have here the single example of an adjective (*lieto*) used as a rhyme-word in Petrarch's sestinas, we see that the word becomes nominalized. Whereas nouns refer to specific things, predicates to "anything," the use of recurrence here gives *lieto* a new concreteness, concealing from the new reader relationships of comparative significance among various facets of what is being said. Feelings, states, and responses appear to be revolving in nonjudgmental order until the very last, where the verb of judgment and action appears: *prego che'l pianto mio finisca Morte.*

To call the lover passive is commonplace and inexact. The nature of his passivity needs articulating. For one thing, his thought processes though fertile and continuous are not expressed as symbolic action. Any potential predicates of action or being that attach to him are nominalized. *Morte* is the only one in rhyme position. It could have been realized within the line as a verb (I will die), but this possibility would give way to persistent reification. In the first six strophes of the sestina, a marked avoidance of active verbs invites their substitution by contructions that show the speaker as acted upon. The lover is debarred from subject-status; *rime* and *stile* are known to him only through a concurrence and complicity of emotions that he harbors. He is unable to use adjectives analytically. Feelings disconnected from psyche, boomeranging perceptions projected on the world, relations drawn through the weakening chain of mediators: This amalgam called man is a sounding board for contending externalized powers.

But his leave-taking launches the poet-lover into something whose sense is disjoined from that of his past. Here is a literal beginning, consisting narratively in the overcoming of the lover by death, which is both a beginning and an ending. The missiles of death hurled at him also include verse, rhymes, and style functioning in a way dissociated from the subject. The materials of textuality appear divorced from his control and little in need of humanity for their patterning. The poem made from such materials becomes an image itself, an object of contemplation abstracted from the physical and causal order of life and death. No center exists in the personality; rather, the lover anticipates another state. He calls it death, knowing that there is no retreat from it. At other times, he calls it Laura—the next dialectical advance from death.

Lieto belongs either to the irreversible past or is negated in the present. It applies to the lover's former existence as an aspirant; his actual lack of happiness; that of those who heard his former poems; the benign glance of Laura; or to the happy past recalled in present despair. It acquires potentiality when the lover invokes his own death (strophe VIII). Recapitulated within the sestina's spiraling movement is the term for temporal measurement, *notti,* related to *morte* by contiguity.

The horizontal process of word combination manifests itself through metonymy, whose principle is contextual. In this poem the figural quotient is reduced entirely to metonymic relations, with exceptions among codified figures (Fuggito è 'l sonno a le mie crude notti). Once a literal signatum has been submerged, like the figure of the poet himself, under the figural signatum (reified emotions and impulses), the maximal context-sensitivity of metonymy supervises the changes of the sestina. It is in fact the contextual locus, the whole poem, and the presence of the contiguity relations facilitated by the context that enables the figural meaning of metonymy to be understood as such and for the poem to be read.

To hypostatize Love, or Death, shows the lability of such figures in respect to their proportion of metonymic aspects. It is an old "rhetorical color" often used in the service of courtliness and ultimately of a phenomenology of self-articulation. Hypostatized love is a metonymy for the absent beloved; it is a functional substitute and a member in a chain of substitutes. To draw attention to doing and redoing, to the iterative process of shaping, the selection, rejection, and correction of material calls for the advent of a metonymic series. The double sestina formally duplicates an antecedent moment, a strategy serving the purpose of extending time, of saying it. The relation it manifests between love and death is one of change, this time viewed *hors de concours* from the transformative forest, through the screen of "style," so that the terms for change apply specifically to poetry itself:

> I: soavi sospiri e'l dolce stile . . . volti subitamente in doglia e 'n pianto; III: Ov'è condutto il mio amoroso stile?; V: Chiaro segno Amor pose a le mie rime; VI: Così è'l mio cantar converso in pianto; VII: doppiando 'l dolor, doppia lo stile; VIII: Amor alzando il mio debile stile; XI: ben riconoscerà 'l mutato stile; XII: muti una volta quel suo antiquo stile.

Death marks off segments of human time, but these are subordinated to the temporal structure of a poem, the action of poetry on external reality. That assumption of Orphic myth not only underlies the unprecedented "stylistic" effort of the double sestina but is the ontological ground of the poem's striving. Orpheus as a prototype of the poetic self is recreated in a confluence of contrasting ideas. The poet-theologian, one of the first three, with Musaeus and Linus, to sing of God (Augustine, *De civitate Dei* XVIII, 14), could also be perceived as acting out of cupidity in his descent into the underworld (Wetherbee 1972: II). But whereas the theologian could not be conceived of in negative terms, it was otherwise with the lover. Hence the nonsymmetrical division of self in Petrarch's Orphic fictions. He directs the malleable data of the myth toward escape from the constraints of choice.

The tensions between a waning medieval culture and another culture about to come into being here condition the figure of Orpheus. Everywhere there are traces of bygone tropes enmeshed in commonplace or elision. This ductility betokens the evasion of poetry from constraint and closure. In another sestina the poet-lover proclaims: "Nulla è al mondo che non possono i versi, / e li spidi incantar sanno in lor note, / non che 'l gielo adornar di novi fiori" (CCXXXIX, 28-30). For the poet composing in a Romance language in the fourteenth century, *rime* in one of its meanings equals poetry. It is a specifically representable term (unlike *stile* or *lieto*) and as such invites consideration of its temporal aspect. From its consecutive arrangement a chiastic, self-canceling temporal conception emerges:

I.	che solea resonare in versi e 'n rime	PAST
II.	I mei gravi sospir non vanno in rime	PRESENT
III.	U' sono i versi, u' son giunte le rime	PRESENT
IV.	alto soggetto a le mie basse rime	
	(reference to Laura's vanish glance)	PAST

V.	Chiaro segno Amor pose a le mie rime	PAST
VI.	Fuggito è . . . 'l suono usato a le mie roche rime	PRESENT
VII.	che trae del cor sì lacrimose rime	PRESENT
VIII.	quando i pensier eletti tessea in rime	PAST
IX.	come Euridice Orfeo sua senza rime	PAST
X.	ov'è colei ch'i'canto, e piango in rime	PRESENT
XI.	Se sì alto pon gir mie stanche rime	PRESENT
XII.	e 'n aspro stile e'n angosciose rime/prego . . .	PRESENT

Note how, in the tornada, the persistently revolving closure of the pattern gives way to the futurity of counterfactual anticipation.

Whereas *lieto* must refer to the past, the other terms invite contemplation of temporal process: *Morte* may be Laura's death or the lover's; *stile* and *rime,* while in the strict sense terms for place, link the distant past with the past in creation at the moment of utterance. *Notti* measures time between deaths. All of these are manifested in their contiguous relation at the expense of nascent metaphor. Nowhere is there an admonition to the reader to be especially attentive to figural content. Reference glances off earlier Italian lyric—reference to the *gentil cor,* which is a principle of the *stil novo,* to other rime or anterior patterns of poetic activity (*aspro stile* and *angosciose rime*). But the older pattern is now submerged within a recapitulating spiral movement. A sequence of words describing transformation, beginnings and endings, weaves through the strophes of the second cycle: VII, 4 *trae;* VIII, 2 *torre;* IX, 2 *torre;* X, 5 *tolla.* What is to be given or taken away varies (the poems "drawn forth" from the heart; Laura snatched from Death; the lover spirited to his second life with her), but the teleology of all these thoughts involves the evasion of natural laws toward what would be a new kind of *fabula.* The "style" that gave birth to these lines is a deep contrast to Dante's use of the same trope:

> Ma dì s'i' veggio qui colui che fore
> trasse le nove rime, cominciando
> "Donne che avete intelletto d'amore."
>
> (*Purg.* XXIV, 49-51)

(But tell me if I see here him that brought forth the new rhymes, beginning with "Ladies that have intellection of love.")

There the transformation value of creation (also envisioned in part as a recapitulative movement) prevails over all constraints of natural law, enabling the living pilgrim and the shade in Purgatory to confront one another in mutual understanding. If we follow the path delineated by the Petrarchan progression from stophes VII through X we arrive at another version of Orpheus. Never does the lover openly beg for death; he asks only that it give him his wish, reunion with Laura, in violation of its law. Surely a finer rhetoric would produce his desire: "or avess'io un sì pietoso stile. . . ." It is noteworthy that *pietoso* can refer either to a style that incites pity or to one that contains it. This versatility contributes to the transparency of a language of persuasion. By such means the reader of the poem becomes engaged in its rhetoric, invited into a seamless thought-sequence. The lover begs a visit to the other world without penalty. It is the kind of experience that Ariosto will later describe as a leisurely tour. Not destined, not anointed, not only "neither Paul nor Aeneas" but also "not" Dante, his sole aim is to retrieve his beloved and live in unending union with her.

The story of Orpheus weaves through the double sestina, but there is no indication of his losing Euridice for the second and last time. His myth recalled through the positive exempla connotes eternity triumphant over ending, loss, and closure. The power to which the lover aspires is that of a triumphant lover, not of a seer, and yet the result in terms of the actual poem is the reverse: Only poetic truth keeps Laura alive. It is to those who acknowledge this kind of truth that he especially addresses himself—to sighing lovers (not warriors), listeners and versifiers alike, those who have intelligence of love now heedlessly conflated into a general representation of passion.

Like the *pietoso stile,* things are both what they are and the response that they evoke in the effort to overcome interdict—here, the space between the dead and the living. Style is action and encompasses death as well as life. The lover prays: *muti una volta quel suo antiquo stile.* For the first time style refers no longer to the lover himself (strophe XII). The entire weight and stress of counterfactuality are brought to bear on invocation of the Orphic miracle: the bridging of the gulf between man and the supernatural. In poetry the terms are translatable into signifier and signified, no longer viewable in the terms of Dante's *dolce stil,* for the rhetorical and conceptual ground is another one. The formal meditation upon beginning and ending is more than apposite. In accordance with the full extra measure of grief, the double sestina offers its equivalent in words.

No retelling of Orpheus could encompass the lover's wish. The kind of authority and reward he invokes are conceivable only in terms of what they are not, leaving endless space to be filled by the recipient of the poem. Just where myth, culture, and doctrine would attempt an answer, this poem concentrates its power of questioning through its very fluctuation' What follows death? And the commitment to that question has to be suspended in action, in an enterprise that is "new." Poetry is like Orpheus returning from the underworld with his beloved. As long as poetry walks ahead, signifier leading signified, it leads the next relationship out of what was previously unnamed, then heads steadily toward the light of meaning without reaching finality. But when poetry turns to look at what it names, all that is left is a named meaning, and that meaning is dead.

Chapter 5

Dialectics of Renaissance Imitation:
The Case of Pontus de Tyard

The redundancies of poetic form tend to prolong the possibility of constructing or deconstructing poems even after some of their many sign systems have fallen into oblivion. That is how poems sometimes survive their own forms or genres—through the hidden unit of mutually confirmed structures.

A semiological approach to a poem should discover a movement whereby the firm assumption of analogy between two orders (easily labeled form and content) gives way to a synecdochic relation within a single order. So long as the natural world is treated as a figure for another order, or poetic form as a figure for a world-view, it is possible to play with metaphorical relations as the pre-Enlightenment poets did, using, for example, the seasons as figures for cycles of various kinds, as of moral experience. Within a Platonic-Petrarchan system, the poet could find in the inanimate things of the world the semblance of himself, the call to show that nature is expressive and contains within itself the meanings unveiled by his poetic voice. His aim was to interpret this Nature through his own forms. The concept of form was charged with a load of metaphysical presuppositions, traceable through the various meaning of Latin *forma* and its relatives to the Greek concepts of form (*morphe, eidos, logos, para-*

deigma, arche, typos, schema) in their proliferating interconnections. A paradoxical structure persists throughout all the Platonicizing permutations of *forma.* The notion has always presupposed a division between shape and substance, model and copy. In one way or another it was assumed that the meaning of what is formed pre-exists the form, stands outside, sustains, and validates it. The authenticity of the formed lies in the adequacy of its correspondence to its source or origin. The formed must copy its form, implying a mode of the aesthetics of imitation, form being both the structuring power and that which is structured.

The phenomenon of Renaissance Petrarchism belongs to the realm of poetic imitation and translation. It coincides in France of the sixteenth century with a veritable epidemic of other translations. In 1548 Thomas Sébillet, theoretician of poetics and of translation, affirmed that "la traduction est aujourd'hui le poeme plus frequent et mieux receu des estimés Poetes et des doctes lecteurs" (the translation is today the most frequent kind of poem and is received best by esteemed poets and learned readers [Sébillet 1932: 187]). The same period that witnessed the rendering of most sacred texts into the vernacular tongue reawakened the "profane" culture of antiquity and divulged its inventions. Whereas at the beginning of the century eighttenths of the books printed in France had been in Latin, now the advent of national languages spurred on every sort of translation. The great *Dictionarium* of Ambroise Calepin (1502) was quickly rendered into many languages and flanked by concordances, and in 1539 Robert Estienne produced a French-Latin dictionary that generated a wealth of technical lexicons. The tactics of mediation between the letter and the spirit of a work were a continual subject of discussion in manuals such as Etienne Dolet's *Manuel de bien traduire d'une langue en aultre* (1540) and Pierre-daniel Huet's *De interpretatione* (expanded in 1680). A special, privileged position was reserved, however, for translations of ancient poets. In many a view, Petrarch had taken his place among them and his works were regarded as enjoying the canonical status of models (cf. Shapiro 1973).

Pontus de Tyard, noble servant of Henri III of France, bishop of Chalon-sur-Saône, composer of rhetorics, author and translator of Platonic dialogues, is best remembered (when at all) for the loosely connected Canzoniere, *Les erreurs amoureuses*, that certifies his assimilation of Petrarch as well as his membership in the Pléiade. Its three books (published in 1549, 1551, and 1555) deploy an array of Petrarchan themes and include direct translations from the Italian. The geography of the beloved Pasithee reveals a land peopled with "medieval" characters who use the phraseology of Italian Platonism

142

of the later age. Such was his admiration for them that the poems run concurrently with his elaboration of an imitation of a translation: dialogues that follow his rendering into French of Leo Hebraeus' *Dialoghi d'amore*. In terms of the value assigned them, however, the poems in true Petrarchesque tradition run behind the prose, gathered under the rubric of "error."

Error is a name for a word deprived of sense and center: elements, soul, body, death, ascent, descent. As the poems confront the crucial questions of form, this staunch defender of the obscurity of Maurice Scève concentrates within their limits the full extent of his departure from the Platonic certainty that sure cognition exists. There the concept of language as speaking of forms of similitude (adjacency, analogy, emulation, sympathy) that contain the undoubted kernel of knowledge (Ideas) yields to a situation—of absence and the lack of a center—in which the object (of love or cognition) is not available for direct perception, thus modifying the stance of the searching *subject*. The main goal for the subject becomes the understanding of signs; the poet as subject is confronted by the diversity of signs and has to assign them objective reference while knowing that interpretation has neither beginning nor end.

Formal experimentation abounded in the Italy of Pontus' time. It attracted poets who were committed to a dynamic conception of art understood as a perennial approximation to fixed ideal limitations. Such ideas were consonant with Pléïade poetics (cf. Castor 1964), which repeatedly trace the line of emanation from a prior unit, personifying inspiration in the Muses. In the case of the Pléïade, a further alliance was sealed between the notion of perfectibility of poetic language and that of translation. The appearance of Du Bellay's *Deffence et illustration* incorporated poetry into an epistemological framework that was most hospitable to the willed development of a national poetics. But it was for Pontus de Tyard to confront and try the sestina against Ronsard's and Du Bellay's condemnation of its "formality" (Laumonier 1923: 668). He remained the only French poet to compose sestinas until the nineteenth century and the precious exercises of Gramont. We have only one more sestina by Pontus, (in *Erreurs* II) of a more nearly Petrarchesque cast.

Far from viewing Pontus' Platonic sestina as a mere solution to problems posed by conditions of form, considering it as a part of translation enables us to glimpse the immense area of *non*-verbal contrivance that is concealed beneath the words. When Mallarmé asked for a reader's card to the Bibliotheque Nationale so that he could copy in their entirety the works of Pontus de Tyard (Dubief 1963), it was no mere ordering of resemblances that he would study, but the rhetorical embodiment of the conflict between subjectivity and objectivity, event and iteration, being and becoming.

The introduction of a Petrarchan poem into the canon of French Renaissance verse shows that translation and imitation were central to the development of that canon. The very title "Sextine" sets up a literal context around the poetic utterance. The poem participates in the double nature of translation and imitation. Like translation, an imitation erects a hierarchy between itself and its original: Since this is not a poem by Petrarch it is to be viewed in one aspect as standing in a relation of courtship to its predecessor ("original"). Indeed the relations governing Platonic hierarchy as a whole are often transposable to relations of courtship in general. The imitative poem delineates a hierarchy culminating in Petrarch's own work (cf. Burke 1969: 208-212), to which it bears a more or less explicit external reference. From the principle of imitation of nature, it is a mere enthymemic slip to derive the principle that the work of a master poet is part and parcel of the scheme of Nature itself. The production of the imitator would be dominated by Memory (the first part of the old Rhetoric), which would guard the limits of possible metamorphoses attempted by an amateur without weakening the intensity of those metamorphoses in the work of a virtuoso. The scheme would not exclude the materiality of Rhetoric, returning in veiled disguise to the draftsman's bench. Summarizing the creations of his contemporaries, the rhetorician Tabourot inserts (1603: cit. McClelland 1967: 131): "Je ne sçay comme j'avois oublié la Sextine, que ce grand Pontus de Tyard et seigneur de Bissy, a le premier d'Italien habillé a la Françoise: qui est une poesie *pauvre* de ryme, et *riche* d'invention. . . ." ("I do not know how I had forgotten the Sestina, which that great Pontus de Tyard lord of Bissy, first dressed in French style, which is a poem poor in rhymes and rich in invention. . . .") The paradoxical status of rhetoric within a Platonizing scheme is parallelled by the double definition of its second "part," *inventio.* The same name used to indicate the quotient of "originality" in a work also referred to the relationship of the poet to a preexistent subject matter that he was said to "invent," or find. As imitator, the poet manipulated systems of signification, acted as the taxonomist of a landscape of recognition.

At the same time, through the act of self-generation, imitation seeks to derange this hierarchy, to make itself present through imputed *similarity* between itself and its "original"; whereas in a contiguity relation, imitation, like translation, can be considered reported speech—the recoding and transmitting of a message received from another source (Jakobson 1959: 43). Such a view would conceive of the imitation as grounded in a dependent relationship to its "original" and tend to conclude that the imitator, if he lives on, does so in his predecessor. Pontus de Tyard's introduction of the sestina into the French language of poetry proclaims its difference from the canonical sestina even as it enfolds itself within the context of the Petrarchan code. Poetic fury seems to grow, in the course of his first sestina, as a branch of the tree of alienation.

Apart from the fact that imitation is a Platonic principle, it dominated the very reading of the Platonic texts. Plato was known to the Renaissance, after all, not in the original Greek but through the filter of or at the remove of the Latin translation by Marsilio Ficino, embellished by his extensive commentary. The result yielded a constantly renewed Plato formed of the analytic and recreative transfer of previous meaning into another language. Myth was acknowledged not only as a fiction imposed upon the world but as a way of apprehending that world, having a radically cognitive function. Permutation entered into play wherever the coded elements of the dialogues were at once broad enough to shape a form and specific enough to produce identifying, lasting verbal expressions peculiar to that form.

The same process operated in the case of lyrical Petrarchism, which emanated from a poet so supple as to serve others to profoundly different temper and outlook over several centuries. In French poetry, the rampages of verbal prodigality, grammatical exuberance, and metaphoric experimentation were checked by the strong normative tendency of Petrarchan classicizing. Nevertheless, the very universality of the original, its resistance to referential interpretation, invited a quasi-theological outpouring of homage along an infinite *via negativa*. The mere experience of this poetry of praise could remind poet and reader of the encompassing primacy of negation in all cognition.

As Kenneth Burke (1970: 18-19) puts it, "The paradox of the negative, then, is simply this: Quite as the *word* "tree" is verbal and the *thing* tree is non-verbal, so all words for the non-verbal must, by the very nature of the case, discuss the realm of the non-verbal in terms of *what it is not.*" Drawing from a chapter in Bergson's *Creative Evolution* on "The Idea of Nothing," he elucidates the fact that "the negative is a peculiarly linguistic marvel, and that there are no negatives in nature, every natural condition being positively what it is . . . Or you can get the point by stopping to realize that you can go on forever saying what a thing is *not.*" Platonizing aesthetics held before poets that mirror of negation, whether or not it became translated into Ideas. For on the other hand, the unity of an Idea passed (by definition) into its human representation in the person of the artist, was humanized, incarnated by experience. It need not, however, lose its right to absoluteness; that would be confirmed by the hierarchy of value dominated by the *greatest* artist, the invisible object of praise. In consequence of this solution, the principle of art as a universal means of knowledge, espoused by Pontus' theoretical model, Ficino, could be transformed into the principle of literary experience, of literature. The artist as creator could be amended to a knower of literature, and invention amended to knowledge, or awareness.

The poetry of praise following Petrarch shows an effort at closure against shifting movements at the hierarchical summit. A theme dear to the Pléïade was the permanence of writing. Pontus de Tyard warns the recalcitrant love-object:

> Si ne dois-tu despriser la louange,
> que tu reçois de moy: car l'escriture
> Plus que beauté mortelle, beaucoup dure.
>
> (*Erreurs amoureuses,* II, ix, 5-7)

(You should not condemn the praise you receive from me: for writing, more than mortal beauty, long endures.)

The search for closure was far more pervasive than the revival of the canonized materialism of craftsmanship. Perfect repetition would constitute closure, and Pontus' exercises in poetic translation are evidence of a search for the suppression of difference through verification by repetition. Translating from Petrarch's sonnet LXI ("Benedetto sia 'l giorno . . .") he produces an index of the difference from repetition, an attempt to repeat in order to make a difference. What remains of the effort is the juxtaposition of pieces of text, as here:

Heureux le mois, heureuse la journée,	Benedetto sia 'l giorno e 'l mese e l'anno
Heureuse l'heure, et heureux le moment,	E la stagione e'l tempo e l'ora e'l punto
Heureux le siècle, heureux le Firmament	e 'l bel paese e 'l loco ov'io fui giunto
Souz qui ma Dame heureusement fut née.	da' duo begli occhi che legato m'anno:
Heureuse soit l'heureuse destinée	e benedetto il primo dolce affano
De l'Astre heureux, qui feit heureusement	ch'i' ebbi ad esser con Amor congiunto
Ce jour heureux son heureux mouvement,	e l'arco e la saette ond'i' fui punto

Sur toute estoille en bon
aspect tournée.
(*Erreurs*, I, xxxv, 1-8)

e le piaghe che 'nfin al
cor mi vanno
(LXI, 1-8; ed. 1968: 51)

(Happy the month, day, hour
moment, century, firmament, under
which my Lady was born. Happy be
the happy destiny of the happy
star that happily made this happy
day its happy move, over every
star turned to its good aspect.)

(Blessed be the day
and the month and the year
and the season and the time
and the hour and the instant
and the beautiful country-
side and the place where I
was struck by the two lovely
eyes that have bound me; and
blessed be the first sweet
trouble I felt on being made
one with Love, and the bow
and arrows that pierced me,
and the wounds that reach
my heart!)

The interaction of the two poems displays a high value placed on repetition and a constantly elusive field of reference. Their idiom is saturated in sheer encomium that depends on yet unrealized repetition. Hierarchies of likeness that seek to reconstruct the absence of the beloved object without the metaphorical violence of naming speak for the imitative accuracy of Pontus' title *Erreurs*. Yet the text does err, deviate from its road. The option of fleeing violence, the flight from the mere periphrase of a name, and the fear of the Sun propel Pontus' sonnet into its game of difference. Unlike Petrarch's beloved Laura, "Pasithee" even when named evokes only praiseworthy thoughts in her lover; unlike Scève's "Délie," she does not have a "speaking" name.

For the poem as communicative act we supply the missing elements; its fiction is definable only as a distant context. One trait of the imaginary world interposed between subject and object is the materiality of the text itself, a self-regulatory process that includes the interplay of anticipation and correction. Petrarchism and Neoplatonism are the maintainers of that distance, the place of discontinuity.

Pontus de Tyard acknowledges this space of alienation when his speaker, experiencing disharmony, attends to the noise of signs as signifiers impeding the message: the ambivalence of a simultaneous communication and noncommunication. The menace is that of form deprived of genre, de-generate forms with illegible senses:

147

La harmonie, aux doux concens nourrie
Des sept accords, contre l'ordre sphérique
Horriblement entour mon ouir crie.

(*Erreurs* I; "Disgrace," 19-21)

(Harmony, nourished by the sweet concord of the seven accords, cries horribly, around my hearing, against the order of the spheres.)

On one level the dualisms of this poetry emerge from the Petrarchan paradox of a conflict of being that represents the simultaneously beneficial and destructive experience of love, yielding the persistent instability of "natural man." The desired object participates at once in an external continuity beyond the poet's reach and in the flux of his "spirit." But the problem of cognitive dualism extends far beyond this local field and far more deeply into the core of Renaissance epistemology.

The entire six-year period during which Pontus de Tyard composed the *Erreurs amoureuses* can be regarded as a time of intense attachment to Platonic doctrine as transmitted through Ficino and Leo Hebraeus. In accordance with this apprenticeship, the image of man as microcosm, the coursing of his blood like the flowing waters, his breath like the wind, his flesh like the earth, embodies a diachronic structure of Platonism within the poems. But these structures of the mind are synchronic in a far stronger sense. They coexist in a present moment, that of the poem, and it is through the external, "present" moment that they make their entry into the sensible world. The diachronic structures of Neoplatonism are actually synchronic ones that make reference to time. The poet deals with flow and transiency in his *Douze fables de fleuves ou fontaines* (Twelve Tales of Rivers or Fountains), where closure and permanence arrest metamorphosis in the creation of mythical time. The movement of Error, the poet's being, carries messages between void and being in soliloquies joining Eros and Logos. Each fable contains the plan for a painting in fresco, impatient for a synthesis of literary and plastic arts that would accord closure to discourse fleeing the terror and authority of the sign (cf. Lebègue 1955).

There can be no doubt of that terror. In its service, observation seeks not to depart from exegesis. Cognition searches in the multiplicity of things for unity and a chain of belonging. A language of the elements exists, running parallel as in the *Fables de fleuves* to human language. To this structure of the mind belong alchemical etymology, Cabbalism, and the formal domain of Neoplatonic reminiscence. The awareness that sheer homophony derives only from chance, and symbol from convention, menaces the allegiance of language to that cosmic order. Then the signifier reveals itself as detached (except on the superior level of pure relation and equation of relations) from its signified, whereas closure would, conversely, ensure that signifier, signified, and the relation binding them are that "parole première, absolument initiale" (Foucault 1966: 56) on which discourse is based and by which it is controlled.

The same metaphor could apply to the cosmos, the body politic, the human body, the "faculties" of the soul, the moral properties analogous to chemical ones (attraction/repulsion). In the Platonic repertoire of dualisms—spirit/body, sun/moon, fire/water, masculine/feminine, solid/liquid, light/shadow, high/low, positive/negative, external/internal—the sign-pairs must relate and refer to one another after the fashion of harmonics on one string. And in each term the signifier belongs to the signified in an ontological permanence that derives from and manifests unity. It has been alleged (Paris 1969) that the crisis of this system was carried into literary expression by Rabelais. Yet its depth is even better demonstrated within the bosom of the Platonic Renaissance itself. Pontus de Tyard as re-creator of the sestina form in France offers an extreme case in point, and it is in illustration of that flight from the sign that his first "Sextine" is to be studied in some depth.

It is no accident that in the sixteenth century poetic experimentation with homonymy and identical rhyme achieved an unprecedented modern diffusion. Nothing makes present more than paronomasia the relational status of words and the capricious connections that arise from their use in alternately denotative and connotative senses. Where the pun comes to replace the armature of syllogistic logic, poetic form encourages construction on the shifting sands of changing relations. Since in the sestina the same set of end-words is used in a rigorously determined order in six of the seven strophes, the first line of each strophe, which repeats the last endword of the preceding strophe, leans on a *contiguity* association between the two lines and with the total context. Lexical reduction turns the poetic flow back into itself, excavating the cumulative meaning from each term. To charge with meaning so restricted a choice of terms and to liberate them simultaneously from the encrustations of conventional limits is a process not of "invention" but of transmutation, consonant with the drift of Pontus de Tyard's metamorphoses. The range of potentially infinite variations is the greater for the strict distribution of invariants. The revolutions of endwords emphasize the fact of dynamic progression, while their free ad hoc arrangement in the seventh (half-) strophe (*envoi, tornada, congedo*) undoes the weary comparison of this poetic form to the circle. This lack of closure is emphasized by its inventors' use of identical rhyme, resulting from the constant appearance in each strophe of endwords that do not rhyme among themselves. The revolutions of mutants occur free from any primary datum of experience. The high concentration upon end words serves to make present the mediation of those terms among themselves.

The cumulative effect of key terms in seeming repetition emerges, however, from a complex field of prior semantic values. Herein enters the found, Petrarchan code, the end result of an anterior process. Across the diachrony of forms, the Platonic and Petrarchan constancy of desire is kept visible, easily bridging the disparity between the available prosodies of language and period. The reading of a Petrarchesque poem involves the gauging of probabilities of verbal association. Petrarch's generic idiolect assumes the right to extend to all it can include and describe. But its hospitality to interpretation should warn of the essentially negative properties of this language.

Although the externals of the poems included in the *Erreurs amoureuses* make them appear synecdochic by bringing the entirety of Petrarchesque production to mind, Pontus de Tyard strains the fiction toward a Platonic paradigm. The first time the lover encounters his lady, he admires her countenance, which becomes his "idol" (I, vii). But she speaks and at once his imagination, understanding the presence of her more nearly perfect soul, recognizes that this countenance is a temple. From then on (in the main), Pontus' language honors Pasithee's virtue, the divinity of the temple, making it possible for the ascent of sheer encomium to conform to that change. From the level of subject/object (lover and beloved), key terms are replaced by their homonymic metaphors, "translated" to the realm of the supernaturally tinged relation between man and knowledge. The enveloping fiction presents the speaker as divided from knowledge by erotic fury, absorbed into encomium. On one hand the pressure of context recollects the primary meanings of words; on the other, the expansion of semantic associations enlarges the remoteness between the signifiers and their contextually present referents. The sestina form dramatically enacts the contingent aspect of discourse.

Elsewhere, Pontus de Tyard displays interest in the contraction of poetic discourse by homonymy and paronomasia, as in this sestet:

> Elle peut bien la terre en verdeur voir,
> Verdeur qui donne aux Laboureurs espoir
> De leurs travaux recueillir les fruits meurs.
> Et ne voulut quelque verde esperance

Me faire voir, comme pour asseurance
De voir finir les travaux ou je meurs.

(*Erreurs* I, xv, 9-14)

(She may well see the earth greening, a green that gives laborers hope at gathering the ripe fruitsof their travail, and she did not wish me to see any green hopes, as if to be assured of seeing the end of the travail in which I die.)

The persistence of subject-object relations here is not concentrated in end-words alone (*espoir/esperance; meurs/meurs*) but also in a non-rhyming pair (*travaux/travaux*). Between these common techniques and the content-substance of his verse lie an essential datum of Pontus' text and the system of operations that make it exemplary of a discontinuity of knowledge. The sestina exemplifies laws of combination that may be modified according to competing norms of versification. By introducing the capital modification of rhyme into the form, Pontus de Tyard essentially reverses the hierarchy of the contiguity relation between his poem and the anterior Petrarchan texts. By introducing rhyme, Pontus evades the entire question of the relevance of semantic features to the determination of "identity." What ensues is the effectuation of a conversion of lexical differences into affinities of sound. Rhyme represents an effort to organize things into phonic resemblances, which speaking across space recall forms of similitude.

Within Romance tradition the use of rhyme draws a measure of strength from evident community with other poems. In the realm of French verse, it was motivated as well by the imperatives of linguistic nationalism, French being of all modern languages the most dependent on rhyme (Wimsatt 1972: 177). The phenomenon of rhyme was a specifically French contribution to the sestina. It constitutes the mark of transference through which the metaphorizing aspect of translation comes to the fore, imposing a new play of sympathies and emulation on the sound-sense relations of the poem. When Arnaut Daniel invented the sestina, it represented one of a number of formal strategies that would lengthen the attention span of his audience from strophe to strophe by increasing the number of lines that would elapse between repetitions of end-rhymes. The poetic line unrhymed with any other in the same strophe recovered some of the dynamic individuality realized in classical meter. The proliferation of sestinas among Pontus de Tyard's Italian contemporaries includes pointed efforts to discredit rhyme as "a vulgar and barbarous singsong" (Trissino [1529] 1969: 12). In the French translation of the form, the seamless strophe is recast into a series of

151

couplings based on orders of sound, into so many accidental encounters of phonemes. The expansion of sense that would radiate from homonymous rhyme is transformed into a relation of reciprocity that emphasizes the fundamental dualisms of the poem's content-forms. The mirror game introduced into the poetic space reveals a bisected world, enlarged, uncentered, finding recourse in the mirage of symmetry. The poem presses toward closure: The synecdochic "richness" of its rhymes (*ame/enflame; oeil/soleil*) shows two intances of enclosure and one linguistic metaphor (*elemens/tormens*), offering a very low specificity of meaning and consequently facilitating the number of words that may be subsumed under one rubric. Just as the rhymes invite the construction of "correspondences," capital letters silently induce the reader to project his thought beyond the word to essences:

    I. Le plus ardent de tous les elemens
        N'est si bouillant alors que le Soleil
        Au fort d'esté le fier Lyon enflame
        Comme je sens aux doux traitz de ton oeil
5   Estre enflamée et bouillante mon âme,
        Le triste corps languissant en tormens

    II. A ces piteaux travaux, à ces tormens,
        N'ont les hauts cieux et moins les elemens
        Fait incliner ou descendre mon âme:
10   Mais comme on void les rayons du Soleil
        Eschaufer tout ça-bas, ainsi ton oeil
        Rouant sur moy de plus en plus m'enflame.

    III. Je voy souvent Amour lequel enflame
        Pour me donner plus gracieux tormens
15   Ses traitz cuisans en ton flamboyant oeil:
        Lors me muant en deux purs elemens,
        Le corps se fond en pleurs quand ce Soleil
        Empraint le feu plus ardemment en l'âme.

    IV. Vienne sécher toute langoureuse âme
20   (Si comme moy Amour trop fort l'enflame)
        Ses tristes pleurs aux rays de mon Soleil.
        Vienne celuy qui comble de tormens
        Se pleint de Dieu, du Ciel, des Elemens,
        Chercher confort au doux trait de cest oeil.

25   V. Le doux regard ou fier trait de cest oeil
        Fait ou joyeuse ou dolente toute âme,
        Et temperez ou non les elemens:
        Aussi c'est luy qui rend froide ou enflame

30   L'occasion de tous ce miens tormens,
                            E qui m'est nuit obscure ou clair Soleil.

                VI. Fuyant le jour de ce mien beau Soleil,
                        Tout m'est obscur et rien ne void mon oeil
                        Que deuil, ennuy et funebras tormens,
                        Tormens si grans que ma douloureuse ame
35   Meut a pitié le Dieu qui tant m'enflame,
                        Mesme le Ciel et tous les elemens

               VII. Plutot ne soit resoult en elemens
                        Ce corps, ny l'ame au ciel sur le Soleil
                        Puisse saillir, que doux ne me soit l'oeil
40   Lequel m'enflame et me tient en tormens.

(I. The most ardent of all the elements is not boiling so when the Sun inflames the proud Lion at the height of summer, as I feel my soul inflamed and boiling at the sweet glance of your eyes, my body sad, languishing in torment.

II. It is not the high Heaven, even less the elements, that have made my soul incline or descend to these pitiable travails, these torments; but as one sees the Sun's rays heat everything here in the world, thus your eyes turning upon me inflame me more and more.

III. I often see Love inflame his burning lineaments in your flaming eyes, to give me more graceful torments. Then transforming me into two pure elements, my body melts in tears when that Sun imprints fire ever more ardently in my soul.

IV. Let every languishing soul come to dry its tears of sorrow by the rays of my Sun (if Love inflames it too much, as it does me). Let him who overcome with torment complains of God, of the Heavens, of the Elements, seek comfort in the sweetness of these eyes.

V. The sweet or fierce glance of these eyes makes every soul either joyous or grieved, and the elements tempered, or not. Thus it is they who make frozen or inflamed the occasion of all these my torments, and that are to me dark night or clear Sunlight.

VI. Fleeing the daylight of this my beauteous Sun, all is darkness to me, my eyes see nothing but grief, trouble, and deathlike torments, torments so great that my suffering soul moves to pity the God who so enflames me, even Heaven and all the elements.

VII. May this body never be dissolved into elements, nor may this soul ever rise upon the Sun to Heaven, before the eyes that inflame me and keep me in torment become gentle.)

The following passage of translation from Ficino could serve as a gloss to the content-forms of this poem:

Sans doute il y a deux espèces d'Amour, l'une est simple, l'autre est réciproque. L'amour est ou l'Aimé n'aime point l'Amant. Là l'Amant est tout mort, parce qu'il ne vit point en soy, comme nous avons monstre et ne vit point aussi en l'Aimé estant de lui mesprise. Ou est-ce donc qu'il vit? Vit-il en l'Air, ou en l'Eau, ou au Feu, ou en la Terre, ou au corps d'un animal irraisonable? Non, parce que l'Ame humaine ne vit point en autre corps que l'Humain. Il vit paradventure en quelque autre corps de personne non aimee? N'y la encor, parce que s'il ne vit la ou vehementement il desire vivre, beaucoup moins vivra-t-il ailleurs. Donce ne vit en aucun Lieu celuy qui aime autruy, et d'autruy n'est aime: et pourtant est entiere-ment mort le non aime Amant. Et jamais ne resuscite. . . .

(cit. Kristeller 1943: 26)

(Doubtless there are two kinds of Love, one simple, the other reciprocal. This Love is that in which the Beloved does not love the Lover at all. Here the Lover is entirely dead, for he does not live in himself at all, as we have demonstrated, nor does he live at all in the Lover, being contemned by him. Where, then, does he live? Does he live in the Air, or in the Water, or in Fire, or in the Earth, or in the body of an animal deprived of reason? No, for the human Soul lives in none other than the human body. Does it perchance live in some other body, that of one it does not love? Not there either, for if it does not live where it vehemently desires to live, much less does it live elsewhere. Thus he who loves another lives nowhere, if he is not loved in return: and in this wise the unloved Lover is entirely dead. And he never comes back to life. . . .)

The passage accedes by analogy to the code by which the poem operates. Yet the poem's application to the task at hand demonstrates that the definition of the semiotic object is part of its analysis. An analysis that takes account of semantics and aims to elucidate mean-ing will necessarily include among its goals the description of the formal class to which the poem belongs. At the same time, as I read Pontus' sestina, I recognize that the cognitive dualism that charac-terizes this very text will be very much with us if we maintain that analysis can be neither wholly objective or wholly subjective. Never-theless, one reading may legitimately aim to encompass what is repre-sented in a work within the larger concern of the relationships between sign and sign.

Pontus de Tyard's use of the key-term *elemens* takes account of the intermingling of Petrarchan-Platonic codes throughout his poem, rendered in translation as separate elements. The surface content presents a conflict of being, encompassing simultaneously "beneficial" and "destructive" experiences of love parallel to an "icy-fiery" alter-nation. The loved object is conceived as renewing the lover's suffering but also as repeatedly restoring his life. *Elemens* is also the single key-term that cannot be taken to refer primarily to the Petrarchan code. The very congeniality within the *Platonic* system of all the end-words emphasizes the close alliance of the two systems. The proliferation of senses among the end-words gives a sense of the multiplication ad infinitum of substances, pointing as far as the radical nominalism of the *Gorgias:* Speech is not the same as any existent thing. In Pontus' metaphysical justification of poetry, *furor divinus* was the first of the four degrees by which the soul was enabled to rise out of the world of materiality and multiplicity and rejoin "le souverain Un, commencement éternel de toute chose." But the poem opens in a characteristic periphrase onto a chain of "errors." The unnamed object, a reduction of the symbolism of the Muses and Apollo, is not synthesized into emblematic status. The poet moves toward analogy and closure: The soul of the speaker is to fire (le plus bouillant . . .") as the eye of the beloved is to the Sun. Rhyme-words call for inclusion within Neoplatonic discourse on the soul. In Ficino's commentary, the hierarchy of terms is made clear: The function of *Soleil* has a primary place in the centrifugal landscape of ideas that reflects creative energy in nature. In the visible world, the sun is to human sight, Plato explains (*Republic* IV, 508), as the idea of good is to man's soul in the invisible world. It is therefore the end-term of cognition but is bound up in both the terrestrial and super-terrestrial realms, at once the symbol of maximal visibility and the ultimate source of earthly light. *Soleil* moves between the two ethical corollaries of Platonic dualism. Now in Ficino's commentary the Sun, fire, and the soul appear as "active causes" in which other things participate insofar as they move, shine, or exude heat. An essential difference exists between the quality of an active cause and the same quality in a participating thing that is of necessity commingled with other elements. Heat is an essential property of fire, contained in its essence, whereas for wood it is a contingent quality produced in it by the action of fire. By analogy, the soul does not live through other things but is life for itself ("Est igitur animae essentia vita"; Ficino 1576). Fire, therefore, constitutes the element that is analogous to the soul.

The Platonic doctrine of analogy here undergoes maximal strain. Soul divided from body returns us to the lover's insomniac watching and purely astrological sense of destiny. Nor could it be alleged that the refining process operated by *Soleil* has vouchsafed cognitive intuition. The transference of absence and loss to the charge of the object simply underscores the prevalence of lexical over deeper semantic values, and the further potential of lability. Error constitutes its own danger by showing that the longing for stability and the proliferation of words are at odds. The spacing of the interval between strophes is an outburst of discontinuity. This retardation and the "repetition" of terms at the beginning of each new strophe embody the fated reticence of the articulating poet.

With the entry into the poem of images of fire arises an ontological principle of motion extended by Ficino from Aristotle's theory of the motion of elements to the entire reach of reality. According to this theory, everything capable of motion possesses a directional movement that conforms to its essence and species. Water and earth descend; fire rises, as does air. To their movement corresponds an inclination born of the substances of these elements. Both movement and inclination are resolved into a state of repose as soon as the elementary body has reached the sphere to which it belongs. Although the principle claims universal validity, Ficino expounds it most often through the contrary motions of earth and fire (Ficino 1576: 308). The subtext of Pontus lies in this theory of natural movement or appetite. Over and above the corporeal world is the human soul, the first in the series of existents that has its natural movement toward God (primary cognition). Ficino compares the appetite of the soul to fire and that of the body to stone (Ficino 1576: 473): "Quia superior locus igni bonus est, ideo an illu movetur ignis et quiescit in illo, non quia movetur et quiescit, bonum."

It is the state of exemption from movement in nature, however, that has determined error, as the second strophe makes known. The spatial movement is revealed as nonanalogous to that of the soul. This seeming contradiction is embraced by Ficinian Platonism. Although the soul is turned toward God as to its natural goal, its behavior in this life is not determined by this inclination. On the contrary, whereas elementary and animal bodies are given over to one form of operation, man may turn his mutable thoughts and activities to the most diverse objects according to his will—to God or to earthly things, therefore either following or opposing his "natural appetite" (Kristeller 1943: 351-356 and passim). Now, since man may and does oppose this appetite, his soul is unlike fire, his object unlike the Sun, variable in substance and therefore ultimately unnameable. Even as the key terms contract new rhyme-relations among themselves, they unveil their fundamental alientation from one another, negating the gemination of sounds. Accordingly, the secondary subject changes from strophe to strophe, each new appearance sustained only by its immediate antecedent, each block of words representing its contiguity relation to the preceding one. The third strophe indelibly links *oeil* and the encompassing *Soleil*, which functions as the instrument of division between *corps* and *ame* in both semantics and prosody.

The ego subject to death desires the immobile otherness of the object and has begun by addressing that object directly. Subsequent strategy includes the interposition of "Amour" between the desiring subject and that Other in a referential shift whereby Amour becomes a metonymy for Soleil. The referential instability extends laterally to comprehend the range of Platonistic signs. In the fourth strophe it is the soul, not the body, that has turned to water, the descending element; and the transparent *celuy* replaces the "I." The rhetorical description of this pattern reveals separation (*Dieu, Ciel, Elemens*). Out of that separation, the variously derived motifs of the poem (presence/absence, light/darkness) draw nourishment by analogy to the lover's desire for self-loss. While the lover denies the presence of sense and ultimate order without the governance of the beloved, they are still present in his formal governance of poetic means.

From this "endoresment by dignification," as Kenneth Burke (1969) terms it (Vienne . . . toute ame; vienne . . . chercher confort), arises the dualistic arrangement of the fifth strophe. This time the effort at closure takes the form of twinning semantically equivalent series of terms, arresting each horizontally at the frontier fixed by the closure of each line. Whereas in the sestina as a whole, sense derives from identities of a formal order (equivocal rhyme, homonym) among key signifiers, here a rival sort of organization obtains, in the equivalences established by signifers on the basis of metonymic or metaphoric relations. Pontus de Tyard approaches the technique of *rapportatio* that lifts words from their place in the syntagm so that syntactically analogous members are placed in co-ordinated series (Lausberg 1971: 120). With a subversive effect similar to that produced by rhyme, rapportatio organizes synonymic equivalences against the larger organization of homonymic equivalences. The two modalities of articulation embody the dualism of cognitive effort, creating an expressive system that reveals the object's withdrawal from possession. In the very body of this poet's world is the active wound of desire, for an object that is never far but always inaccessible. With great irony the main referent ("le doux regard ou fier trait de cest oeil") suggests total fixity; it is the metonymic shift that links the referents and enchains them in contiguity relations.

The pain that penetrates this poem is less the product of absence than of emptiness—the imposssibility of fixing reference and, therefore, of repetition, or re-presentation. The signifiers are suspended between representation and signification, testimony of the epistemological break between word and thing. The poem's myth invites proliferating difference, for like the rhetoric that surrounds the signifiers, the myth is under the control of suspension. The thematic domain upon which rhetoric operates—the establishment of the object's "uniqueness"—ironically enhances the display of subject-predicate relations. The "unique" object has a precise reference, but its value depends on the suppression of that reference, on its remaining unique.

Pontus de Tyard lengthened the tornada to four lines so that each line would rhyme with another, displaying to the last the fragmentation of the form into smaller complementary entities. The asemantic aspect of rhyme provides the vehicle for the articulation of tangential linguistic relations. The final evocation of the lady's *proximate distance* brackets her yielding (discovery, knowledge) and the lover's death, each process activated by fire. Now the lady's glance "stands for" the Sun, which may destroy and refine the lover's body into the two pure elements, water and fire, while the soul ascends to its source and final abode in the sun. Yet the lady's eyes (synecdochic *oeil,* indeed) had passed for that Sun; the merging of *Soleil* and *oeil* is now revealed as the last of the poems' metamorphoses. Rhyme has a chaotic effect on the old form. In this confrontation of resemblances some lines play off one against two key terms, summarizing the loss of centrality undergone by the poem as a whole. The rhyme scheme has in fact produced a different successive order of end-terms for each strophe. Analogously the metonymic shift effected within the semantic potential of each key term reveals the instability of the signifier. Error is its own danger, and the obscurity of this work can be penetrated only by recognition of this constant shift of reference. Obscurity, at the very origin of this poem, figures the infinite relation of word to tenor. The expansion of sense that would emanate from the identity of a single word becomes rather a deceptively reciprocal, nonlogical relation of a pair, a tautology verified on the levels of single word and syntactic sequence. The heroic attempt to neutralize the contrast of Suns has taken place under the auspices of an irremediable subject-object dualism, hence the unsuccessful interpolation of the object, discontinuity, parenthesis, and the recurrent release of the thought of death.

From the dimension of imitation (translation, encomium) the poem progresses to the manifold complications of shifting reference. It reveals that no other than contextual meaning can exist, that any entity or sign is defined relatively. The lexical referents of poetic signs are contextual meanings taken severally. This sestina constitutes an extreme case in point, no matter how the poet might seek to stem the fluidity of its revolutions with his strategies of agreement.

It is the destiny of the Platonizing lyricist to remain entrapped in the dualism of subject/object theories of cognition. In his hierarchy of values, the highest rank is occupied by the full, actual presence of object in the acts of his consciousness. From that actuality radiate the possibilities of imitation, of translation, of necessity involved with the conceptualized data of prior experience. But only the fullness of presence abstracted from the indivisible flow of life ruptures the ambiguity of Platonistic man. Both knowing subject and object of knowledge, he is thereby able to realize an order of being that is nondiscursive and nondualistic, in which knower and known are not to be regarded as entities but as the two terms of a single act. The wanderings of the poet yield up translations of words from the "lower" realm of subject/object, lover and beloved, to that of meditation on meditation perceived as its own end.

From another, compatible viewpoint, intersubjectivity, or common, shared acknowledgment, appears as the certifying agent of cognition and of the highest cognitive value. Within this principle are encompassed the myriad "imitations" on which the lyric of the Renaissance conferred honor. Expressibility of content and the intersubjective communicability of meaning follow. Underlying both principles is the search for the beginning, for a self-subsistent content.

The sixteenth century witnessed a radical deviation from the search for absolutely certain cognition, an epistemological crisis in Christian Platonism that detached literary discourse from the certain pursuit of the beginning of knowledge (cf. Foucault 1966). That pursuit gave way to the rudiments of a sign theory that took cognizance of knowledge as a linear, enchained structure, having no starting point and no final conclusion. The realization that every cognition has its antecedents and results by which it is determined, that no parts of cognition constitute its simple data, that indeed no single datum possesses its cognitive sense, portended that every meaning could be seen as coexistent with other meanings to which it owed its own intellectual or emotional content. In consequence, meaning could be grasped solely through the other meaning, never directly.

The moment of Pontus de Tyard finds the poet conceiving still of a "hidden" meaning, one obscured when the rays of his Sun move obliquely. But already a turning toward a theory of signs menaces the dualism of subject and object; hence, the translation of individual, "revolutionary" poetic forms into rhyme and the search for closure. The sestina is evidence of contextual awareness. But whereas sign theory would discover the formation of any cognitive relationship into a *triadic* representation and into an enchainment of triads, the *pontifex maximus* of Neoplatonism for the Pléïade knows only that the object can be neither free from interpretation nor fully present, and in those moments hears the cacophony of signifiers.

Chapter 6

The Pastoral Sestina

1. Introductory

Formative ideas transposed from one context to another have in common a certain generosity of outline, a plenitude that enables poets to accommodate within them, before the ideas fade, empirical data, epistemic variations, and perennial figures of human imagination. This comprehensive hermeneutic value was achieved by Renaissance pastoral. Its outstanding preference for the sestina resides partially in the redundancies and in the preponderance of the signifier. The mind of love, erotic and impassioned, usurps the foreground of the pastoral. Since it is the inner states that find their classic symbolism in the shepherd, the speaker's declaration of his stance uncovers the source of his invention, and in pastoral it is a unilateral stance of desire.

So it is that pastoral poetry is one of passion and suffering, not of action as evinced by bodily movement. The special connection between the sestina and the pastoral derives chiefly from the intersection of linear and cyclical concepts of time, the cyclical predominance bodied forth in the revolving arrangement of end-terms, the linear inevitably connoted by the enveloping reality of poetry itself, unfolding sequentially in time. The shepherd describes his own poem's birth into consciousness, drawing from Orpheus the seer and sage, and from Orpheus the persuader, making new the infinite reproducibility of meaning and signification as set forth in the pastoral world. This quality produced a descent of Petrarch among the shepherds that alters the landscape of modern poetry. Of all the metamorphoses of Petrarch filtered through Virgil's *Eclogues,* the first Arcadia of the vernacular tongue, that of Jacopo Sannazaro, exerted the major influence, setting into motion waves of pastoral poetry in many languages and awarding a place to Sannazaro among the few moderns of Raphael's Parnassus. That Sannazaro was buried near Virgil meant, of course, that his readers could be counted on to respond with full recollection to the Virgiliam evocations that abound in his work, reinterpreted through Petrarch. Obviously, however, it means far more. Sannazaro indicated a direction of translation, repetition, and permutation recognized in its own turn, providing a clear answer to a question itself long asked and understood. He set a current tone for a form of life found everywhere at every time, with figures of speech that made their way in the Christian tradition, linked forever to speculation about origins and about love, drawing to itself a preponderance of eroticism. "Arcadia was forever being rediscovered" (Curtius 1953: 187); the latest way was through Petrarch.

To be satisfied with this explanation is to trivialize the depth of meaning in pastoralism. When Heidegger defined the poet as the "shepherd of Being" ("der Hirt des Seins") it suggested Orpheus drawing the world toward him as his flock, embodying the relation of form and idea in its philosophical dimension. So rich a yield of condensed meaning is unexpectedly hard to interpret, so well does it exploit the resources of an apparently simplified language and an underground network of associative imagery. For Heidegger, the focus on man as he understands himself in his historical environment was translated into the search for an understanding of understanding itself, and in order to arrive at it, the philosopher becomes aware of an intrinsic escapism that is contained in all understanding. The task of philosophical hermeneutics is to retrace the escape-route of human understanding, and to unearth what is being repressed in its course. The historical presuppositions of understanding have to be uncovered.

Pastoralism is largely a poetic expression of aesthetic Platonism that subsists in Western society into our time (Cody 1969: 20 ff.). A poetry of poetry, it has deeply etched into its being the link of song with sexuality and with other forms of initiation. Beginnings and endings, admittance and leave-taking, as well as the redundancies of their expression, provide the conceptual framework that is reflected in the sestina scheme. That the mythology embraced by many Renaissance poets stressed transformation (conclusion and survival, death as one thing and rebirth as another) provided for them a tropological frame for the language of beginning and ending. It has been aptly remarked that Plato, "though never a pastoral writer in the strict sense, seems to have been its originator" (Parry 1957: 29). The assumption lies very deep that the ancient cosmos is assumable again and again in ever-widening orders. The poetry describing this movement may well be spiral, gyrelike in organization, rendering the sestina a particularly apt means of unfolding pastoral logic. Its cyclical configuration can diagram the passage of days, seasons, and their corresponding zodiacal movements, which pastoral celebrates, while its infallibly linear direction can be rooted in the Golden Age and promise the reconciliation of historically created contraries "after the world." This patterning also clarifies the sense of the abundant impossibilia and adynata to which pastoral poetry naturally recurs, with especial emphasis in the sestina.

The continuous presence of the pastoral poet is easily joined to other figural senses of *pastor:* poet, lover, and theologian coexist with the literal shepherd. The tropes could never permanently fade since they were revived again and again in texts. Orpheus embodying this continuous process of resurgence was a type of Renaissance shepherd (Cody 1969) who could represent a changing but eternal love. To cast the mind's eye over its shapes could yield all those types of madness distinguished in Plato's *Phaedrus:* the madness of poetry or the Muses, of ritual, of prophecy, or Apollo, of erotic possession, or Venus.

Pastoral poetry produced a concentration on the sense of place, or moral geography. Spatial configurations determine the isolation of the ideal pastoral abode; its enclosure serves as a retreat. Since the ascent of the mind from delight in physical beauty to its contemplation begins in a willed alienation, the growth of that virtuous inwardness is nourished by a stepped construction of solitudes. These are valued in pastoral above any sort of worldly life. Another stratum of alienation arises, consisting, for a Platonic culture dominated by a courtly ethos, in the accommodation of the idea of the perfectible inner life to the circumstances of the courtly or urbane person. A symbolic existence profoundly at variance with external realities could be created out of the fictions of pastoral; its endurance would be sustained by desire feeding upon itself.

Many of these concerns find their most appropriate expression in the sestina. Its strenuous beauty surpassed empirical reality and exemplified the human power of reordering the experiential world, and could comprehend an estrangement from externals entailing the very loss of self—the voluntary abdication of will. The sestina's process of conscious alienation, often demanding the erotic abandonment of reason, is a form of action akin to a remarkable physical feat. The same action betokens surrender, as well—to the movements of sun and moon taken as measures of poetic time, telling and re-telling myths of soul, immortality, and rebirth. From a historical standpoint, the poem surrenders to the demands of courtierliness and courtship; therefore it would find a most hospitable matrix in the sestina with its deathless yearnings built into the revolutions of uncentered contiguity relations. The inwardness that Plato and the New Testament commend could search for a supernatural "center" and uncover hero-worship, instead turning from God-worship to the sacredness of class. God as ultimate point of reference would represent an end-point of desire; on the other hand, the King, having no immortality, would represent desire unending.

This dyad helps greatly to explain the predominance of mourning in Renaissance pastoral sestinas. It is divided between the grief of unrequited love and mourning for a deceased ruler. Either of these two missing centers acquires a regenerative power in and for poetry. For the next step beyond death is memory, and the mnemonic value of pastoral is manifest, hence the insatiable appetite for its repetitions that conditioned so much of Renaissance text production. To tell and retell fables of the shepherd's life was to narrate through sublimation and subterfuge a turning from the temporal to the eternal, to state and restate a sense of eternal value. Pastoral poetry stubbornly maintained the convention of a lost oral and musically oriented culture. Idolatry of the memory-images so transmitted took the place of activity in pastoral. The poetic muse, daughter of memory, represents there the ultimate hope of pathos—a fiction that results from emotion.

Petrarch furthered the ability of poetry to create a lie against time and show that within poems it can be controlled and conquered, subordinated to attitude, willed into the future, and finally converted like all content-substance into an element of poetic structure. Although he did not exploit the social uses of bucolic gatherings in his Italian poems, he introduced a speaking and responsive "Nature" that echoed poetically expressed feeling and showed the connection between echo and memory. Apart from the narcissistic traits of poetic echo, it did more. Given the distinction between visual mirror-images and the temporality of acoustic ones, it is important that echo is itself a form of memory and the transmission of memory.

The frequent corelative procedures Petrarch uses in his poetic works generally, and with an extra quotient in the sestinas, are joined by the recurrences of rhyme-words. Scholars have long noted the tendency within pastoral poems toward coordinated and correlative constructions (Alonso 1961; Lopez Estrada 1948), particularly in the generative Italian poems. In pastoral poetry, the Petrarchan intensification by repetition and emphasis is extended to the confrontation of death in elegy. Affective images are heaped up by way of compensation, to suggest a true "beyond." Progress from sexuality to death is itself a contiguity relation as well as a change, and death is the final form of change. Simultaneously, death is the most violent of rhetorical disjunctions, the only human event in which the crossing between thought and knowledge is beyond communication. Incremental repetition functions as an antinoetic safeguard, nearly a talisman, against the destruction wrought by death, which is at the same time recognized paradoxically as the origin of beauty in the world. As corroboration from outside the mediating self, it replaces validation by experience. Then the poetry of feeling turns backward again, becomes a poetry of conduct, hero-worship, and collective memory.

Oxymoron, hyperbole, and adynaton mythologize the loss of original justice, miming the desire for an unity of origin (as of intention and language). Toward the aim of that impossible recovery the consciousness of a received culture may operate as surrogate. Renaissance pastoral represents both an ontological and existential recuperation of an antique culture that actually had been revived from a previous state of assumed disarray and near oblivion. Hence the reading of the Orpheus myth of regeneration pertained to the genesis of pastoral poetry itself and at the same time remained near the core of its *materia*.

The interpenetration of physical and moral landscape invites the workings of a semantic more than a syntactic imagination. The point of many poems is that man is not synchronized with the rest of creation, because of his power of conjuring. A minimal vocabulary appropriates to itself polysemic significances whose recurrence shows the unity in multiplicity and multiplicity in unity, both dependent on context. Recorder of metamorphoses and of flow, the pastoral poet may be fixed in an ancient hope of Paradise and know simultaneously the inevitability of change in the world. The sestina with its invariable set of rhyme-words in varying order moves analogously between the multiplicity of sense or context and the unity of sound.

The quotient of introversive semiosis in poetry, heightened in the case of the sestina, tempts comparison with that in music. Far more pervasive in music, semiosis in both is linked ineluctably to temporality. "Orphic" sestinas often take cognizance of this communality by

164

reviving the discussion of poetry as music, as if they were identical. To do so is also to maintain the connection between the oral and the written, or composed. In this context of self-reference, the importance of novelty is demoted. Whether language is reduced to essentially lexicalized reminiscences matters less than the endless need for permanent bliss, which is infinitely expressible.

This poetry of connotations is open, as well, with respect to the antique culture that serves as its model. The appearance of guileless, or rustic, simplicity shows a distrust of the *language* of learning or of scientific proof as a means of self-knowledge. Petrarch led here also, in a knotty treatise that inveighs against natural philosophers and other kinds of *doctores (De sui ipsius et multorum ignorantia* On His Own Ignorance and That of Others). Since the erotic world of Neoplatonistic pastoral finds Virgil a follower of Plato (this, too, in Petrarch's treatise, Capelli 1906: 72), and since the stance of privileged retreat from the world is fundamentally necessary to it, the sense that understanding must occur without prior demonstration often appears to confer iron closure on the poems. But this is a hermetic screen, although one to be pierced by strangers only. The artifice of amateurism is important not only to the courtly frame of the poems but even more to their implicit or explicit discussions of anteriority, seen as the dyad nature/culture.

In a historically recordable world, the dialectic of nature/culture is to be viewed as partially arising from a temporal dilemma, and in the sestinas the resulting tension calls out to the surviving idea of the theological *pastor* for resolution. Since this, too, denotes a missing center, the sestina gravitates toward "imitation" by analogy. Double sestinas, for instance, arranged as singing contests between two competitors, each speaking a strophe in alternating order, may embody two diverse phases of the dialectic. The case of Sannazaro is the more apt in that his *Arcadia* (1502-4) initiated a wave of such works in Europe. His chief shepherd, Sincero, has a "speaking" name that signifies a protest against artifice, in favor of "nature."

In the double sestina (*Arcadia* IV; ed. Mauro 1961: 29-31) the two contestants, Logisto and Elpino, are accompanied by a rustic pipe, and the whole is described as *suono* (sound or music). Two of the rhyme-words (*rime* and *pianto*) are Petrarch's, and the recollections and recapitulations of Petrarch amount at times to a contest with him as well. Petrarch's rhyme-words anchor the poem to the matter of poetry, while the rhyme-word *giorno* measures the daily and seasonal round of external affairs, as well as the cyclical against the linear event of singing. The more desperate of the two mourns his enclosure within a landscape of exile and wandering:

165

Logisto: Lasso, ch'io non so ben l'ora ne'i giorno
che fui rinchiuso in questa alpestra valle,
nè mi ricordo mai correr per campi
libero e sciolto . . .

(Strophe III)

(Logisto: Alas I do not know well the hour or the day I was closed in this
alpine valley, nor do I remember ever running free and unbound through
the fields.)

Passing over the multiple Petrarchesque locations, the drift of the
prosody, and the Petrarchan topos of marking the fatal day and hour,
we find embedded here his play with the name Vaucluse (or "enclosed valley") to signify the paradox of latitude and imprisonment.
Near the end of the poem the other speaker, Elpino, takes up the
chant:

ma pur sperando uscir de l'aspra valle
richiusa intorno d'alti e vivi sassi,
e ripensando al ben che avrò quel giorno,
canto con la mia canna or versi or rime.

(Strophe XII)

(But still hoping to escape from the harsh valley enclosed by high, living
stones, and thinking again of the good I shall have one day, I sing with my
pipe now verses, now rhymes.)

The first sufferer's inability to remember the day of his confine-
ment within the enclosed valley reinforces the sense of an alienated
memory, but also of a basic discontinuity that may signify, as well,
the close of a cultural cycle and the resumption of a new one. The
combined emotions resulting from banishment and imprisonment
come to resolution by the second speaker in the activity of singing,
which is directed toward another new day.

Sannazaro chose to merge the contraries of his two voices with
little apparent dramatic reason. At the close of the sixth strophe,
again near to the missing center, Elpino announces that a voice has
promised him hope and good fortune. By contrast with his preceding
speech in the present tense, this is rendered gradually into the historical past:

Ben mille notti ho già passate in pianto,
tal che quasi paludi ho fatto i campi;
al fin m'assisi in una verde valle
et una voce udii per mezzo i sassi
dirmi: — Elpino, or s'appressa un lieto giorno

166

che ti farà cantar più dolci rime.

(Strophe VI)

_____

(Certainly a thousand nights I have spent in weeping, such that I have almost made swamps of the fields. At last I seated myself in a green valley and heard a voice through the stones saying to me: Elpino, now a happy day is approaching, which will make you sing sweeter rhymes.)

It is here that time as the measure of motion and change enters the discussion. In both speakers' utterances, the tendency to subordinate time and make it relative has contended with the passage of time leading to death as closure. Even there, memory succeeds death, with mention of the sepulcher to be honored. But in this crucial place, which critical opinion has heretofore found perplexing and unmotivated, the poet makes free with tense and hints at temporality as a universal synchrony dominating all being and change, binding men and gods under the aegis of cosmic force no longer enslaved to seasonal or other recurrences. The shepherd's life and the reconciliation of its contraries are realizable in the world only through the transfiguration of time; and I suggest that this moment constitutes an adynaton with respect to all external conditions. The intrusion of such a moment corresponds on one hand to a further removal of conflict (through a third "speaking" voice) but also as far as the nature of the poem is concerned, to a promotion of adynaton as a structural support for the whole sestina. It is following this announcement that Elpino is fully able to fall back onto the powers of Orphic poetry, to make woods and rocks dance and birds perpetually sing, in other words, to create a perpetuity of presence for song.

This poem, like other pastoral having little reality behind it except art and imagination, has often been accused of "insincerity" (Poggioli 1975: 98). It may well be in anticipation of this accusation that the poems as well as the larger works in which they generally are situated call for not one or two, but a *company* of the exiled. The expedient finds historical support to the extent that such a company furnishes a model of idealized court life. Beyond this contingency, however, the business of "truth-in-poetry" makes a subject of the poem the logical and temporal insolubility of nature versus culture. Nature and culture ultimately correspond, as one to one, with the prevailing conceptions of time as cyclical and linear, respectively.

Nature, taken as the whole semantic constellation revolving around liberty and the absence of man-made constraints, corresponds then to cyclical time that is the mythologized background of such a state, unbroken by event or closure. Culture accordingly would signify the combined banishment into linear time and imprisonment within the closure imposed by event and death. The sestina as an embodied cognitive act only alludes to the chaos behind regression into mythical pre-temporality, only suggest a fusion of contraries within the abyss of the beginning. It makes sufficiently evident, though, that the dyads nature/culture, solitude/company, country/ city, shepherd/urban dweller, choice/reconciliation, arms/letters at any stage repose on dialectical, that is to say, shifting ground: "Dopo Dio comincia la bellezza," wrote Pico della Mirandola, "perchè comincia la contrarietà" (After God begins beauty, for then begins contrariety [*Commento,* ed Garin 1952: 495]). On a simpler level, the shepherds Logisto and Elpino caught in a prison of Petrarch's making can choose only his means of escape. Cyclicity spiraling into linearity, through maximal formal discipline, best illustrates how forms adjust to the larger lines of cultural force.

The interpretation of the Petrarchan sestina model according to pastoral modes took wing in the England of Sidney and Spenser and the Spain of Montemayor, Cervantes, and Lope de Vega, with somewhat more determination than in Italy. The strength of the movement reached seventeenth-century Germany, creating an instance of belated interest, as far as literary fashion was concerned, that adds a special function to the sestina as recapitulation and crossing of temporal conceptions. Martin Opitz (1597-1639), the earliest composer of a sestina in German, isolated a trait that marks it off from other categories of poetry. Opitz's indefatigable efforts to make German poetic achievement catch up, as he saw it, with that of other nations (Forster 1969; Friedrich 1966) included his importation of an Italian opera to Germany. The demise of the iambic, octosyllabic verse of the Meistersänger is attributed to his influence (Friedrich 1966: 162 ff.). A work he composed at the age of twenty has a speaking title: *Aristarchos sive de contemptu linguae Teutonicae* (1617; translation). Opitz translated Sidney's *Arcadia* (1638), pointing toward a German pastoral literature as well as providing a practice-text for an "ennobled" form of the German language. His *Buch von der deutschen Poeterey* (1624; Book on German Poetic Composition) formulated the requirements of a perfectible rhyme-system that he applied strictly in the greater part of his own poetry. Again the book advocates a sweeping reform of German in the light of Romance poetry.

A pastoral romance of his, *Schäfferey von der Ninfen Hercinie* (Pastoral of the Nymph Hercinie) drawing largely from Sannazaro's *Arcadia,* involves three 'shepherds," whose names betoken aspects of pastoral: Büchner, Nüssler, and Venator, loosely translatable as Book-man, Nut-gatherer, and Hunter, (Riesz 1971: 162). These gentlemen on a day's excursion of wandering and versifying come upon their friend Opitz and compose poems together. But they also make a discovery of many lines cut into the bark of a tree, complete for their inspection. Moved by their treasure, they jointly "rhyme" a sestina.

The discovery of the poem is emphasized in the succeeding narration, which otherwise deals with different though related material. The season is late autumn; in the poem it is winter, pointedly disjoined from the youthful "springtime" of the beloved. The sestina is new, its content-substance old; even as the larger text turns toward an evident literary future the poem recurs to the recent past of pastoral, with its own layers of imitation.

At a time when Malherbe was the standard of poetic imitation, this Francophilic poet (Forster 1969: 71) would have had to conceive of himself as composing in a kind of *style antique*. This experience may be viewed as part of the "baroque experience of contradiction" (Warnke 1972: 44), but more particularly as a manifold instance of poetic recurrence: to the repetitions of rhyme-words, the reawakening of dormant topics, and the recourse to an old form. The beginnings and endings within the sestina that, as Bembo had noticed, confer on it an extra measure of "gravity," are reflected in context. Mirrored in Opitz' preoccupation with belated reform is the recapitulation of form itself.

The insertion of sestinas into larger works of verse or prose, or combinations of the two, occurs in a context akin to that of pastoral. The Iberian Golden Age accorded the sestina a larger measure of narrative status by including it in experimentation with verse-forms in drama. Sestinas mark the suspension of linearity, arresting the development of action, and punctuating the flow of dramatic discourse. In three of Lope de Vega's plays, for example, a sestina marks the end of the expository first act. Only one of these plays is a pastoral (*El remedio en la Desdicha*). Additionally, where the action is delayed just before a conclusion, or characters ponder diverse courses of behavior, a central personage delivers a monologue in the sestina form, integrating the poem fully within the action. At certain moments the sestina recapitulates action that has recently taken place (Riesz 1971: 138-139). Like the double sestina in Lope de Vega's *Arcadia*, the poems are love-laments.

In the tragedy *A Castro* (1587) by the Portuguese Antonio Ferreira, the chorus mourns the celebrated death of Inez de Castro in a sestina. Her murder is first announced there:

> Ja morreu Dona Ines, matou-a Amor;
> Amor cruel! se tu tiveras olhos,

Tambem morreras logo. O' dura morte,
Como ousaste matar aquela vida?
Mas naõ mataste: melhor vida, e nome
Lh deste do que ca tinha na terra.

(Ferreira, ed. Marques Braga 1953: 289-290)

(Now lady Ines is dead; Love killed her. Cruel love! if you had eyes you too would die on the spot. O hard death, how did you dare to kill this life? But you did not kill: you gave her a better life and a name that will endure as long as the world.)

Like the pastoral sestinas, this elegy recapitulates the cultural and literary forms that generated it. The rhyme-word *terra* is used in a number of Petrarchan senses: as planet, human flesh, the soil of burial, the world of discourse. *Vida* and *olhos* are rhyme-words in the sestina by Luis de Camoens (text in Riesz 1971: 228). *Amor* and *morte* are paired as contiguous forms fo self-effacement. Verbal paronomasia contends with the cyclical order of strophes toward a restructuration of time. As in pastoral, the commemorative sestina refers to memory on many levels, and its relation to the referent, the deceased person, is of pure otherness, an indexical semioticity. The poem as willed and invincibly principled is the immutable form through which the dead may come to life. It is only in the futurity of memory that the poet calls the balance: There he plants the trace of a futurity of the past.

The following sestinas have been chosen to indicate the directions in which form adjusted to larger lines of cultural force. I will show that pastoral continues as the dominant mode of contemporary sestinas.

2. Sir Philip Sidney: "Since wailing is a bud of causeful sorrow"

Unlike the model provided by Sannazaro, Sir Philip Sidney's *Old Arcadia* (1590-1593), containing three sestinas, is little concerned with the celebration of love in an ideal world of retirement. This is no ideal country, but one in which the workings of government are uncovered frankly and openly. Arcadia for Sidney contains no center of Platonic values such as the cave in Sannazaro's romance. Nor is there the elevated temple to any god, as in Montemayor's *Diana*. Here the meeting of the shepherds is largely commemorative. Under the protective shadow of Elizabeth and in honor of her dual qualities of Gloriana and Belphoebe, rituals of courtship are accomplished in agreement with the *Defense of Poesie*, where Sidney holds that poetry exists "to show the misery of the people under hard lords or ravening soldiers," if conversely asserting the right of the poor and weak to protection and the duty of the strong to protect them. Closer to pastoral as it appears in the *Arcadia,* the composition equilibrates "what blessedness is derived to them that lie lowest from the goodness of them that sit highest." A pyramid of assumptions regarding courtship underlies such a program, comprising the subtleties of sociopoetic alliance, as well as the direct stimulus of noble patronage.

The *Old Arcadia* turns to Plato's *Symposium* and *Phaedrus* for reflections on virtue and reason, beauty and love, all framed within the rhetoric of courtship. But the fusion of the public and the private, the outer and inner worlds that we find there is not to be confused with the Platonism of the Italian works that probably was a stimulus to Sidney, such as Castiglione's *Libro del Cortegiano.* Though an active Protestant statesman, Sidney wrote his *Arcadia* for the understanding of lovers, and far more than the pragmatics of the semi-retiring Castiglione, Sidney's book constitutes a devastating commentary on the Platonic-Petrarchan vision bequeathed to him. Turned now to the search for balance between the demands of the heroic life and the inroads of passion, the old *locus amoenus* is the site of complex experience, argument, and predicament. Polarities of the active and contemplative life represent its innermost conflicts, and the theories of the imagination that buttress it not only connect poetry with love and leisure, manifesting poetry's narcissism, but carry with them the implicit and carefully enunciated *telos* of moral action—to move the audence in the direction of virtue. To summarize: The cardinal points of courtship and symbolic action become forcefully attached to the lament of pastoral exile and wandering. This accounts for the static, oracular weight of a number of poems as well as for their carefully redundant reproduction of meaning.

The distrust of *otium* in pastoral is not to be taken for granted, despite precedent in Virgil's *Eclogues.* Yet it neatly distinguishes Sidney's form of pastoral from that strain created by the store in Petrarch's *Canzoniere.* Models for the symbolic development of Sidney's terms could be found in Petrarch's word-play, as well as in the chains of discourse emanating from the poetry of earth and desired centrality vying with the transcendental searcher. Reaching far beyond Petrarch's groundwork, though, in Sidney Petrarch's imagery found allegorical treatment that can profit from the infinite reproducibility of meaning to effect a radical transposition of values.

It is significant of their place in the total context of the work and as signs of metamorphosis and evolution that the eclogues, which contain the far greater element of pastoral, occur at the transition points from one book of the *Arcadia* to the next. Although these are pastoral poems with short prose links in the manner of Sannazaro's model, this similarity facilitated the play of Sidney's work against the conventions of Italian erotic pastoral. The process of recapitulation counterposes the most recent state of Arcadia to its pervious state, displaying the contiguity relations inherent in both external and internal aspects of literary structure. Bringing into its spiral movement the classical reminiscences that abound in Sannazaro, then the work itself of the Italian poet, Sidney's book furnishes a commentary on these that ultimately is preeminent in the hierarchy of pastoral values. Love is far less simple in Sidney's world. Although the Golden Age, the death of shepherds or their heroes, the praise of the country over city, are still structural principles, the echoes of Virgil and of Theocritus are no longer romanticized. The twelve eclogues of the *Old Arcadia* are nearly all laments, but behind them resides the force of highly charged superlatives that ready the field for another dimension of critique of Virgilian shepherds and then, Petrarchan lovers. Even as it summarizes the inherited topoi of pastoral to its date, the work is catapulted into a new realm of invention.

The notion flourishes in Platonistic pastoral that the rational soul may undergo a death and new life, lost and found again in the fire of love. The return of Venus Urania, the absent "beloved" of the *Arcadia,* would signify such an event. Sidney's double sestina (*Old Arcadia* I), a variant of the Orphic model provided by Petrarch, works out a verbal conquest of death and reinforcement of Eros. Its large mevements are so patterned that the elegiac beginning is a ritualistic invocation, followed by an expansion of enjambments and other suspensions (sometimes of two or three lines in a strophe), as the persistence of repetition inflates complaint to its climax. There ensues a measured return to the somber note on which the poem began, this time enhanced by a new wave of knowledge and awareness.

The pastoral echo effect is a striking feature that binds together the elaborate resemblances between strophes alternately spoken by two figures, Strephon and Klaius. A recent, masterful reading of the poem by Alastair Fowler (1975: 43-58) illuminates the process of question and answer, pairing and comparison in a Platonic *askesis* that has its roots in the invocation (bound by the repetition of a whole line in strophes I and II) to Pan and his satyrs. The conditions are set for an allegory of the descent and subsequent reascension of the soul. Fowler points out that Klaius' invocations have a Christian source (Alanus de Insulis, *Anticlaudianus* II, 3) which would complement the mythical (or cyclical) one. In accordance with the pattern of resemblance and disparity, "Sidney's Echo, 'tired in secret forests' by the music of the shepherds, mythologizes the sestina's form"

172

(Fowler 1975: 49). The object is (Venus) Urania "whose parts maintained a perfect music." Desire for her is externalized again in persistent assonantal, lexical, and syntactic echo as well as in larger units of structural resemblance. The younger of the two speakers, Strephon, is associated with what is wild or passionate, and Klaius with what is civilized, orderly, and rational. Fowler contrasts the emphases of the final pair of strophes that show Strephon's self-absorption and Klaius' social concern for the general loss of Urania. By having the *Old Arcadia* begin with their complaint, Sidney makes the advent of the hero Pyrochles follow immediately on the fading of the mythicized world and the beginning of Urania's absence. Their mourning, alleviated by hope of her return, is the sign of a shared love for a beauty encompassed by Justice, or integrity. The role of Pyrochles then becomes clarified as that of a Christian hero inspired by a Christian Muse, always subtended by the Neoplatonic Venus.

Fowler's brilliant and much-needed interpretation of this poem calls for little more than clarification of it as a sestina, that is, as the locus of the meeting of the two kinds of time and an ensuing debate, externalized to some degree, about the dominance of closure. Although the formal resemblances throughout are manifest, they do not create a chiastic result: The turning point of the poem occurring as near as possible to its center is the succession of Klaius' voice to Strephon's in the recognition of new light and possibility. The "rigid grammatical parallelism" between their speeches, pointed out by Kalstone (1965: 81), actually subserves the unveiling of a series; the parallelisms only mask progression and a fundamental asymmetry not only in the diction and prosody but in the nature of the speakers and their roles. Klaius, after all, invokes Mercury, the inventor of music; and when he brings music into being himself, it is a harmony of the passions momentarily realized in acoustic form.

The persistent metaphor of music and its suggestion of harmony and order represents cosmic and natural order, to be achieved through askesis. The sestina scheme is deeply embedded in the execution of the metaphor, the lament for lost music taken up mainly as the poem moves toward its end. Strephon curses the inventors of music while Klaius fears madness through the demands of order. Nowhere more than at this crucial point does the control exercised by the sestina scheme function as a sign of the contention of subcategories of will. Klaius himself "was once the music" of the valleys, this later replaced by cacophonous "cries." Now "the nightingales do learn of owls their music"; a realized adynaton in a context of chaos. In this way within the poem, a moment of utter disintegration occurs only to give rise to new cycles of order. The spiral movement of the sestina

173

comprehends even those beginnings and endings that in a different context appear decisive and final.

Sidney's choice of the sestina for meditation on "music" as chaos and disorder is not coincidental. Its harmony is imaged as centered (enclosed by valley, strophe IV) or centerless (and echoless, as in reception by the gods' "silent ears," strophe I), while the poem gravitates around the deprivation of a center, Urania.

The paradox described in the realm of music is not the only one to be found here. A fundamental pastoral complaint, the avoidance of the city and its constraints, appears in Strephon's speech, where he refers to himself as formerly "free-burgess of the forests" (strophe III). This kind of image represents a structural reversal of the older, bourgeois concept of the freedom of the city that had developed during the high Middle Ages. From this perspective, the city would have been a place of release and recreation from the constraining effects of agrarian or feudal life. The idea of the free city helped to legitimize capitalism and further literary awareness, as well, of the individual as subject. Here Sidney's paradox presupposes a prior reversal, to "freedom of the wilds," an image that has already replaced the city with the pastoralized landscape as the superior locus of collective aspiration and fellowship of the sort to which Klaius repeatedly alludes. Sedimented in the landscape of this eclogue is the *hic sunt leones* of urban concentration. It is a monitory image that conveys the notion of closure in either aspect, for both city and country represent necessary barriers.

But this image as it conditions the poem has its own frame, as well: the ambiguity of the adynaton as it dominates, for example, the entire seventh strophe:

> Strephon: Meseems I see the high and stately mountains
> Transform themselves to low dejected valleys.
> Meseems I hear in these ill-changed forests
> The nightingales do learn of owls their music.
> Meseems I hear the comfort of the morning
> Turned to the mortal serene of an evening.

It is ultimately the poetic imagination or musical impulse that connects the three members of this impossibilium. Through the filter of semblances produced by figures the transformation of externals into music progresses. The consolatory aspect of this power, in the neo-Petrarchan mode shared by Sidney and Spenser, evokes Orphic claims for poetic autonomy. In the interstice between the departure of Urania and her return, the sestina demonstrates the recurrence (hence the partial absence) of catastrophe and heralds ultimate

174

repose through the very conditions of language: its referentiality and its fanning of desire.

In a time that finds imagination identified more or less with figurative speech, this tendency is linked to metamorphoses of things as they are described in pastoral. The given situation of the wanderer in wood and field evinces the pains of self-imposed exile, for instance, but in Renaissance poems evokes the exile following the Fall, so that the pastoral trope, which is meaning transmuted into style, evokes history as well as myth. The same hyperbole subserves laments for all departures: That of the beloved, the ruler, the celestial or terrestrial Venus, all the disjunctions that portend the origin of earthly Arcadias in loss. Read in context, the Arcadia poems emerge as the dramatized form of response to this deprivation. The contraries of heroic responsibility and passion suffered at leisure, complaints of lost honor and love, actually turn out to be coupled as the two faces of one kind of active experience. Thus the opening moment of Sidney's work, where the heroes Pyrochles and Musidorus reach Arcadia and abandon their military undertakings for the love of the indigenous princesses, blurs the dyad of action/contemplation.

The world where sport, dance, and poetry are the only valued kinds of action is a timeless one in that it draws from an archetype of perfect bliss, a paradise for poets. Courtship inserted into this world has reference to relations that can be visualized only as being without end. Heroic quest, by relative contrast, is imaginable as event and the source of events. They are the manifestation of linear time as opposed to the cycles of amorous pursuit and satisfaction. Only a debased and attenuated Virtue mediates between the passions and their philosophical evaluation. At the same time, the poetry of love depends for its Arcadian vitality on the enduring connection between passionate intensity and ideas of permanence and value. Within the narrative sequence, the "Greek" warriors appear with their heroic past essentially behind them and pastoral leisure ahead. In the new world, they constitute an intrusion of external realities that uncover a dearth of energy within the old idyll in the Italian style.

The *Old Arcadia* is set within the limits of a temporality regulated by presence and absence. The persistence of hyperbolical anteriority creates a state of continuous past. Ceremonies mark the despair of separation from a felicity at once the order of Original Justice and the simplicity of that order. From loss ensue delights and then disorders of "mind," and the moral evaluation of events—ending the harmony of the spheres before the Fall (embodied by Urania)—is represented through the absence of cosmic and social order, through all that is only adumbrated in the poems. Wealths of ordered concepts

175

that are now excluded from the universe are understood as present only within the poems.

Not every feature of the ideal polity is lacking. The poetry is often public and occasional, alluding to shared intimacies of culture. But as we turn to the consideration of the rhetorical status of public imagery, it is impossible to avoid the sense of a continuous weighing and measuring, a temptation to find differences. Renaissance poets are apt to use paradox as a sort of mathematical formula in whose intersections a particular condition may be fixed, yet conflicts between impetuous youth and restraining age, indulged pleasure and rigorous duty are complicated greatly by socialization, through the essentially urbanized culture of pastoral. The state of being that is peculiar to characters thus beleaguered (as well as to work that encloses them) condemns them to retrospection.

Those who have not known love are excluded rhetorically or are evoked as objects for future transformation. Change, however, can be noted only in retrospect. Through figures of doubtful knowledge emerges a sense of irremediable alteration through expression. This dyad represents the tension between externality and internality, their respective assumptions including a division between the poem as private icon and as public symbol:

> Then do I think indeed, that better it is to be private
> In sorrows torments, than tyed to the pompes of a pallace,
> Nurse inwarde maladyes, which have not scope to be breathed out ...
> (*Arcadia* XIII, 102-104, ed Robertson 1973)

Sidney's own vacillation between the alternatives of public affairs or devotion to writing (Connell 1977: 10 ff.) reflects this fundamental division. So do his pondering of beginnings and endings, of circularity and event, of eschatological time and mythical time, which are germane to the *Arcadia*'s central concerns:

> For before there was a heaven or an earth there was neither a heaven to
> stay the height of the rising, nor an earth which in respect of the round
> walls of earth, could become a centre.
> (cit. Harrison 1930: 712)

Centerless space coincides in this view with beginning—and with endless time beyond knowledge. It is, of course, the glory of that height and centering that is the lost desideratum of the Arcadians. Pre-text and prehistory are their only recourse for the purification of passions, even as they fall back on the mercies of blind Cupid. As the shepherds invoke original Justice, paying court to their own poetry of praise, their inventories of sorrow are unqualified. Nothing is conceded to the explanatory, modifying phrase, for their loss is known and shared. The metaphors of line and cycle, of outside and inside set scenes of mourning as islands even within the enclosed valleys of the privileged country. Catalogues and litanies are enough, for it is the juxtaposition of things, their significant adjacencies, that best embody the imperatives of openness and closure and their extension into the fundamental tensions within pastoral.

Composing the divisions of mind that are translated into some degree of symbolic action, the Arcadians mourn the omnipresence of change in the world, and perceive this change as loss. This assumption partially explains why this poetry resides not as much in images or ideas as in the quality of incantation. Reconciliation of discord and contradiction is achieved in death, so at some level death is always an initiation, comprising ending and beginning. Death-rites are then a step toward the good inner life, a tempering of mind to the omnipresence of conflict. The power of song alone will survive death as a voice. That song will provide a public voice for the private event. The poem travels between the abstract conception and concrete example, and finally, through its own being as art, declares for pleasure: Even in sorrow the senses give, without taking, the trace of mythical time to the sympathetic imagination.

This transfer is accomplished through figures. The gnomic aspect of pastoral is made known through the veil of mythical time in the linear progress of speech. Sidney's often orotund diction in the first sestina of the *Arcadia* winds around the single one of his rhyme-words that contains an important degree of ambivalence: *Nature*. For the rest, the rhyme-words belong to a harmonized field of public symbolism. Sidney evades their tautology with an increment of near-repetition. The sestinas are embodiments of retrospection, and as such turn upon an inward spiral. The content of each poem shows imitation itself as a form of retrospection, and of musing on the past of pastoral.

I have referred to courtship as an essential teleological aspect of Sidney's poems. The additive series that are a necessary feature of the sestina, the catalogues of ordered feeling and emphasis, are subject to alliance with a hero-system at whose apex is a (departed) ruler. The symbolic action of arms is transformed into the encompassing action of song, within and without the narrative. Their common project is defying death. Toward this end the Petrarchan expedient of intensification by repetition appears magnified in the sestinas. Sidney is credited (OED) with the introduction of the word "sestine" into the English language and is probably the first known English poet to have composed one. Hence courtship in these poems is both a statement of allegiance to his predecessor and a self-statement by association (contiguity). The quotient of innovation exerted by Sidney on the Petrarchan forms concerns not only Petrarchan dichotomies of the inner and outer lives but also repression itself. What and how much is made new? To what extent does a poem externalize "nature"? In so doing, how much is "nature" altered?

On the death of the redundant but much mourned King, Agelastus, "noted among them as well for his skill in poetry as for an austerely maintained sorrowfulness" creates his elegy. It is to be found among the few poems strewn within the prose of Book I:

I.   Since wailing is a bud of causeful sorrow,
     Since sorrow is the follower of ill fortune,
     Since no ill fortune equals public damage,
     Now prince's loss hath made our damage public,
5   Sorrow pay we unto the rights of nature,
     And inward grief seal up with outward wailing.

II. Why should we spare our voice from endless wailing,
     Who justly make our hearts the seats of sorrow,
     In such a case where it appears that nature
10   Doth add her force unto the sting of fortune,
     Choosing alas, this our theatre public,
     Where they would leave trophies of cruel damage?

III. Then since such pow'rs conspire unto our damage
     (Which may be known, but never helped with wailing)
15   Yet let us leave a monument in public,
     Of willing tears, torn hair, and cries of sorrow.
     For lost, lost is by blow of cruel fortune
     Arcadia's gem, the noblest child of nature.

IV. O nature doting old, O blinded nature,
20   How hast thou torn thyself, sought thine own damage,
     In granting such a scope to filthy fortune,
     By thy imp's loss to fill the world with wailing!
     Cast thy stepmother eyes upon our sorrow,
     Public our loss, so see thy shame is public.

25   V. O that we had, to make our woes more public,
     Seas in our eyes, and brazen tongues by nature,
     A yelling voice, and hearts composed of sorrow,
     Breath made of flames, wits knowing naught but damage,
     Our sports murdering ourselves, our musics wailing,
30   Our studies fixed upon the falls of fortune.

VI. No, no, our mischief grows in this vile fortune,
     That private pangs cannot breathe out in public
     The furious inward griefs with hellish wailing;
     But forced are to burden feeble nature

35   With secret sense of our eternal damage,
     And sorrow feed, feeding our souls with sorrow.

   VII. Since sorrow then concludeth all our fortune,
        With all our deaths show we this damage public.
        His nature fears to die who lives still wailing.

                              (ed. Robertson 1973: 284-285)

The verbal device of stated candor establishes sincerity as a convention, integrating the notion of the impromptu and immediate with the measured content. Sidney achieves a regular correspondence of metrical pattern and syntax, furthering the realization of a reordered actuality. Time as a structural principle is abstracted from flux, just as consciousness contemplates itself against a "natural" background. In a sense, the control of temporal flow is the first stratum of a multilevel scheme of repression.

Beginning with ritualistic invocation in groups of coordination and opposition, the poem progresses to its declaration of external representation. The additive series competes with chiasmus: open against closed structure. "Wailing" is the symptom of "sorrow." which was caused in turn by "ill fortune;" the progress is arrested by a comparison of simple magnitude: "Public damage" eclipses all other "ill-fortune" in sheer size. From there on chiasmus takes over: That of rhyme-words and their proximate terms "public damage/damage public" and of conceptions. The second appearance of "sorrow" in the first strophe represents the *manifestation,* not the original form of feeling. Counterposed to "nature," it forms the complete figure taken together with "inward grief . . . outward wailing."

The bulk of terms is drawn from a Latinate lexicon but one rarely used otherwise to dramatize Petrarchan lament. Sannazaro's harmonious theater is invoked, now by contrast with the life of action, government, and loss. The singer Agelastus emerges with a substratum of the "Athenian senator" still attending him. Unsponsored by an ultimate figure of authority, the lamenting "public" knows the precarious element of its sorrow. Of course the participation of nobles in Arcadian rites remains at their core. Summarizing the order of causal relations at a point near the would-be center of the poem, figures of repetition usher in the referent of all this failed power: Lost is "the noblest child of nature." It is curious that no panegyric is included in the lament. If we reflect that Mannerist poets were overwhelmingly conscious of the political implications of their art, of its power of courtship and reiteration of standing, it is legitimate to inquire after the nature of the speaker's avowed sincerity. At

179

several places, chiasmus closes off speculation: "Public our loss, so see thy shame is public" (24); "And sorrow feed, feeding our souls with sorrow" (36), denoting an equilibrium of the internal and external that is belied by the language of good intentions.

The turmoil of love leads to games of disguise. "Rustic" and "noble" wedded in one image represent one of the chief categories of desire in early lyric. Poetry often protects this kind of subterfuge, which masks the sunken elements of class-distinction and privilege. Akin to the language of sensuous idealism in the speech of Platonizing theologians, the elegiac sestine provides an accommodation of soul and immortality with change and the absence of change, which is death. "Likeness" turns into "sameness," the inner and outer voices falling into harmony. Yet such apparent concord is not the whole picture. When Sidney's fifth strophe invokes "a yelling voice," "our sports murdering ourselves," "musics wailing," these aural images are the obverse of pastoral harmony, just below the surface of accommodation. The trope of poetry "a monument . . . of willing tears" reduced the polarity of distinctions while increasing the totality of resemblances. Poetry is then fully unmasked as action, analogous to presentational rituals of other kinds. Metaphor by replacement is a chief vehicle, and the varieties of relevance imposed on it sublimate previous worlds of feeling to present courtship. The poem seeks public sanction for desire. Therefore it works to repress and evade, as well as state, elements abstracted from the category of "nature."

The place of *nature* as a rhyme-word in the first of Sidney's sestinas depends on a deeper sense of metamorphosis at the core of "nature" itself. In his *Apologie,* Sidney discusses the exclusivity vouchsafed to the poetic art: "Onely the Poet, disdayning to be tied to any such subjection to the works of Nature, lifted up with the vigor of his owne invention, doth growe in effect another nature . . . not inclosed within the narrow warrant of Nature's guifts, but freely ranging onely within the Zodiack of his owne wit" (VIII.). The trope of the zodiac gives the firm sense of limitation at the core of invention. Sidney comprehends within the term *nature* on one level, what is characteristic, hereditary, suitable, originary, and on the other, all that is in creation, or "totality." In dramatic form, discordance within nature is conveyed in the poem by cacophonic sounds, underscored in the surrounding narrative by "shrieks" and "drunken commotion." The poetic self is given back as a kind of death instinct.

If repression is the power source for resonant and controlled moral debate incorporated within pastoral, then in accordance and in cadence with the smaller-scale model of repression, the decline of the Duke from agent of authority to its victim must be seen as a fact of nature that makes it possible for poetry to ascend the tragic heights from an initial smallness of motive. Pastoral's special sensibility insofar as it progressively excludes the world of fact stands in a complicated relation to "nature," rendered by Sidney in the tropes of feeling and of the sublimation of feeling. It is the latter kind of figure that aids in Sidney's unmasking of pastoral.

The fictions of this poem are tropes of control and release. These pivot around the rhyme-word *nature*. The aspects of nature understood as force: Fate, destiny, necessity, even "fortune" (combating another aspect of "nature"), constraint and limitation—in other words, the estranged aspect of nature—prevail. The basic dyad of those elements in life that are humanly controllable and those beyond man's capacity for domination molds rhetorical form; for us, this ideology is no longer so fully assimilated and requires examination. "The nature of anything comprehends its original, innate character, its spontaneous behavior" that "can be contrasted with what is made to be or do by some external agency" (Lewis 1975: 45). Although the distinction will not hold for natural philosophers, it emerges daily from the experience of the practical world. For the anthropocentric pastoral poetry of the Renaissance, nature as given could easily comprehend among its meanings that which is untouched by man. A parallel in contemporary literary parlance would even extend to the blank page in which no word has been "ploughed." Nature can be "all that is not man-made," since man as agent stands out among all other interferers. This sense of the term is one that includes all others, even those curtailed or petrified figurative senses involving personification. Sidney uses certain meanings that call to mind their etymology. The first appearance of the term gives us "nature" as the collectivity of traits that are peculiarly human, reflecting the identity of human "kind" (Lewis 1975: 28); here, the need is to externalize and thus eliminate grief. But in the second strophe nature is a "force," a direct movement immanent in things, and distinct from the particularized "fortune" that selects from them. In the fourth strophe the trope gravitates even more strongly toward personification: "the noblest child of nature" recurs to the connection with *nasci*, its noun *natus* and *natio*, race or nation. This meaning leads to the personification carried throughout the following strophe, of Nature as stepmother whose "shame" is in the deprivation of her children. The next sense could substitute "description" or "character" for "nature." It is the final one before the tornada that most intrigues us because of its complexity and pivotal status. None of the previous senses agrees with this instance; nor does the adjective "feeble" easily attach itself to other common meanings.

Throughout the poem the otherness and the divinity of nature cohere with its various meanings, even those that include the given character of man.

"Neither a heaven to stay the height of the rising, nor an earth which . . . could become a centre"—Sidney wrote of eschatological time, surrounding the linear time of the world's history. This is the chaos that later was created into cosmos. Lewis cites Milton's use of the idea: Chaos as "the womb of Nature and perhaps her grave" (*Paradise Lost* II, 911, cit. Lewis 1975: 40). The cosmos can then be called nature.

If this is the meaning of the term, it summarized the argument implicit in the sestina form. In it is to be found the intersection of cyclical of mythical primeval time, or pre-time, and linear time, or history. The adjective "feeble" would evaluate the fragility of the world. Beyond the opposition of the controllable and the fated is inclusive closure within the planet, defined by its beginning and possible ending. Again, however, the tornada does not permit of final closure, rather picking up one of the former, discarded senses ("character") of "nature."

The opposition of the "natural" and the "man-made," or artificial, as a fundamental element of the dialectic of pastoral, comes under consideration also with respect to Sidney's two views of man: as a speculative and as a practical being. That man ever lived with no form of social organization is a seductive belief to all who would wish him to have obeyed no laws but those of "nature"; on the other side, his pre-civil condition, in the state of "nature," might be perceived as a state of chaos. The beginning of civil society, which is the beginning of linear time whether it is evaluated as a good or as an evil, is presumed to have as its precedent the "state of nature," which would also return if civil society were abolished. Now pastoral is often able to conceive of an insertion of a realm of freedom, feeling, and wildness uncatalogued in time within the wider limitations of societal closure. But as soon as it is recorded, that time falls within the sway of the known and knowable. What remains beyond the margins on either side is the immemorable and unknowable, in both past and future. What is known and therefore recorded in Sidney's poem is the contention of different kinds of power. The absent "Basileus" signifies that no single power gains and holds ascendancy. Rather, the poem revolves inward toward things remembered that are as such inexhaustible, and hence escape closure.

3. Edmund Spenser: "Ye wastefull Woodes! bear witness of my woe"

The arrangement of Spenser's sestina, which dominates the August section of his *Shepheards Calendar* (1579), helps to inform it with the fundamental assumption that the pastoral world is the product of a special, enclosed sensibility that has consciously excluded the world of fact. As they did in Virgil (Damon 1961: 281-289), the woods, birds, the Spring itself, listen to the unhappy swain. Furthermore, they are to function as more than an echo chamber ("Wherein my plaints did oftentimes resounde"). Although the emptiness of the forest ("wastefull") otherwise made it possible for it to provide the main metaphorical link between sylvan habitat and poetic inspiration, now the pastoral poet associated with mythical creativity demands that they "waile," "drawe neere," that the owls ("ye banefull Byrds") respond to his cries with ever more "yrksome yelles." Whereas the shepherd previously had listened to the sounds of nature and found in what he heard a stimulus to music, in the moment of this new song he no longer follows nature's sounds but invokes them within his own. This reformulation of metaphor prefigures the alienation which the singer declares, near to the center of the poem, to be his chief desire: "Here will I dwell apart," the prosody following the semantics.

I. Ye wastefull Woodes! bear witness of my woe,
    Wherein my pliants did oftentimes resounde;
    Ye careless Byrds are privy to my cryes,
    Which in your songs were woont to make a part:
5   Thou, pleasaunt Spring, hast luld me oft asleepe,
    Whose streames my trickling teares did oft augment.

II. Resort of people doth my griefes augment,
    The walled townes doe work my greater woe;
    The forest wide is fitter to resound
10 The hollow Eccho of my carefull cries:
    I hate the house, since thence my Love did part,
    Whose wailefull want debars mine eyes of sleepe.

III. Let stremes of teares supply the place of sleepe;
     Let all, that sweete is, voyd; and all, that may augment
15   My dole, draw neere! More meete to waile my woe
     Bene the wilde woods, my sorows to resound,
     Then bed, nor bowre, both which I fill with cries,
     When I them see so waste, and finde no part

IV. Of pleasure past. Here will I dwell apart
20 In gastfull grove therefore, till my last sleep
    Doo close mine eyes; so shall I not augment
    With sight of such as chaunge my restless woe,
    Help me, ye banefull Byrds! whose shrieking sound
    Is signe of dreere death, my deadly cries

183

25 V. Most ruthfully to tune: and as my cryes
    (Which of my woe cannot bewray least part)
    You heare all night when Nature craveth sleep,
    Increase, so let your yrksome yelles augment.
    Thus all the nightes in plaintes, the days in woe,
30 I vowed have to waste, till safe and sound

    VI. She home returne, whose voyces silver sound
    To cheerefull songes can chaunge my cheerless cries.
    Hence with the Nightingale will I take part,
    That blessed byrd, that spendes her time of sleepe
35 In songes and plaintive please, the more t'augment
    The memorie of his misdeede that bred her woe.

    VII. And you that feel no woe, when as the sound
    Of these my nightlie cries ye heare apart,
    Let breake your sounder sleepe, and pitie augment.
                                    (Spenser 1852: 278-9)

The teleological consolation that the lover imagines he may hear
the forests intimating is none other than the sound of his own voice,
reminding us that visions of a purposive universe and a pantheon that
presides over human destiny are a projection of human desire.
Cuddie, who performs the song, is not its composer but reproduces
the song Colin made, and even prefaces the performance with a line
echoed in the poem:

> Cud: Then listen ech unto my heavie lay,
> And tune your pypes as ruthfull as yee may.
> . . . my deadly cries
> Most ruefully to tune . . .
>   (Sestina 11, 24-25)

The *Shepheardes Calender*, dedicated to Sidney, was Spenser's
choice of a self-introduction as poet (Nelson 1963: 31), in which the
composer, "Colin," insistently maintains the modesty of a shepherd
boy, though his rustic friends are lavish in his praise. This screening
relationship between author and text is verbalized throughout the
Renaissance as a concomitant of the modesty topos. It signifies textual independence. If we arrange into a temporal order the external
detachment of poem from poet and the Orphic power manifested
within the poem, we may infer a transference of that power from
person to text: The omnivorous teleology of poetic form can take
the most resistant elements of extrapoetic experience into itself.
    Yet the pastoral poet holds carefully to the humilis/sublimis para-
dox. He is ambivalent towards the poet-shepherd in the text who
suffers together with the torments of unrequited love and the ache of

unfulfilled ambition. The ancestor of the *Shepheardes Calender* is the *Kalender and Compost of Shepherds*, translated from a fifteenth-century French original in 1503 and 1508. Spenser assimilated into his work the chapter of the weaker precursor entitled "Of the Commodity of the twelve months of the year with the twelve ages of man" (Nelson 1963: 36). The sestina in particular, whose form urges retrospection, is "the only deliberate imitation by Spenser" (Harrison 1930: 715). It forms the link between Sannazaro's *Arcadia* and the *carte du tendre* of pastoral love as drawn by British poets.

The emblematic seasons of the *Calender* are commemorated by twelve eclogues for the twelve months. The rich rhetoric of Summer surrounds the August sestina, its abundance challenging the imagination and coercing it into additive series. At various times the shepherd functions primarily as a poet, or as a seer. In the sestina he seems entirely a lover, but the sunken imagery of Orpheus persists, counterposed to the rustic round of two other characters. Growth, maturity, and decay, in whose organization life is reflected and debated, engage a vocabulary of change, mainly of increase.

Two rhyme-words, *augment* and *resound*, involve increases of inner turmoil and outer expression, respectively. None of the rhyme-words names a material substance, and there are two verbs among them, placing full stress on symbolic action. Verbal energy is Spenser's most salient departure from the Italian model. The co-presence of change and permanence challenges previous notions of what a sestina should be. While retaining the *capfinidas* Spenser re-arranged the internal portion of strophic succession so as to reverse the pincer-movement of the last four lines of each strophe: 6 1 2 3 4 5. The measuring of time in segments is subverted by the use of "sleepe" in rhyme-word position, a labile marker of time that creates a new standard (sleeping-waking) independent of astronomical manifestations. Spenser's abandonment of *retrogradatio cruciata* favors the scheme set by the Spaniard Gutierre de Cetina (1518-1554) (Riesz 1971: 155-157) in Cetina's double sestina, and by way of compliment, he translates one of Cetina's rhyme-words: *quejas* (cries).

In conformity with the round of the season and toward the aim of making the poem's revolutions unrivaled by centripetal movement within the strophe, Spenser determines a scheme in which the same rhyme-words succeed one another, except at the capfinidas. This formal reorganization has serious consequences for the sestina, which now contains six end-stopped reiterations of the same series. The tendency toward greater asynchronism is encouraged by the frame of the poem itself, the capfinidas functioning only as frames, although they vary more in their order than the "picture" does. To borrow further from the language of painting: Heightened expressionism pulls the imagery up to the surface of the picture plane, demoting concerns of perspective.

Lacking in the elements of formal organization that otherwise call attention to centerlessness in the sestina, the poem turns to asynchronism in the relation between syntax and metrics. Spenser explores the figurative implications of metrical variation as no composer of sestinas did before him. Enjambment within strophes infuses with syntactic energy lines that are end-stopped with verbs or other objects. The receding object is thus rendered through a heightened expressionism: "The forest wide is fitter to resound / the hollow Eccho"; ". . . all, that may augment / My dole, draw near;" "More meete to waile my woe / Bene the wild woods"; "Here will I dwell apart / in gastfull grove"; "the more t'augment / The memorie of his misdeede." The second half of the poem also contains a number of enjambments that pivot on lines end-stopped by nouns; by this time a climactic moment has already been achieved.

In the nineteenth line of the poem, the initial one of the fourth strophe, we find its essential barrier—that between remembered delight and future grief. The line is broken by final punctuation at its caesura. Following this rupture, the enjambment is strengthened by the late placement of the adverb ("therefore"), reminiscent of Petrarchan flow. As a Renaissance theorist wrote, if the transience of human life and its patterns of mutability are at issue, the "run-on" line shows the hastening of the end and promise of permanence: "Thus when we read a sonnet in which every verse represents for us an end, that is, corruption, our intellect suffers; and on the contrary, when we read another which has its verses running on into one another, it takes pleasure, for from them it derives an indefinable promise of eternity" (Vincenzo Toralto [1598], cit Weinberg 1961: I, 229).

The vocabulary of change gathers speed after the multiple enjambments beginning with the interstices of III and IV and continuing within that strophe. That turning point enunciates also the moment of the lover's death. The remainder of IV introduces not only the explicit mention of change but carries it into the matter of poetry itself. The image of the owls, "baneful Byrds," converts one of the chief metaphors for human song into cacophony. To this "shrieking sound" the poet compares his own "deadly cries," simultaneously the signifier of death and of disharmony. The lover invokes this conversion of his song, heaping upon it the paradox of "ruthful" or harmonious tuning. The overarching scheme of enjambment continues into the fifth strophe, encapsulating both parentheses and a further line. Change and multiplicity are thereby held within the unchanging unity of the poem. The eternity of change most effectively conveys the idea of perpetuity and openness. The poem's dilemma, that of any Christian poem, accommodating the idea of a world without end or beginning with the eschatological account of creation, has a provisional solution in the echo.

This expedient is manifested in the permutations of rhyme-words as well, lexically and contextually altered. "Sleepe" has its first appearance in the varient "asleepe"; "resound" and "sound" divide the poem in half until "sound" is favored in the tornada. The most versatile term is the Petrarchan "part" (cf. Petrarch CCXIV): Used synecdochically as a noun in four instances (strophes I, III, V, VI), it is transformed by a prefix into an adverb (strophes IV, VII) and appears also as a verbal infinitive with an alteration of sense (strophe II). In every case, even those with the meaning of "partaking" or "participation," it functions to denote separation. A similar quotient of change appears among the members of a comparison that runs in the present song, that of cacophonous owls, the "silver sound" of the lady's voice and its power to transform, in turn, the singer's plaint into good cheer. Alternations of night and day are no longer key terms. The act of making the world resound, choosing the elegiac treatment of death as finality, utilizes the recurrences of the sestina form to the utmost. The "auditory imperatives of Arcadian song" (Damon 1961: 295) renew the inclusive relation of content-substance to form.

We have reason to ask if the speaker is a sylvan dweller: He has declared that he "hate[s] the house" for the absence from it of his beloved, and hinted thereby of an eventual return to the city. Is the wood, then, only a stopping-place with ultimate reference to an extrasylvan source of authority and value? A hazy imprecision is enough: We recognize the open door leading out of pastoral (which may include the return of the beloved). The absence of the object was imperative. The green world is a foil for amorous concerns that have nothing to do with sylvan or rustic existence in itself. Taken as one of an open series (like any line within the poem), the "memorie" of the first nightingale and the myth related to it, Spenser's poem subordinates its numerous innovations to its sense of temporal succession as a reverberation of the songs of hypostatized sylvan gods.

4. W. H. Auden: "Paysage moralisé"

Auden composed seven sestinas. Besides the two discussed here, we have a group of four, collectively entitled "Kairos and Logos"

(1941). These constitute a capsule view of human history as construed in the dichotomy of the title. The first sestina deals with the ancient world, the second with the advent of Christianity, the third shows a telescoping of temporality in its concentration on the Reformation and wars of faith. The final poem in the group recapitulates moments of the past where critical time and opportunity (*kairos*) intersect with the discursive element in myth (*logos*).

The translation of human anatomy into landscape proved to be one of Auden's most persuasive means of charting psychic geography. He prepared a large map of his moralized country for a course he taught at Swarthmore College on Romanticism, with a gloss worth citing extensively:

> Beginning with the Fall from Paradise (Eden) into This World (or from Essential into Existential Being), the chart tabulates in the center column the characteristics of Dualism of Experience or Knowledge of Good and Evil in This World. . . . The first category is Primary Symbol: in the center of the page, this is City; verging to the left, still in the center column describing This World, is Forest; in the left-hand Hell (of Pure Deed) it is Common Night and at extreme left, Sea. Verging to the right in the center column it is Mountain. . . . For the category of Order the center is a Differentiated Unity or Civilization, with Rivers and Country verging left to the Hell of Monist Unity (Water) and Barbaric Vagueness, while Roads and Towns verge right to the Hell of Dissociated Multiplicity and Decadent Triviality. . . .

(cit. Spears 1963: 248-249)

The map is tempting material for analysis of irony-and-tension, and a number of tensions are manifest—between center and periphery, unity and multiplicity, stasis and flow, City and country with their concomitant "barbaric vagueness" and "decadent triviality," are end products of inroads upon landscape. Treacherous roads and streams erode centers. The inroads of desire on reason reproduce the conditions under which Auden as composer of sestinas locates his conflicts and rings his changes upon the tone world of English pastoral.

Whereas the map shows these concepts as polarities and refers to religious myth, openly displaying its didactic purpose, the poems exhibit a sunken imagery in which the referent may easily drop out of sight. Topography, though a leading concern, has in the poems to elucidate the diagnosis of poetry with its distilled experience. In numerous instances islands stand for escape and isolation, cities for society, water for belief, valleys for passivity or innocence, and mountains for effort and decision (Spears 1963: 142). These are, of course, topoi with explicit connections embedded in the history of pastoral, and Auden enters into dialogue with his own Neo-Victorian sense of time and place. In a sustained analysis of Romantic attitudes, *The Enchafèd Flood,* he summarizes the abandonment of the age of the "Just City": "The City walls of tradition, mythos and cultus have crumbled" (Auden 1962: 67). Pastoral would then constitute an extra layer of postlapsarian wandering, following in cycles upon the first dispersal. Auden goes on to depict the flight of "survivors" to the "Garden of Happy Island," which would represent a "Prelapsarian Place" of innocence—always illusory. Like the myth of Orpheus, pastoral is linked to renewal and vegetation; like the resurgences of the myth in Italian and English pastoral, Auden's versions are compounded by the willed suspension of time incurred by dreaming. The poems vacillate between their private and their social uses, well distant from the frank enunciations of that conflict by Sidney, but expressing an analogous regret for unity and centrality.

Moral geography as poetic practice is easily traceable past Petrarch, as the title of one of Auden's sestinas, "Paysage moralisé," gives us to understand. Evocative of the medieval topographies of the soul, they were extracted, as it happened, from the myths of transformation in the *Ovide moralisé.* The assignment of value continues but its results are radically different. Throughout the Middle Ages, the City as a center of value remained substantially uncontested, even in the face of constant comparability with the Heavenly City. Variously translated into the earthly and the heavenly Jerusalem, and in the tropes of psychomachias as well as analyses of architecture and of civilization, the city was a place of safety, a source of the amenities of culture and harmonious coexistence. The principle strain of British pastoral lyric comes through Sidney and Spenser from Petrarch, and shows a gradual development away from the idealization of the city. With the onset of Romanticism, urbanity as virtue is reversed, and escape from the city begins in earnest. As Spenser took over the complaint ("The walled townes do work my greater woe") and Sidney translated Petrarch ("I that was once free-burgess of the forest"), they provided a diachronic ground for Auden's eventual ambivalences toward the industrial society of modern England.

The spiral form of the sestina turns with failed concentricity toward the core of its origins, the pastoral wanderer reappearing as a dramatic figure on the verge of adopting quasi-arcadian rhetorical schemes for his own. Whereas the Renaissance poet used pastoral as a means of measuring the private and the public in terms of desire and heroism, in Auden both alternatives are reduced, often, to an ambivalence regarding "culture." His collection *Homage to Clio*

(1960) contains the poem "Dame Kind," whose eponymous nature-goddess is defended against the exclusive lady of Romance lyric:

> She mayn't be all She might be but
> She is our Mum . . .

The magnificent amalgam of earth-mum with unmistakable overtones of the British monarch must be preferred to the "hypochondriach / Bluestocking from Provence."

In his chart, Auden declares that he would replace the Wanderer by a new "builder, who renews the ruined walls of the city" (Spears 1963: 153), thereby reconciling inner and outer worlds through their very interpenetrability and convertibility. The first of the two sestinas I will discuss is often read as an expression of that promise. Its title, "Paysage moralisé," first appears well after the initial publication of the poem (*Collected poetry*, 1945). *On This Island* (1937a) contained it, entitled simply by its first line.

Paysage moralisé

I.   Hearing of harvests rotting in the valleys,
     Seeing at end of street the barren mountains
     Round corners coming suddenly on water,
     Knowing them shipwrecked who were launched for islands,
5   We honour founders of these starving cities,
     Whose honour is the image of our sorrow.

II.   Which cannot see its likeness in their sorrow
     That brought them desperate to the brink of valleys;
     Dreaming of evening walks through learned cities,
10   They reined their violent horses on the mountains,
     Those fields like ships to castaways on islands,
     Visions of green to them that craved for water.

III. They built by rivers and at night the water
     Running past windows comforted their sorrow;
15   Each in his little bed conceived of islands,
     Where every day was dancing in the valleys,
     And all the year trees blossomed on the mountains
     Where love was innocent, being far from cities.

IV. But dawn came back and they were still in cities,
20   No marvellous creature rose up from the water,
     There was still gold and silver in the mountains,
     And hunger was a more immediate sorrow;
     Although to moping villagers in valleys
     Some waving pilgrims were describing islands.

25 V. 'The gods,' they promised, 'visit us from islands,

Are stalking head-up, lovely through the cities;
Now is the time to leave your wretched valleys
And sail with them across the lime-green water;
Sitting at their white sides, forget their sorrow,
30   The shadow cast across your lives by mountains.'

VI. So many, doubtful, perished in the mountains
Climbing up crags to get a view of islands;
So many, fearful, took with them their sorrow
Which stayed them when they reached unhappy cities;
35   So many, careless, dived and drowned in water;
So many, wretched, would not leave their valleys.

VII. It is the sorrow; shall it melt? Ah, water
Would gush, flush, green these mountains and these valleys
And we rebuild our cities, not dream of islands.

                                 (Auden 1937a: 22-3)

The issue of centrifugal movement against centering and presence addresses itself in this poem to the "concerned reader" willing to pore over the process of myth-making. Diction conveys that art, love, and peace should not be thought of as divested of their content or words of their teleology. As sketched by the poet, the reader belongs to a "we" that "seeing . . . hearing . . . knowing," draws the consequences. These are quickly shown to be no more, however, than the conditions for a commemorative occasion. We are reminded of the assumptions of audience in the first sestina of Sidney's *Arcadia.*

The place of the poem is, of course, an island. It follows the contour of England but also encompasses an escapism and isolation to be classed with other "islands," those of romantic love or other kinds of self-absorption. From here it is not far to the ground of the pastoral sestina in elegy. "Sorrow" is the only rhyme-word that is not a term of place in its primary sense. The ironies are mild, the narrative unstressed and full of conditionals, gerunds, adjectivized verbs, and attenuating verbs of being. The founding of cities is presented as a "reining in" near the "brink," the symbolic action of the poem quickly glossing over the activity of "building." Under the eyes of death, being is disclosed as temporality. Yet a synchronic meaning emerges from the unchanged poetic structure, its pentameter taming the question of the degree to which atemporal structure underlies cultural phenomena (like "cities"). This is a poetry born of cultural saturation, a poetry where we may discover embedded recollections—oratorical and artifactual—of ordered opposition and coordination. The oratory that constructs a verbal frame around its content also displaces strong denotative meaning.

If we glance at Auden's first strophe laid next to the first strophe of Sidney's, their communality is manifested through relations of consequentiality and a feeling of inevitability:

Hearing of harvest rotting
    in the valleys,
Seeing at end of street the
    barren mountains,
Round corners coming
    suddenly on water,
Knowing them shipwrecked who
    were launched for islands,
We honour founders of these
    starving cities,
Whose honour is the image of
    our sorrow.

Since wailing is a bud of
    causefull sorrow,
Since sorrow is the fol-
    lower of ill fortune,
Since no ill fortune equals
    public damage,
Now prince's loss hath made
    our damage public,
Sorrow pay we unto the
    rights of nature,
And inward grief seal up
    with outward wailing.

The enthymemic structures of Sidney's poem can be cautiously applied to Auden's. None of the actions listed depends on a previous one but the act of "honouring" as image-creation. What emerges is rather a map of sensory data that together lead to knowledge. And yet the elegy for the "central" is attached to an unmistakably public object: Like princes, the "founders" stand for centralized power. In Auden that power is transferred to the cities themselves. Auden stresses historical discontinuity in the interstices between the first two strophes, where instances of elegiac "sorrow" are measured. The series "image-sorrow-likeness-sorrow" denotes "our" and "their," building layers upon prior loss.

Historical pretensions to causality are unmasked. The structure of history, this poetic space tells us, will not be the same tomorrow, because the very traces of today will have been added to its domain; something new will have to happen. But today's islands are tomorrow's cities, and the reverse obtains as well: Final judgment, then is infinitely suspendable. The "they" of the poem shifts from "founders" to the "pilgrims" (strophe IV), raising yet another cycle of voyaging within the sweep of the first, this time culminating not only in the usual losses of life or attrition but also in arrival at already decaying "cities."

"Water" and "islands," lexically opposed, reveal semantic affinities through contiguity: Dreaming of one entails the other. Similar relations obtain between "mountains" and "valleys," here subsumed into coordinates, both barren, menacing, and resistant. From the first, "cities" and "islands" are opposed; it is only across temporality that their ground is revealed as identical. Even as the speaker declares for the tradition of modernism that builds out of the destruction of its immediate antecedents, he returns to the mythic time that is impervious to change and succession. Such terms as "learned cities," "pilgrims," the evocations of the white and lime-green that dominate many paintings of myths of origins in our museums, even the topoi of the ship-allegory (to be dealt with in this study as a subgenre of the sestina) reiterate both learned and ceremonial recurrences and the bonds between them. The rebuilding of cities is shown in one aspect as an encrustation, sharing in the temporality of cultures and of their inheritors. All is framed by culture: Enclosure is inevitable. Nostalgia for openness and liberty, for "being far from cities," the dream of man as innocent ("each in his little bed") are fundamental topics of pastoral and also of its history, grounded in a lore long that of cities, in myths of their founding and building, and the welcoming of artificial barriers such as walls. The sestina generically is concerned with reflection on limits, and therefore, at the base of mountains or the edge of the wilderness, commands the effort to reconcile being and knowing. The sorrow of disillusioned founders is and is not the same as that of their mourners. Atemporality within an enclsoure of innocence remains a dream ("Where every day was dancing in the valleys, / And all the year trees blossomed on the mountains" betrays the compromise of measurement). Only the shifting object of desire— now cities, now islands—is reflected in images that keep time with flux.

The "marvellous creature" that did not rise "up from the water," Proteus or sea-monster that he is, the untapped riches of the mountains, and the hunger all exemplify the obverse results of desire. No rhetorical finality is admissible, only addition to a store. The stimulus to new migration can never be the monster himself, or the god, but the poet-pilgrim (or Proteus-substitute) who urges action by casting his rhetoric out to the founding of new Romes and then records it. That cycle with its intermittent "closures" is nothing without eternity, in the light of which alone they are what they are. The tornada (in the poem's one perfect enjambment) captures the conditional possibility—also a memory—of deluge, a thawing of remembrance and history. The possibility of transcendence held up for an instant in the vision of the gods is only the mirror-image of the seeming impossibility that concludes the poem: An apocalypse leading to the next greenness.

5. W. H. Auden: "We have brought you, they said, a map of the country"

In a critical work, *The Dyer's Hand* (1962), Auden draws a parallel between Christianity and the notion of punctuality: "The notion of punctuality, of action at an exact moment, depends on drawing a distinction between natural and historical time which Christianity encouraged if it did not invent" (cit. Spears 1963: 164).

At about midpoint in the sestina, a man crosses himself as he passes near a forest. His trip to the country has provided an invitation, incorporated within the poem, to dip into rustic life. But the locus of pastoral is also that of transformation, spells of unearthly magic, and confrontations with obscure divine and demonic forces. The manifold conception of "wood" with its various literal and metaphorical implications furnishes instant associations:

"We have brought you, they said, a
map of the country"

I.   We have brought you, they said, a map of the country:
Here is the line that runs to the vats,
This patch of green on the left is the wood,
We've pencilled an arrow to point out the bay.
5   No thank you, no tea; why look at the clock,
keep it? Of course. It goes with our love.

II.   We shall watch your future and send our love.
We lived for years, you know, in the country,
Remember at week-ends to wind up the clock.
10   We've wired to our manager at the vats.
The tides are perfectly safe in the bay
But whatever you do don't go to the wood.

III. There's a flying trickster in that wood,
And we shan't be there to help with our love.
15   Keep fit by bathing in the bay,
You'll never catch fever then in the country.
You're sure of a settled job at the vats,
If you keep their hours and live by the clock.

IV. He arrived at last; it was time by the clock,
20   He crossed himself as he passed the wood.
Black against evening sky the vats
Brought tears to his eyes as he thought of their love;
Looking out over the darkening country
He saw the pier in the little bay.

25 V. At the week-ends the divers in the bay
Distracted his eyes from the bandstand clock;
When down with fever and in the country
A skein of swans above the wood
Caused him no terror; he came to love
30   The moss that grew on the derelict vats.

VI. And he has met sketching at the vats
    Guests from the new hotel in the bay;
    Now curious following his love,
    His pulses differing from the clock
35 Finds consummation in the wood
    And sees for the first time the country.

VII. Sees water in the wood and trees by the bay,
     Hears a clock striking near the vats;
     This is your country and the home of love.

(Auden 1937b: 122-3)

The sestina in *The Orators* (1932) is one of only two poems that Auden retained from the section called "Journal of an Airman" for his *Collected Poetry*. The subtitle of the little work, "An English Study," conveys a double meaning, the information that the book deals with England and the lingering connotation of English literature and schoolboy composition. The second meaning is reinforced by the general context: The term "orators," for one, designates "headmasters, teachers, clerics, propounders of false doctrine and defenders of the system generally" (cit. Spears 1963: 47). These often are parodied throughout the work, in patient expository style. The Airman, by contrast, is an outsider, hence an appropriate focus for conflicting ideologies.

Narrative prevails throughout, emphasizing the irremediable externality of reported experience. The inner/outer dichotomy subdivides into a number of apposite dualisms: affective/pragmatic, private/social, rebellion/obedience. The subject of the poem is bound to the "orators" by ties of several kinds — affection, common social background, probably a former dependency. In the course of the narrative he is freed from his prior existence and connected more explicitly with art, seen as the champion of the fullness of life, opposed to the repressive agency of reason. The background of mostly inchoate nature, even without recourse to the topographical scheme of Auden's consciousness as set forth in his map, must be recognized as suggestive of topographical features rendered into categories of the mind. Within the sweep of the sestina, they become ordered matter, the open and indefinite enclosed. Together with the existential and immediate elements (such as the monologue of an approximate half of the poem), they are rendered artificial.

The clock is an actual point of reference for the contextual transformations of the rhyme-words. Topography becomes personalized in the first strophe, when it is not perfectly certain that the speakers do not share with their addressee a common enemy. They point out

195

the advantages of bathing in the bay, which they have marked with an arrow. They value this occupation and its position outside the "wood," which they characterize as dangerous. To this evaluation they attach their "love," which binds together the first two strophes. The speakers in the first half of the poem mark time, "your future," "years," "week-ends" in increasingly punctilious order. In genteel fashion they look at the clock, refuse their tea, and bring their talk to a close. The social aspect is pointedly juxtaposed to the internal norms of meter dominating them with diffuse syntax.

As in our other sestina, objects do not summarize thoughts but reflect and and complete them. Through the veil of nonpoetic or un-canonized poetic objects, a nascent universe of pastoral comes into being. The "flying trickster" evoked in the warning against the wood and its "fever" emerges in the second half of the poem, made explicit by the "skein of swans," a much more appropriate metaphor for poetry. It is "time by the clock" at the moment of transformation. The passage *near* the wood is differentiated from *traversal,* yet the sketch of sacral gesture recalls the warning and mimics the transformations of pastoral and romance. Suggestive properties conferred on places and times replace the clear lineaments of change and confession. So the inner world of the subject must be inferred from his actions, and the reader performs the work of alignment. As Hoffmansthal wrote, to find ourselves we must not stop at our innerness; "we are to be found outside" (cit. Staiger 1951: 44).

From an external measure imposed externally, time becomes an emotional and physical inner movement on which things have no bearing. The leveling of an assortment of objects to poetic appropriateness within a narrow context is part of the poet's escape-device. Without passing through the wilderness, the subject experiences no fear of the swans and is soon able to transform the "vats" into a seemly, moss-covered ruin of a sort popular during the Enlightenment years, otherwise evoked by "guests sketching." For the pastoral of poetry, he who would partake need undergo only such initiation as is required of him by "pulses differing from the clock" (by parentheses). The rough and forbidding things are ordered into an ornate landscape without the soil of gardening.

Anthropomorphic in its promises of love and renewal, the country neutralizes violent latencies, as in the chiastic "water in the wood / trees by the bay" of the tornada. The "he" is neutralized as well, first in a series of verbs of reception "has met . . . sees . . . hears"), a weakening point of reference as the poem draws to a close. Objects are knowable only through their interrelations. At the end of the poem, "country" appears in a near-patriotic guise, as national land, the England of the "study," summation of poetry itself. The "airman" as bourgeois rebel can detach himself from man's earthbound condition and emerge triumphant in the inner/outer struggle, but only if the clock striking is his internal one. What this means in terms of viable behavioral categories is, to be sure, elusive. From the world of gods to the world of work, all is lower-case now, humanistic, and circumspect. Implicit is a recognition of the successive deprivations suffered by withdrawal throughout centuries to increasingly precarious ontological claims. As this sestina pulls into the present tense we know the speech of a man who acquiesces in the potential overthrow of his class, and we hear the rhythm of his retreat.

6. The Modern Sestina: W. S. Merwin and John Ashbery

Lexical recurrence and stanzaic progression each display the perplexities of temporality in poems. Poets of our time are often thought of as resisting recurrence and pointing forward in sequences with no restrictive order. Open form appears to be the order of our day. But the atemporal life of nature against the time-bound consciousness of man continues as fundamental to poetic creativity. Out of the ashes of a world—even a post-Enlightenment one—of well-made structures and meters, of lived experience formerly transmutable into materials for a curriculum, emerges a fascination with time and attachment to the past. These far surpass concentration upon "the poem itself" or simple avoidance of the capillary distractions of literary documentation. Although most contemporary sestinas have been composed by poets with a sensible link to *docta poesia* (W. S. Merwin, John Ashbery, Richmond Lattimore, and Douglas Hall are important examples), the choice of the sestina has an internal focus. Producing an articulation of consciousness regarding tradition and artifice, sestina poets also mark their own time.

Glances backward and forward reveal the tremors of an ego distracted again and again from the only possible source of undisputed satisfaction, the living moment. This perennial situation of language makes us heirs and perpetrators of many formulaic bits of loftiness and sonority whose focus is easily underwritten by exterior, modish conventions. We would expect this discouraging state of things to persist into sestinas. What has generally prevented it is a feature inherent in the form itself, a continuous pointing beyond itself toward a successive phase of knowing. The "object" stands just beyond reach, in a teasing contiguity to the poem, and the pincer movement of rhyme-words progresses inward under the pressure of a constantly self-renewing context. Directionality emerges as a main problem, one of function and meaning, and one the poet confronts willingly, for the rules of the game remain unchanged.

Beyond the sense of the written word alone, writing is a means of intervention of human culture into nature. To plough a field is to write upon it, and ways of life represent "inscriptions" upon the world. Although the words and the entities they control undergo diachronic mutation in structurally undetermined aspects, the structures of the sestina are atemporal. If an unchanging structure of mind may be inferred eventually from poetic language, then the poetic world a at any given moment is the product of that interaction. The meanings of individual words—flashing, iridiscent vestiges of the evolving consciousness behind them—appear in sestinas as latent values.

A number of contemporary sestinas draw attention to form by means of their titles: "Sestina" or "Poem." Even the latter title is prediction of response. Whether or not they deal openly with "writing," artifice and narcissism lurk in their background. The impulse to reunite with an idea of its own form is characteristic of the individual sestina. The absence in our time of a clearly definable audience has the effect of universalizing the receiver of the poem, which may recall the fluidity of the public in Petrarch's lifetime, in its elasticity as to social class and its rapid growth. Concerns of present-day readers find points of tangency with poetic discoveries that can be attributed to his work: the intersection of conceptions of temporality; the privileged reality of the passing moment and transitory phase; the acute self-awareness of poetry now often raised to the status of a basic, distinguishing feature; the determination of the crucial importance of contextual relations for words.

The notion that interpretation evolves along with other kinds of change—that it is not a matter of recovering some meaning that serves as a center governing structure, but rather is an attempt to observe and participate in possible meaning—is for us largely a product of the Petrarchan years. The innovations of syntax in the manifest structure of Petrarch's sestinas come into play. The syntactic function of a term can be forcibly detached from its purely referential meaning, guaranteeing the energy of the larger entity to which it belongs. Petrarch's effect, achieved through such disposition, was not only to qualify the semantic import of an entity but to suspend it, achieving the equivalent of a prolonged dissonance in a cadence about to be resolved (cf. Contini's example: *Primevera per me pur non è mai* [Contini 1951: 19]).

Called repeatedly back to the sounds of words, the poet relearns that sounds are capable only of distinguishing meaning (the diacritic function [Shapiro 1976: 28 ff.]). Where phonic identities act on semantic nonidentities, poems are unveiled as tissues of signs derived from various codes, chains of signifiers and signifieds having no center convergence but poetic contingency. In contemporary poets, contiguity relations may be reflected not only in the choice of grammatical categories, verbal tenses, or convention. Replaced within the new context, even public symbols lose their singly definable meaning or set of meanings, showing irradiations of sense that reflect "otherness" before anything else. Adjacencies of content defy principles of causality. When the semantic elements of the poem are presented in a succession that overlooks internal causality, the poet has to address the question of whether context is "continuous and graduated or discontinuous and piecemeal, linked in space or reconstituted at each instant by the driving force of time" (Foucault 1966: xxi).

Every sestina belongs simultaneously to the paradigm of "the sestina" and to the syntagm of renewal. The frequent sorties into pastoralism by our poets accordingly find a power in formal order that authorizes the spontaneous character of poetic creation. In our age, shame and glory reside, as current critical idiom has it, in its belatedness. The overflow of involuntarily assimilable information furthers the notion of the telos of poems in the silent and "unwritten." "Reference must be viewed as a circular process, or better, as a spiral or whirlpool in which any absolute referent (like text in a religious sense) is an effect of arbitrariness, i.e., is an axiomatization of experience" (Bouissac 1976: 128). To this awareness of the arbitrary stopping point, analysis of internal structure, conventions, and relations to "literary" habits of mind are a poor counterweight. American poets, in the main, have stayed on the periphery of that danger, keeping options and forms open, as A. R. Ammons puts it (1965: 8):

> I see narrow orders, limited tightness, but will
> not run to that easy victory:
>   still around the looser, wider forces work:
>   I will try
>   to fasten into order enlarging grasps of disorder,
>   widening scope, but enjoying the freedom that
>   Scope eludes my grasp, that there is no finality of
>   vision, that I have perceived nothing completely,
>   that tomorrow a new walk is a new walk.
>   (A. R. Ammons, "Corson's Inlet," 11. 120-128)

It becomes the task of the critic to penetrate the aggregations of randomness in an act of faith. Teasing eruptions of unforeseen and cryptic meanings, as in John Ashbery's work, convey to the reader permission to hope his faith was not futile, that although new meaning behind the wall of words is not entirely manifest, its signifiers show the meeting of desires and the fleeting contact of otherwise alien minds. In the case of the sestina, dominant tones tend to issue from the belated and the transitory, achieving elegiac quality. Interpretation involves the awareness and decoding of a tradition of filiation; then the poem emerges as one *not* only about itself, rescued from circularity by its intertext. Scrambled texts—that is, texts showing considerable linear displacement of grammatical parts, texts preserving shreds of their precursors, ungrammatical poems—are iconizations of intention, which is unidirectional and moves forward even as implicit comparison moves backward (to an anterior referent).

7. W. S. Merwin: "Sestina"

Sestina
for Robert Graves

I. Where I came by torchlight there is a dawn-song
    Leaves remembering, sudden as a name
    Recalled from nowhere, remembering morning,
    Fresh wind in high grass, cricket on plowshare,
5   Whisper of stream in the green-shadowed place,
    Thrush and tanager keeping season.

II. Have I not also willed to be heard in season?
    Have I not heard anger raised in a song
    And watched when many went out to a wild place
10   And fought with the dark to make themselves a name?
    I have seen of those champions how thin a share
    After one night shook off their sleep at morning.

III. In a stony month a long cloud darkened morning.
    Their feet gone white, shuffling the cold season,
15   The breath of some was worn too small to share.
    Have I not heard how fragile then grew song?
    Gray water lashed at the island of one's name.
    And some stayed to flutter empty in that place.

IV. What road is it one follows out of that place?
20   I remember no direction. I dreamed of morning,
    Walking, warming the tongue over a name.
    And a few of us came out of that season
    As though from sleep, and stood too bleak for song,
    And saw hills and heavens in the one-dawn share.

25 V. Whom shall I praise before the gray knife share?
    I have gone like seed into a dark place.
    Whom shall I choose to make new with song?
    For there will be sinking between night and morning,

200

Lisp of hushed voices, a dwindled season,
                    The small lights that flicker at a name.

         VI. Where again shall I walk with various name?
                    Merciless restlessness falls to my share.
                    Whose house shall I fill for more than a season?
35   I woke with new words, and in every place,
                    Under different lights, evening and morning,
                    Under many masters studied one song.

         VII. A breathed name I was with no resting place,
                    A bough of sleep that had no share of morning,
                    Till I had made body and season from a song.
                                                           (Merwin 1952: 48-9)

The speaker is a survivor. "Remembering, he rambles over heroes
and songs, evoking the bard and the mead-hall in the simplicity of his
diction. Echoes of other spring-beginnings collaborate with the poet's
own voice as he recalls the birds' task of "keeping season." Whatever
there is of pastoral belongs entirely to the past. The songs he had
heard may have been his own or those of others; the battles were
certainly ones in which he did not participate as warrior. Memory is
encapsulated within memory. The entire duration of night, for
example, is recapitulated within a dramatically narrow space ("Where
I came by torchlight there is dawn-song"). The coupling of *dawn* and
song recalls a genre, the *alba* (or dawn-song), a genre that lies at the
core of early Western lyric poetry. The shift in time shows it reverse,
for the speaker has progressed forward into the past. This freedom of
tense and mood shifting between memory and anticipation evokes
the eternal present of poems, but goes beyond pastoral in that it
follows a continuing journey ("Where I came . . . What road is it
one follows . . . Whom shall I praise . . . Where again shall I
walk") of "merciless restlessness." Lexical constants such as *morning*
and *season* anchor the movement to measures while the *place* remains
generic. One rhyme-word, *share,* appears variously as noun and verb,
its first instantiation in a decidedly biblical (*plowshare*) register. The
totality of these reminiscent elements commands speculation on
what is anterior to the poem. Whereas the plowshare is still, the poet
has written into it the (inevitably literary) cognition of wars among
men and between men and elements. Witness, not of death but of
departures, the speaker suggests mythical time and simultaneously
history (battles known).

The arrival of the speaker in the beginning ("Where I came") constitutes the *end* of the time preceding the poem. In the midst of the
dialectic of memory and invention, no clear beginning can take place

("I remember no direction . . .") on the level of discourse. Already the scene on which he appears is pastoralized by the swords we posit as preexistent to the plowshare. The intrusion of this man-made object into a background composed of natural detail suggests also that the residue of human "culture" is gradually becoming assimilated into the cycle of growth, change, and decay inherent in nature. Merwin evokes a postheroic "place" of former glory returning to an earlier phase of the cycle, toward its pristine state. Prehistory is a "a name / recalled from nowhere," beyond memory. The plowshare grew still long after the sword was exchanged for it; now the music of novelty (cricket, whispers of leaves and grass) has as its counterpoint the seasonal birdsong.

The first two strophes are strongly connected by the first line of the second, which binds the analogy of poet's and birds' song. Now the term "willed" enters the sestina context, challenging cyclicity (and recalling the sestina's roots in Arnaut Daniel and Petrarch). The speaker as poet bears witness to the residue of shattered life through his memories of departure and return. Here the sestina scheme becomes strained ("I have seen of those champions how thin a share"), hyperbaton accommodating the demands of rhyme-word order. The statements cast as questions ("Have I not . . .") establish a rhetorical relationship that assumes the speaker's vindication by his listener, and his agonistic turn of speech strives to match the exploits of the "champions," then dies with them in elegiac periphrase.

The third strophe opens with the "stony" image honored by Dante. The speaker draws a relationship between the death of heroes and that of poetry or fame, revealing poetry (as in classical rhetoric) as a branch of rhetoric together with history. The "gray waters" of forgetfulness erode man's island, and forgotten souls "flutter empty." Throughout this strophe, anaphora points to the absent heroes. Then too, as at their departure, the speaker experiences song as a passive receiver, not as poet. He stands at one remove from even that marginal degree of participation. In the fourth strophe he can remember no "original" connection between his presence in the lost country and his future. He asks what escape he found from the desolate place of the dead, knowing only that he has migrated again, testing repetition ("warming the tongue over a name") and recapitulation ("And a few of us came out of that season"). The survivors (not of battle but of decay) are revisited awakening to new beginnings encompassing earth (hills) and heaven.

Alliteration, coming to fill the lack of dual rhyme (plowshare/place; morning/evening; season/song) is recalled in its role in the epic, binding together fabled synchrony and an eternal present. The plaint of the Anglo-Saxon Wanderer comes to mind, as the speaker takes up the question of the nineteenth line ("What road is it one follows") to unite it with questions in the next two strophes ("Whom shall I praise . . .? . . . Whom shall I choose to make new with song? . . . Where again shall I walk with various name? . . . Whose house shall I fill for more than a season?") The tranquillity needed for poetic creation is intermittent, parentheses between cycles of wandering. Like a seer, the poet has retreated into a "dark place" that fuses the metaphors of death, of sleep, with the secondary sense of germination and of sexual transport ("like seed," "sinking between night and morning"). All the activities of creation are compressed into these temporal boundaries. Poetic energy is opposed to "sleep," the common condition of fields and poets lying fallow.

The yearning for centrality, a "house" to fill, the search for permanent attachment, harks back to the medieval tropism, repose being the goal that retrospectively would make sense out of effort. Yet the poet boasts of his Protean variety: his "new words," travels and changes, the "many masters" under whom he "studied one song." Here is the secret of the Many in the One that unites the discontinuous phases of his journey. Inaction and action are interchangeable, in that each is indispensable to creation, and poetry arises not out of a twinning attachment to the action it describes, but precisely when that false closure can be denied without fear. The sestina's spiral movement recapitulates moments in Western poetry and of the sestina form in particular, involving the old word-pairing, alliteration, and semantic oscillation that characterize it from its inception forward. Phases and loci of memory and tradition, "many masters," also denote a port never quite reached. Closure is thereby revealed as a goal to be shunned.

The tornada with its astonishing ending in the past perfect ("Till I had made body and season from a song") reestablishes the true relation of the poet to his work. It puts an abrupt, arbitrary end to change, but locates it in so distant a past as to assure us that the cycle of exile and creativity is infinitely repeatable within the boundaries of the poet's life. The pastness of heroism is revealed as detached from the body and season of a song—this knowledge perfectly coterminous, however, with the sestina itself, hence ready to be lost again.

Another sestina by Merwin, "Variation on a Line by Emerson" (Williams 1977: 280-281), deals with the topic of concealment and revelation, taking its departure from the Emersonian dialectic of fate and will. In this context the paradisiacal dream of synchrony delights the evening of the speaker's life:

Let a kind diction out of the shadows tell,
Now toward my slumber, a legend unto my face
Of sleep as a quiet garden without malice
Where body moves, after the bitter light,
A staid dance among innocent solitudes;
So let me lie in a story, heavy with evening.

(Strophe IV)

The markers of "evening" and "light" are ambivalent with respect
to terms for ostension (face, tell), and terms for internality (solitudes,
malice). Repetition and cyclicity are the destiny of things belonging
to both classes. The poem bristles with barriers—doorways, measures,
roofs, gardens. But the speaker dreams of an unfettered flow:

But I dream of distances where at evening
Ghost begins (as no migrant birds can tell)
A journey through outlandish solitudes,
Hair all ways lifted, leaves wild against face,
Feet trammeled among dune grass, with spent light,
And finds no roof at last against wind or malice.

(Strophe V)

The intersection of the linear and the cyclical raises the old questions about poems: "Oh, though all breath be seasonal, who can tell /
A story like new grass blown in sunlight?" (II, 5-6). Searching for the
spontaneity that designates newness, the speaker engages nature in
poetic speech and then perceives the impossibility of response. He
returns to the humanity that alone possesses the power:

Sir, who have locked your doors, but without malice,
Or madam, who draw your shawl against evening,
By the adumbrations of your thin light
What but this poor contention can you tell:
Ceaseless intruders have demeaned your face
And contrived homesteads in your solitudes.

(Strophe VI)

For better or worse, the poem tells us, over time, our life and
body are subject to invasion. No part of the world is without artificial
barriers (just as any matter can become a song). But the barriers are
there to be infringed. The poem's manifest sense of audience and its
search for a firmer sense of its own reality and for reestablishment of
its public premises counterbalance the will to closure, and tenuously
overcome it:

Tell me who keeps infrangible solitudes
But the evening's dead on whose decided face
Morning repeats the malice and the light.

(Strophe VII)

8. John Ashbery: "Poem"

The sestinas of John Ashbery—three in the early collection *Some Trees* (1956), one in *The Tennis Court Oath* (1962)—seem a prominent exception to the preoccupation with time that characterizes the diachrony of the form. His archaeological layers of diction, from biblical to colloquial, seem to take no measure of sequentiality. Modalities coincide or collide, and the work reveals a reliance upon the provisional in encounter, perception, and reception. There is an extreme, however, at which patterns await events. In Ashbery's sestinas, form successfully gives material a sense of place, conveying the possibility that a lost unit of perception can be redeemed through artifice in the imposition of patterning on poems.

There is, as Ashbery knows, no unmediated language for the present ("This past / is now here," he writes in *Self-Portrait in a Convex Mirror*). His agrammatic structures question the authority of grammatical assumptions—for the modulations of tense and the inflexions of verbs construe an individual, social, and cultural past. Standard patterns of history are points of departure, but it is the spatial and temporal coordinates of the act of poesis that replace the past-present-future axis or vertebrae of coherence. Abrupt shifts of reference as well as of tense, multiple corrections, and self-sabotage easily puncture the straw-clichés and public vocabulary of many of the poems. Ashbery's poetic syntax breaks through the petrifaction of old idioms, scattering them into their parts. The finished work is its own death, "a cloth over a birdcage," he says (*Self-Portrait* 1, 76), troping on the old analogy of poem and birdsong. Art's permanence, then, is one of its chief dangers. Here we recognize a poet well capable of assessing the (ironic) aptness of sestina form to his concerns:

> Our time gets to be veiled, compromised
> By the portrait's will to endure. It hints at
> Our own, which we were hoping to keep hidden.
> *(Self-Portrait* II 79-80)

To resist formulation, remain flexible and ductile, is the telos of Ashbery's elusive diction. The complete poem apologizes by evasiveness. Poetic creation as activity, not as the fixation of content, would reside in perpetual openness. We may ask why he was attracted to poetic forms with other than simply sequential organization: Experience in his work often amounts to massed kitchen-middens of artifacts, devoid of any recognizable expository traces of consequence and cause.

In an informally expressed view, he discusses his attraction to the sestina:

These forms such as the sestina were really devices at getting into remoter areas of consciousness. The really bizarre requirements of a sestina I use as a probing tool . . . I once told somebody that writing a sestina was rather like riding downhill on a bicycle and having the pedals push your feet. I wanted my feet to be pushed into places they wouldn't normally have taken. . . .

(Kalstone 1977: 172)

It is as though the distant reaches of the present ("consciousness") were accessible only to an alliance of unyielding form and aleatory object. Against the constraints of form, the flow of images demands to be disentangled as far as decorum is concerned, but when that is satisfied, may display its fitful coherence without further "requirements." The hidden foundation of all the necessary adjacencies in sestinas is function. Attempts to read the "Poem" under some hypotactic shelter fail, and two antinomic structures emerge: a poetic structure that is whole and a narrative structure that is fragmented, much like a matrix of fossils.

If we examine the components of the "Poem" I have selected for the elucidation of this museum-culture, we can identify many elements from our own cultural environment: Objects, costume, patterned social behavior. By cultural environment we understand not only things but systems of relations among them, for example, ritual, which would produce a prior notion of compatibility or incompatibility regarding certain situations. Ashbery's "Poem" presents us with signifiers that point in one way or another to the fundamental categories through which we perceive our universe as a meaningful system. Then having assumed the cosmological view, we have to re-identify the constituents themselves.

"Poem"

I.   While we were walking under the top
     The road so strangely lit by lamps
     And I wanting only peace
     From the tradesmen who tried cutting my hair
5   Under their lips a white word is waiting
     Hanging from a cliff like the sky

II. It is because of the sky
     We ever reached the top
     On that day of waiting
10   For the hand and the lamps
     I moisten my crystal hair
     Never so calmly as when at peace

III. With the broken sky of peace

206

Peace means it to the sky
Let down your hair
Through peaceful air the top
Of ruins because what are lamps
When night is waiting

IV. A room of people waiting
To die in peace
Then strike the procession of lamps
They brought more than sky
Lungs back to the top
Means to doom your hair

V. Those bright pads of hair
Before the sea held back waiting
And you cannot speak to the top
(It moves toward peace)
And know the day of sky
Only by falling lamps

VI. Beyond the desert lamps
Mount enslaved crystal mountains of hair
Into the day of sky
Silence is waiting
For anything peace
And you find the top

VII. The top is lamps
Peace to the fragrant hair
Waiting for a tropical sky

(Ashbery 1956: 36-7)

Stanzaic progression even in simpler poems poses complex problems of meaning. A first reassurance is the framing of distinct stanzaic openings and closures by sestina rhyme-word order, but it is attenuated by the total lack of punctuation. The reader is teased into making connections himself, subverting the surface randomness. "Waiting" marks time; the poem's first verb, "walking," marks space. For the rest, any goal or center is represented by "top," always involved in either a past or a predictive situation. Beyond "top" lies "sky," present in many accepted meanings: As spatial delineation of the earth (strophe I), as heavenly agency (strophe II), as heavenly nonbeing, possible indicated by thunder (strophe III), as air (strophe IV), as the determinant of light in the world (strophes V, VI), and of weather (strophe VII)—each subsisting on conventions preestablished yet permitting of an immense range of semantic relationships.

The activity of "waiting" imports a memory of at least the image of what is being awaited. If we read the fifth line of the poem in the present of the time of composition, then the rest of the first strophe identifies the topics to be remembered, made present at the time of their occurrence. Thus the time of the event and the time of recollection are collapsed together, not telescoped (with the sequential order therein implied) but crushed into one. Grammatical data have no more room. The reader as interpreter has more to do than settle that kind of question; he has to gather in the dispersed fragments of a universe of discourse. The play of abstract nouns representing values with concrete ones that display a mysterious specificity clearly places the burden on the specific: "Lamps," "hair," the "tradesmen," the "procession" among others call for reference. The poem mocks anaphora: "Their" in the first strophe, "your" in the third and fourth, "you" in the fifth and sixth, expose emptiness and loss. While affectivity is rendered mainly by adjectives ("only peace"; "that day"), or even by conjunctions ("And I wanting only peace"; "And you cannot speak to the top"), the adjectives are there to reject any complete flattening of value and to reveal occluded glimpses of memory ("ruins," "a roomful of people waiting / to die"; "those bright pads of hair"). Semantic closure and disclosure are the more bewildering in that there is a "we" as well as an "I," and because many terms are terms for value capable of invoking opposites (peace, sky, waiting, and top roughly answerable by war, earth, motion, bottom). Manneristic repetition, as of "peace" in the third strophe, creates a litany of longing for repose and centrality as the "we" proffers suggestions of communality and even of ceremony emanating from a shared ideology. Having noted these features that link "Poem" to the manifestations and functions of sestinas (rather than to their "history"), that is, to the constants that can be isolated in its synchrony, the reader is still faced with the necessity of reading.

Presences definable chiefly in terms of their interrelations tempt Ashbery's tendency toward indulgence and sheer play. But the absent terms I suggested above are pre-text, an understood, that makes sense of what is there. A prior chaos of contention and sensuality would serve as the missing past for present striving toward a superrealm of plenitude ("sky," "top"). An astute observer has noted Ashbery's recurrent "myth of diminution" (Kalstone 1977: 191). We recognize it now against a landscape containing a procession. Like a revenant from the carnage of human sacrifice, the speaker remembers a progress "under the top," in the first strophe very close to "sky." Sacrifice would encompass the hair-cutting and the final word, "waiting." In the second strophe, "sky" in its acceptance of "god(s)" becomes a locus of causality, "hand" and "lamps" instrumental in the ceremony. Earthly demand for peace "means it" to the sky, the touch of slang conferring unprecedented dynamism on the motion, immediately counterbalanced by the distracting internal rhyme hair/air. Modulations of syntactic inference form a question at the end of the third strophe, which again seems to point to the relative weakness of the sacrifice against the fatality of time's measure ("night"). Those who wait to die, next, correspond to the engulfing night, showing the space of alienation between the strophes. "Hair" is the only human element, again associated with sacrifice, particularly in tandem with "doom" and "bright pads." Assuming the unity of the single experience described, the receding sea could have the secondary sense of low tide. Friezelike, the entire ceremony takes place under the remoteness of "sky" ("And you cannot speak to the top / It moves toward peace"); the "bright pads of hair" could alternately be seen as synecdoche for the sacrificed being, shrinking from death. This reading would be augmented by the metaphor of stars as "falling lamps" opposed to "the day of sky" or sun, twice enunciated by way of compensation for the inaccessibility of "sky" and even of the perceivable "top" that moves beyond human grasp. That movement only reproduces the movement of the sestina toward an inaccessible center. "Hair," we have seen, most strongly connotes human sacrifice, including arrangement, massing, and cutting. It is "mine" and "yours," and finally belongs to the massed multitude. Its last appearance is in a benison ("Peace . . ."), but it has already served to reflect light ("crystal hair"), like the lamps in their turn. In the last three strophes, one of the sudden temporal alternations toward the present takes hold and obtains, drawing the poem to the end of ceremony and rectilinear time, which would also be the end of "revolution" both within and outside the poem. All of the "top" that can be seen is reflected light; exploration is done. Something of the chiastic antagonism of earth and sky ("With the broken sky of peace / peace means it to the sky") survives as the *architectonic* of a larger, vanished mythical context. The poem is a sacrificial offering to the encroachments of entropy on the sestina-scheme: Incantation propitiating forces that are internal as much as external. But if this reading is as valid as it is coherent, the powerful evocation of mass ceremonial, that if successful would not noly propitiate gods but draw men into renewed communality, recreates the twofold cyclical and progressive movement of poem and the ritual to which it is bound, to end *without* an end, in waiting.

Chapter 7

The Ship Allegory

1. Petrarch LIII: "Chi è fermato di menar sua vita"

The ship-allegory in Petrarch's fourth sestina finds its way to paradox. Terms for release and constraint mark the passage of time, which is translated into the flow of things in space. The deceptive presence of semiautomatic allegorical patterns screens an exploration of that overt content:

> Chi è fermato di menar sua vita
> su per l'onde fallaci e per li scogli
> scevro da morte con un picciol legno
> non pò molto lontan esser dal fine;
> pero sarebbe da ritrarsi in porto
> mentre al governo ancor crede la vela.
>
> L'aura soave, a cui governo e vela
> commisi entrando a l'amorosa vita
> e sperando venire a miglior porto,
> poi mi condusse in più di mille scogli;
> e le cagion del mio doglioso fine
> non pur d'intorno avea, ma dentro al legno.

(ed. Ponte 1968: 45)

(He who has decided to lead his life
on the deceiving waves and near the rocks,
separated from death by a little ship,
cannot be very far from the end;
therefore he should retire to port
while the tiller can still control the sail.

The soft breeze, to whom I entrusted both sail
and tiller, entering upon this amorous life
and hoping to come to a better port,
carried me to more than a thousand rocks,
and the causes of my sorrowful end
I had not only all around but also within the ship.)

Leading from the general to the particular, the poem signals the speaker's attempt to organize what he knows of his life's voyage into a past and what he hopes of it into a future, to attribute to himself the potentiality of full understanding at its closure. Past and future, corresponding roughly to *vita* and *morte,* attempt their determination through an unusually high proportion of verbs. These presuppose the speaker who conjugates them, but the only existing time and tense for him is the present. Here again the integration of conventional topoi shows itself to be a constructional device, opening further avenues for interrogation of that present.

Since a sign is perceived in the present, past and future are signs whose interpretant is always at the next remove. Hence the appropriateness of the sestina's system of contiguity relations for the poetic embodiment of the journey. Weak metaphors snap into place: The effort to purify the language of lyric entails forcing it back towards metonymy, finally to that of sheer extension.

The speaker begs God for meaning. He deludes himself that meaning is found in the sense of place, not in the *relations that control* the sense of place. Everything stands for movement or stillness: *vita, fine* linked by the *vela* (sail) and obstructed by three kinds of closure: *scogli, porto,* and *legno* (in its foregrounded sense of "boat"). The body-metaphor extends from this uncertain sense of place (strophe III, *cieco legno;* strophe V, *fraile legno*). This sailor in media res sees both sides at once. To compose poetry is "to set sail." For the Romans, *vela dare* served as a metaphor for the creation of a poetic work envisioned as a journey (Curtius 1953: 129), and the ship-allegory of composition became widespread throughout the Middle Ages.

But nautical metaphor was proper to introductions (Curtius 1953: 129), and summoned reader and listener at the inception of an

211

inward voyage. Dante admonishes the reader who cannot follow in his wake to turn back (*Par.* I, 6-9); it is the poet who sets the pace. But this sailor makes of his journey a means of measurement, and in so doing raises the independent status of time, for instance, noting its catastrophic acceleration by the winds of desire hurling him forward ("la vela / ch'anzi al mio dì mi trasportava al fine"). Laura, who makes it evening "before vespers" (CCXXXVIII), has come to reside *within* the phantasm-forming mind given over to passion. The association of closure with the body (*legno* as boat, then wood, ultimately *hyle* or sheer matter, completing its metonymic representation of the Petrarchan *selva*) and openness with the soul become blurred, despite reminders of danger. If the *scogli* connote the sirens who inhabit them, how much better it were for the sailor to be delivered from his journey. And yet the only life the poem knows is its own continuance:

> S'io esca vivo de' dubbiosi scogli,
> et arrive il mio essilio ad un bel fine,
> ch'i' sarei vago di voltar la vela,
> e l'ancore gittar in qualche porto!
> Se non ch'i' ardo come accesso legno,
> si m'è duro a lassar l'usata vita.

(Strophe VI)

> So may I come out alive from these perilous rocks
> and my exile reach a good end,
> how I yearn to furl the sail
> and cast anchor in some port!
> Except that I burn like kindled wood,
> it is so hard for me to leave my accustomed life.

Vita attaches partially (as *vivo*) to the new life of salvation, then to the old one of earthly struggle. Along a trajectory of desire the poem proceeds, essentially unmoved by the promise of a "better port" glimpsed beyond its reach, for the obstacle is internal: the lack of principle of governance within the lover. The optative mode ("S'i'esca . . . sarei vago . . .") is successfully countered by privative constructions arising from it ("Se non che . . ."). The policing of the will would culminate in centrality and repose, yet the poem is motivated by the inflated sail of enamorment. Against the indexical "insegne di quell'altra vita" (strophe IV) it describes an icon of desire. "L'aura soave," metamorphosed to a violent wind, causes both the body-ship's deviation from its appointed course and the excess fullness that produces the poem. Now the verbal correlate of Laura is revealed as a transforming agent, messenger between the members of Petrarch's duality. The alternations of terms for openness and closure give way to the paronomastic revival of the old trope of winds.

Vita reminds us of the poem's character of extended metaphor. It is the single term that conveys constant reference to external context. And the poem strives to reconstruct a life out of figures of speech. But like the tropes, the life has lost its figurality. It is precisely in the bound context of the time-honored "nautical metaphor" that we most clearly perceive the poem as a substitution. Metonymy, complaisant to extended allegorical discourse, dominates medieval texts because it gives overt expression and specific external reference to a hierarchy of relations—relations that can be contracted by things independently of the trope itself (Shapiro and Shapiro 1976: 10-11). The paronomasia on Laura's name exists to revivify, metonymically, the ship-allegory. Laura's intrusion into the store of texts internalized by Petrarch transforms the nautical discourse contextually, hence metonymically, refreshing the senescent connections of its meaning.

The lover begs not only for meaning but for ending:

> Signor de la mia fine e de la vita,
> Prima ch'i' fiacchi il legno tra li scogli
> drizza a buon porto l'affannata vela.
>
> (Strophe VII)

> (Lord of my death and my life:
> before I shatter my ship on these rocks
> direct to a good port my weary sail.)

The ship is expressed as one of its constituents, *vela*, showing a dominance of figural meaning. But it also asserts the unchanged hierarchy of the constituents, the two signata *vela* and *legno*. It was for later poets to attach the ship-allegory to cases of total, oneiric domination. In this sestina, the essentiall metonymic character creates momentary questions to be answered in silent knowledge by the reader, affirming a subordination of words to anticipated "essences." The figural power of Laura is sufficiently diluted to invite the next step, metaphorization of the whole text as story. Poems by two poets who stood in complex relationships to Petrarch evince that kind of result: Michelangelo and Ungaretti, each poem displaying the contest of will over contiguity, or closure.

2. Michelangelo Buonarroti: "Crudele stella, anzi crudele arbitrio"

As the block of marble encloses the living statue, verbal material conceals within itself a poem to be disclosed. Muscular dynamism, the ethos of the *difficulté vaincue*, carves form out of blocks of im-

213

manent force. Michelangelo was considered by his contemporary Francesco Berni as an "anti-Petrarch":

> Tacete unquanco, pallide viole,
> E liquidi cristalli e fiere snelle:
> E' dice cose e voi dite parole.

(cit. Ferrero 1935: 4)

(Be silent forever, pallid violets and crystal liquids and swift beasts: You say words but *he* says things.)

It is telling that this view of Michelangelo depends on tropological comparison of his work with Petrarch's. Their common features are taken entirely for granted, and rightly so. The caprices of fortune throughout Italian history have undergone considerable analysis but the sediment of Petrarchesque lyric subsisted. By the time that witnessed the composition of Michelangelo's poems, from the 1530s throughout his life, poetic revelations of human weakness would seem to have presented nothing new to the lyric imagination. Petrarch's concern with the impossibility of centrality and fusion has so served a number of imitators as to obscure from us what quotient of Petrarchism came to Michelangelo directly from Petrarch. But the radical differences of Michelangelo's poetry completely subordinate any assumptions of communality. Petrarchan form was the crucible for sixteenth-century lyric, and it did provide the outlines for the poem to be discussed here. Berni conveys to us that the tropes of idyllic or elegiac hedonism, however, are missing from Michelangelo; missing also are a number of Petrarch's screen-words. In the rush toward meaning, Michelangelo's language encompasses the code of Petrarchism for its emblematic convenience, conferring on it an unprecedented, explosive disposition.

The series of existential crises that forms the substance of Michelangelo's poems inscribes attempts to free that self of emotional weight, of an overweight content that bends the backbone of form. Symbols (in which the signans/signatum relation is understood conventionally and acquiesced in) refer variously to the voice of heroic Christianity in Dante, or to the divided will of Petrarch, now infused with the contest of *virtù* and *fortuna* that is in turn the dialectical ground of Renaissance literary argument. The understanding of will is the *telos* of Michelangelo's one complete sestina. Based on tropes so outworn by his time as to constitute a *lingua poetica*, it is composed from an agonistic stance, rejecting in its progress whatever does not engage the speaker's entire, innovating persona:

I.   Crudele stella, anzi crudele arbitrio

che'l potere e 'l voler mi stringe e lega;
nè si travaglia chiara stella in cielo
dal giorno (in qua?) che mie vela disciolse,
5   ond'io errando e vagabondo andai,
qual vano legno gira a tutti e' venti.

II. Or son qui, lasso, e all'incesi venti
convien varar mio legno, e senza arbitrio
solcar l'alte onde ove mai sempre andai.
10   Così quagiù si prende, preme e lega
quel che lassù già'll'alber si disciolse,
ond'a me tolsi la dote del cielo.

III. Qui non mi regge e non mi spinge il cielo,
ma potenti e terrestri e duri venti,
15   che sopra me non so qual si disciolse
per darli mano e tormi del mio arbitrio.
Cosi fuor di mie rete altri mi lega.
Mia colpa è, ch'ignorando a quello andai?

IV. Maladetto (sie) 'l di che io andai
20   col segno che correva su nel cielo!
Se non ch'i'so che'l giorno el cor non lega,
ne sforza l'alma, ne' contrari venti,
contra al nostro largito e sciolto arbitrio,
perche (. . .) e pruove ci disciolse.

25   V. Dunche, se mai dolor del cor disciolse
sospiri ardenti, o se orando andai
fra caldi venti a quel ch'e fuor d'arbitrio,
(. . .), pietoso de'mie caldi venti,
vede, ode e sente e non m'e contra 'l cielo;
30   che scior non si può chi sè stesso lega.

VI. Cosi l'atti suo perde chi si lega,
e salvo sè nessun ma' si disciolse.
E come arbor va retto verso il cielo,
ti prego, Signor mio, se mai andai,
35   ritorni, come quel che non ha venti,
sotto el tuo grande el mio arbitrio.

VII. Colui che sciolse e lega 'l mio arbitrio,
ov'io andai agl'importuni venti,
fa'mie vendetta, s'tu mel desti, o cielo.

(ed. Girardi 1960: 39-41)

(I. Cruel star — or rather, cruel will that binds and ties my power and voli-
tion, nor does any clear star turn in the heavens from the day it unloosed
my sails, wherefore I vagabond and wandering went forth as an empty
vessel turns at every wind.

II. Now I am here, alas, and I must vary my boat's course according to the incensed winds, and without sovereignty clear the high waves where I ever did turn. Thus here on earth is taken, bound and tied that which was already unbound by the tree whence I took for myself heaven's gift.

III. Here it is not heaven that sustains and pushes me on, but potent, earthly and hard winds, for I know not who unloosed himself, to give them a hand and remove me from my discretion. Thus outside my net another binds me. Is it my fault that I went to him, unknowing?

IV. Cursed by the day I went along with the sign that was coursing above in heaven! If it were not known to me that (birth)days do not bind the heart or force the soul into contrary winds against our proffered and unbound free will, (for . . . [it] disclosed the proof to us)!

V. Then if ever heart's grief unloosed ardent sighs, if ever I went among hot winds praying to Him who is beyond constraint, . . . pitying my hot winds, heaven sees, hears and feels, and is not against me, for he who binds himself cannot free himself.

VI. Thus he who binds himself loses his freedom to act, and no one ever unbound himself, safe. And as a tree goes erect to the heavens I beg of you, my Lord, if ever I did go, let my will return to its place under yours, as that which labors under no winds.

VII. He who unbound and binds my force, causing me to go to the clamoring winds—you would make my revenge, O Heaven, since you gave him to me.)

A phenomenon unique to this point in the history of the sestina, the presence of verbs as rhyme-words, underscores the reduction of existence to elemental struggle. The speaking subject is the passive ground of that struggle, since he embodies a state of contrariety perceived as resulting directly from the Fall. An innovation in the contemplative statements of Pico is the value to be attributed to contest. If we consider the mythic time of Eden as a static presence here, we may think of divine contemplation without contraries as the habitual intention and purpose of the lover's self-critique. But the impetus of the poem transcends this position: It makes no division between intellectual and "vulgar" love, as would be made by the great majority of Renaissance Platonists. Beauty involves a tempestuous relation between that desideratum and the desirer, and the entire focus narrows on action. The sestina turns directly on a dialectic of "binding" and "loosing," epitomized in the rhyme-words themselves, a progression no less compelling for the fact that "loosening" is in the historic past, "binding" in the ahistorical present. Nowhere do the determinate content-forms of the Petrarchan sestina receive a more direct and original treatment. Carried about on contrary waves, the subject can externalize and reify the elements of the contest of will and fates. Michelangelo's most accomplished editor informs us that the very paper on which this poem was discovered in manuscript (dated 1532-34; Girardi 1960: 168) is scarred and erased so that the emergent poem had largely to be reconstructed out of the knowledge of others.

This sestina is not philosophical or doctrinal in any discursive way. At the same time, its general lack of imagery is paraded by the rhyme-words. Against the powerful drift of Cinquecento poetics, the verbal rhyme-words are no longer stable resting points for the creating imagination, but points of departure for action. Dependent as they are on person, number, time, and mood, they are even more context-bound than nominal terms would be. *Lega, disciolse,* and even further, *andai* reenact the restless torment of the soul that seeks to free itself from a self-imposed bondage. Each represents a segment of temporality that moves the nominal subject as much as it is moved by it. One is tempted to suggest that the subject falls under the sway of an overwhelming determinism. In virtue of being third person verbs, *lega* and *disciolse* emphasize the suffering of the passive subject, whose love must be accompanied inseparably by pain. Even *andai* denotes confused errantry. Although some terms strongly evoke Petrarch (*sciolta* in Petrarch's sestina CCXIV, for example), where Petrarch's use of the word retains its adjectival passivity, Michelangelo's makes present an unprecedented quantity of sheer movement. The finite verb forms, even as they attract kindred terms (for *lega: stringe, preme, regge, sforza.* for *disciolse: tolsi, tormi, largito, sciolto, scior;* for *andai: errando e vagabondo, gira, varar mio legno, solcar l'onde, correva, va retto, ritorni*), are themselves "bound," and the explicitness of reference to binding and closure is all the more striking in that the poem attacks the matter of will as anteriority.

Devoid of the benign or reticent femininity of Petrarchan usage, *venti,* the old pun for Laura, appears in this sestina in a form of extreme vehemence. *Potenti, terrestri e duri, importuni, caldi:* All of these features are decidedly masculine. The winds' function of mediation is abrogated by their contrariness of direction, severing the connection between motivation and action. The initial line has already denied the continuity of the ship-allegory, and the rest of the poem bears out the allegory's intermittent value. Nor do the correlative procedures of Petrarchesque poetry prevail. Here the opening lines mislead us only as much as a quiet harbor misleads a new sailor.

The meaning of *arbitrio,* the abstract noun that most drains the poem of image, varies greatly according to context, however predetermined its inter- and intra-stanzaic position. In the first strophe it represents the beloved's abuse of power, successfully opposed even to astrological movement. Yet the messages of the stars are twice the cause of self-correction; the lover is not ready to relinquish this way of marking time. In the second strophe, *arbitrio* denotes the sovereignty over the self that the beloved steals from his lover. *Il mio arbitrio* in the third strophe represents *discretionary* power over that self. But in the fourth strophe the conception of self-determination enlarges to comprehend humanity at large. It is the full theological idea of free will ("nostro largito e sciolto arbitrio"), which is used implicitly and Dantesquely, to measure the speaker's deviation from that path. The fifth strophe refers *arbitrio* explicitly to God, as being beyond constraint or "binding," beyond denomination even (as the diction reverts to Petrarchan address, God is designated by *quel*). The sixth strophe compares the divine faculty of judgment with the human one. The tornada opens out again into generality: *Arbitrio* here has the primary sense of force. All of these meanings have in common the connotation of power, whatever their reference.

It is just where the content dwells on the self-shackled will that the poet unshackles the form. The inwardly directed pincer movement of rhyme-words is turned violently outward in the fifth strophe: from 6 1 5 2 4 3 to 6 1 5 4 2 3, in the second, or central segment of the strophe. "Scior non si può chi se stesso lega," the poet exclaims, reproducing the act of submission that logically precedes the composition of a sestina. But it is possible to strain the form to test its plasticity, and this kind of torsion is revealed in the embodied paradoxes of self-restriction. The break in the dominant order of the sestina-scheme enacts an overflow of will.

Floods of words acquire form only when confined between banks, but in Michelangelo's experimentation with the sestina the form-content dichotomy emerges as far more complicated than the relation of "substance" to "expression," and certainly gives the lie to notions of unidirectionality. Unlike the figurative arts, where content is taken to be the object represented in the *materia* as it has been shaped by the form (the sculpture *David*), in a poem, the content is not language but what the language stands for, its reference. Furthermore, the language itself, though it is "arbitrarily" materia in relation to poetic form, is itself a set of forms in relation to its referents. So the form of a poem is "a form [the poet] imposes upon his mass of forms . . . by shaping it as a whole to a structure and a meaning determined by himself. The form he imposes is the peculiar total character of the speech he makes" (LaDriere, in Preminger 1965: 815) The original and vital poetic principle affirmed by this sestina is the form imposed on poetry by the laws of its own origination, the power of execution that creates and constitutes.

Power and the transfer of power figure largely in the organization of the poem. It would seem that power culminates in the reference to God, but that assumption is thwarted by the final transfer of power to the beloved in the tornada. Catalyzing the lover's desire, he now binds his judgment. The incantation to God develops something of the character of an order. God pities him, the lover declares, if ever he has prayed. Man is errant as of his Fall, which dominates the sixth strophe. It was that first unbinding that made possible the lover's present self-imprisonment in his own Vulcan's net: "Così quagiù si prende, preme e lega / quel che lassù gia 'll'alber si disciolse." What is the priority of will, if man is indeed condemned to it?

The story of the first temptation weaves through the lover's plaint, and the crossing of his astrologically plotted destiny with will turned to desire is prevented only by the creator's interdict ("Se non ch'i' so che 'l giorno el cor non lega . . ."). The lover's birthday as the sign of the intersection between his cyclically recurrent star and his uniquely formed and constituted persona is a locus of uncertainty and questing. His drama entwined with the omnipresence of original sin in the world produces negativity in the shape of interdict. Kenneth Burke suggests that in Dramatis terms the propositional negative be replaced in analysis by the hortatory negative, that of command:

> This slight modification would shift our problem from the "Idea of Nothing" to the "Idea of No." And perhaps since "no" is a principle rather than a paradoxical kind of "place" or "thing" (such as "Nothing") we are not so pressed to conceive of it in terms of an image.
>
> (Burke 1970: 20)

The underlying idea is that language can most profitably be approached in terms of action rather than in terms of knowledge, or in terms of form rather than in terms of perception (Burke 1970: 38)

The disjunction between *cielo* and *venti*, their causal dissociation and near-opposition (as in the third strophe), is an appropriate subject for discussion in Dramatistic terms. It is not constant in kind or degree. At times cielo refers to astrological destiny, at others to God, and at one crucial place, to supraterrestrial space ("come arbor va retto verso 'l cielo"). Sin loosed into the world is related directly to another major aspect of this poem's composition: the sweat of toil and, mutatis mutandis, all human striving under which the various kinds of purposive action may be grouped.

Petrarch had blessed the day of his meeting with Laura. The earthier Cecco Angiolieri, writing not long before, cursed the day of his birth. Michelangelo extends the old topos into the realm of action. The serpentine syntax of much of the poem, with its many incisions, only further prepares the reader for something yet more unusual, the

plea of the tornada for revenge on the beloved and for the final torsion of the direct line of power by God.

Action, or motion, is at once the focus and the means of exploring
the mystery before us. Action alone (Creation and the fall of man)
underlies the avowed morality of this sestina and its lashings of free
will. The principle of negativity, rejecting solutions as the poem progresses in time, includes at least implicitly the rejection of temptation. But neither syntax nor correlative semantics would fulfill the
aims of a logical argument. For example, the three lines beginning in
Così do not arise from any previously enunciated consequence. Again
their import is demonstrative, or dramatic, rather than sequentially
coherent. They convey the notions, respectively, that what was unbound in Paradise is bound on earth; that the speaker is bound by his
beloved; and that since he has thus bound himself he is no longer
free. As the poet had surrendered to the confining forms of the
sestina, so does the lover willingly bind himself until the crucial
"turning" of the tornada, which contains an essential facet of meaning and the only escape, in revenge.

Scripture renders the power vested in the keeper of Christ's keys
as that of binding and releasing: "Whatever thou shalt bind on earth
shall be bound in heaven; and whatsoever thou shalt loose on earth
shall be loosed in heaven" (Matthew 16: 19). Michelangelo has already
reassembled the respective values allotted to these actions in the context of heavenly agency. Now it is according to just that intervention
that the lover hopes to recover his freedom of will. Superimposition
is the method of metaphor, and the transference of power to the
secular beloved proceeds by the encroachment upon territories
claimed by his opposite. Despite its unrealized possibilities of theological or philosophical discourse, this poem begins and continues
with a problem of act, or form. Its issues are more ontological than
epistemological, but ontology and epistemology—not statement
only, but a way of seeing—end by implicating each other.

A parallel to this relation arises with the striving of individual
human action against the unfathomable priority of motion. When the
sestina-scheme is momentarily set in reverse, action seems to menace
the order of pure motion. Yet the order of motion is implied and included within the realm of the poem's own action. The rules of the
game still delineate its nature, although the poet acts, insofar as he
can move, within its purposes and limitations. Pathos ensues when
the speaker fails to translate will into action. Individual action on the
level of discourse contends with rule-governed motion. On the level
of fabula, the tropes of power, desire, and restitution strain toward
an Edenic, unknown content. The lost eternity of mythical time is

220

concentrated outside the poem, in the moment before Adam and Eve lost Paradise. That assumption secures the anteriority of Will in the universe. From a Freudian standpoint, the tropological pattern of the poem would invoke a corresponding pattern of psychic defenses. As Burke puts it, "People," and for the speaker of this poem, *cielo* as God, "are entities capable of 'symbolic action'; to varying degrees they can be addressed, 'reasoned with,' petitioned, persuaded. 'Things' can but move, or be moved" (Burke 1970: 40). But the capfinidas of this sestina show chance present in sameness. Their twists around the exaltation of will describe a crisis, in the true sense of a turning point, one that betokens iconoclasm, certainly as regards the duration of outworn Petrarchan tropes.

3. Giueseppe Ungaretti: "Recitativo di Palinuro"

The ship-allegory points to a world of contending forces where the poet, or speaker, projects his own future and casts out his past in a constantly disjunctive movement. The continuity of discourse is counterposed to the idea of centrality, repose, and a promised land of private or historic memory. Ungaretti's sestina returns the allegory to a cultural country of the mind, thereby achieving a new coherence in the linkage of allegory and myth. A rich source for the poet who finds his meaning in freedom and solitude, the typological model is Aeneas' departure from Troy and search for his *Terra promessa*, the title of the collection containing the sestina.

It would be grossly simplifying Ungaretti's discourse here to claim that he is using Petrarchan idiom to retell the Virgilian story. His return after much experimentation to canonical forms ends a long wandering from the precincts of Italian tradition. The poems of the *Terra promessa* became the subjects of autocommentary over fifteen years. The sestina, entitled "Recitativo di Palinuro," belongs to a period of Ungaretti's career in which the operatic use of the word was certainly familiar. In reaction to a reductionistic phase in his own development that had produced a virtual cult of the poetic fragment, Ungaretti took up the old forms again and with them their communality with the Petrarchan and Christian context. For the obverse of the promised land is perpetual exile, violently traversing historical and cultural boundaries while defining them. Seekers know that the route back is sealed by apocalypse. In choosing the sestina, Ungaretti deferred to the preeminence of context in poetry, both in the matter of poetic form and that of "influence." But it is not a unilateral adherence to the tradition of Petrarch: Rimbaud's *bateau ivre*, too, and the expanded connotational fields of Symbolist poetry haunt this ship of the soul. The poet, an island to himself, uncovering the harmonics of the word, comes gradually in the *Terra promessa* to a confrontation with the Arcadias of his mind.

Ungaretti called the *Terra promessa* "il canto dell'esperienza consumata," implying an existential vision of the world that translates through phenomenological experience the overarching experience of time. His poetry is a recapitulation of experience in an effort to surpass it. The Petrarchan aspect of this kind of poetry is manifest, but with a capital difference that supersedes historical, cultural, and intertextual factors. Here the will can break the icon of inertia, destroy the false paradises of the mind, and turn the cult of words to pragmatic use in a decision to overcome the dominance of the myth of repose.

Elements of Petrarchan "Orphism" are here: The fictional speaker, Palinurus, is a shade in the afterworld, making present that of which he is still capable. But unlike that of the lover in Petrarch's poems, the speaker's narrative, sufficiently "bound" in order to form informational sequences that would not permit of another ordering, can proceed from the certain and complete viewpoint of the dead. At the same time, the poetry of self-consuming experience turns inward, seeking centrality in self-knowledge. The problem of dealing with Petrarchan language is recognized, but so is the distance traveled from that source. In Ungaretti's work, the Flying-Dutchman fate may have as its points of arrival and departure a city (Alexandria), a friend, an image of flow (rivers), Queen Dido, or the uses of the poem. The voyage repeated many times throughout his career is assimilated, assumed into the intimacy of his language and of other poems of his that dealt with voyages of hope and remorse:

> Va la nave, sola
> nella quiete della sera.
> Qualche luce appare
> di lontano, dalle case.
> Nell'estrema notte
> va in fumo in fondo il mare.
> Resta solo, pari a sè,
> uno scroscio che si perde. . . .
>
> ("Pari a sè," *L'Allegria* II, 1-8)

(The ship goes alone in the quiet of evening. Some light appears from afar, from the houses. In the extreme of night the sea bottom goes to smoke. There remains alone, equal to itself, a rustling that is lost.)

From the early phase of his career Ungaretti revealed navigation as the poet's destiny, its rules unvarying but infinitely manifested, like "i paesaggi erranti del mare" (the wandering landscapes of the sea [*Terra promessa*, Chorus IX]). The sound of the memory is the only sound heard equal to itself alone. Following any sojourn the old captain turns back to the sea, aware of it as a signifier of cosmic fatality:

> Como prora bionda
> di stella in stella il sole s'accommiata . . .

("Ogni grigio," L'Allegria)

(Like a blond prow the sun takes its farewell, from star to star.)

The heartbreak of exile perpetually replenishes the memory. Through the very lack of lasting repose, days and nights are renewed. But the non-Petrarchan departure provides the poem's finality, for it is through *event,* not meditation, that existence is interpreted. The desired island—bucolic, fabulous, awaited—proves to be that of death and immortality.

The store of Palinurus, Aeneas' helmsman, extends over three books of the *Aeneid.* We recall that the material of Aeneas' quest and founding of Rome provided a typological orientation for the story of Christ. Aeneas' still undiscovered Rome is to Palinurus the promise made to the human soul of centrality beyond that of dreams. This narrative by Palinurus from beyond death still attempts to "seize the moment" in the fullness of its meaning.

"Recitativo di Palinuro"

I. Per l'uragano all'apice di furia
Vicino non intesi farsi il sonno;
Olio fu dilagante a smanie d'onde,
Aperto campo a libertà di pace,
5   Di effusione infinita il finto emblema
Dalla nuca prostrandomi mortale.

II. Avversità del corpo ebbi mortale
Ai sogni sceso dell'incerta furia
Che annebbiava sprofondi nel suo emblema
10   Ed, astuta amnesia, afono sonno,
Da echi remoti inviperiva pace
Solo accordando a sfinitezze onde.

III. Non posero a risposta tregua le onde,
Non mai accanite a gara più mortale,
15   Quanto credendo pausa ai sensi, pace;
Raddrizzandosi a danno l'altra furia,

Non seppi più chi, l'uragano o il sonno,
Mi logorava a suo deserto emblema.

IV. D'augure sciolse l'occhio allora emblema
20   Dando fuoco di me a sideree onde;
Fu, per arti virginee, angelo in sonno;
Di scienza accrebbe l'ansieta mortale;
Fu, al bacio in cuore ancora tarlo in furia.
Senza più dubbi caddi ne più pace.

25   V. Tale per sempre mi fuggì la pace;
Per strenua fedeltà decaddi a emblema
Di disperanza e, preda d'ogni furia,
Riscosso via via a insulti freddi d'onde,
Ingigantivo d'impeto mortale,
30   Più folle d'esse, folle sfida al sonno.

VI. Erto più su mi legava il sonno,
Dietro allo scafo a pezzi della pace
Struggeva gli occhi crudelta mortale;
Piloto vinto d'un disperso emblema,
35   Vanità per riaverlo emulai d'onde;
Ma nelle vene già impietriva furia

VII. Crescente d:ultimo e più arcano sonno,
E più su d'onde a emblema della pace
Cosi divenni furia non mortale.

(For the hurricane at the top of its fury I couldn't feel sleep come near. Oil overspread mad leaves, then an open field to peace's freedom; the feigned emblem of infinite outpouring, mortal, dashed me down by the neck.

Then in my body I felt mortal struggle, descended to dreams of an uncertain fury that misted over depths in its emblem and, astute amnesia, soundless sleep, with distant echoes came poisonous peace, vouchsafing peace to the waves alone.

The waves offered no truce as reply, never more rapid in a more mortal struggle, than when the pause of the senses seemed peace. Then, the other fury evilly rising, I knew no longer which, hurricane or sleep, reduced me more to its own wasted emblem.

The augural eye then unleashed an emblem giving of my fire to waves of stars; it was by virgin arts an angel sleeping; it increased my mortal desire for knowledge. At the kiss, still at heart it was a worm in fury. With no more doubts or fears I fell, and with no more peace.

So did peace flee from me forever. Through strenuous fidelity I decayed into an emblem of despair and, prey to every fury, I was shaken and reshaken by cold insult of waves; I grew gigantic with an impetus that was mortal, madder than waves, mad challenge to sleep.

The more erect I was, the more sleep bound me, behind the hull of peace in pieces, mortal cruelty destroyed my eyes. Defeated pilot of a dispersed emblem, vainly I strove with the waves to regain it, but in my veins petrified fury.

Rising from the last, most arcane sleep, and higher than the waves, and emblem of peace, thus I became fury non-mortal.)

This sestina is the summation of the ship-allegory in Italian poetry. It recovers kinesthetically the connections between will and passion, passion and knowledge, and records the mortality of the search for their ordering. The reader of the poem, cast upon the mixed currents of Ungaretti's syntax, has to perform the task of recovering meaning and thus cede to the demands of a search analogous to that of Palinurus. It is like all narratives retrospective and, like all, nonreversible if meaning is to be preserved. But more important than the hermetically strung syntax and the mutual reinforcement of complexities, the sestina demands an introversive movement that frustrates linear narrative. The intersection of linear and cyclical time as motion tear at the Virgilian subtext, without which the poem retains the greater part of its secrecy.

Words here search out their Latinate, etymological senses and encounter secondary, current ones. Although Ungaretti provided a strophe-by-strophe explication, he evidently assumed in his reader sufficient thirst for knowledge or simply, cultural solidarity with his poems' universe of discourse, for the poet to omit more than the telling reference. What remains beyond the limit of comprehension in this poem of a broken voyage—as, perhaps, in Dante's Ulysses and Petrarch's own forlorn sailor—is the mystery of divine judgment that determines human destiny. All characterizations of experience (for instance, as "moral" or as "natural") follow upon that prime mystery, and remain ultimately dependent on it.

Palinurus' death is predetermined by the quarrels and compromises of the gods. He is to constitute the sacrifice, sealing an agreement between Venus and Neptune that one Trojan alone will not reach the land that is to be Rome. How far the roots of Virgilian *poiesis* reach into the subtext of doubt that underlies poetry of state is a prosaic, not a poetic question. It is clear, however, that Ungaretti closely follows the *Aeneid,* bypassing the existential indecision that characterizes Petrarch's anti-hero. Turning to the far more dominant memory of Latium, Ungaretti opens out the temporal motive of his sestina, toward a superseding of Petrarch effected via his own instruments.

Many times over a proven and skilled helmsman for Aeneas, first in his fleet, Palinurus has read the stars well. He is able to predict the

225

seriousness of a storm and the need to break a perilous journey. It was through his acumen that the fleet stopped at Dido's realm and through his persistence that it did not dally on the way. Both dreams and other means of divination (*sogno* and *scienza* for us) have never failed him. But at the predetermined point, Neptune sends Somnus, who takes the shape of a human companion, to lure Palinurus to rest with sweet words. Against his struggles, Sleep confuses him with mirages and throws him into the sea still clutching part of his helm. Feeling his ship drift, Aeneas, watchfully awake, comes to take the helm and steers the ship safely to Cumae. There addressing the Sybil, Aeneas convinces her to allow him to visit the realms of the afterlife. He invokes Orpheus and also the success of his own lyre, as he pleads with her (*Aeneid* VI, 165-177). In the underworld he meets the shade of Palinurus who recounts the manner of his death, the struggle with engulfing waves, and his murder by denizens of the rocks who threw him back into the sea, to be again the property of waves. He begs that Aeneas find and bury his body so that his shade may cross the river Styx and achieve rest. This plea, then, marks the second cycle of Palinurus' search for a promised land. It is denied, as the Sybil declares that the gods' decree may in no wise be subverted by prayer. Uninvited, the shade of Palinurus may not enter repose, but it is given some compensation: His name will be remembered as the name of the place whose inhabitants put him to death. The rock known to all of its cities will be called Palinurus, guaranteeing the perpetuity of his name.

The cyclical suggestions of this episode could not have eluded Ungaretti. Beyond it in linear sequence lie the wealth of its cultural associations and its kinship not only with the triumphant journey of Aeneas himself but with the ontology of the Christian model for the first and second death—not for Virgil's prosaic exegetes alone but for the poet of the *Commedia,* who kept all mortals but one from the secrets of afterlife and all from surviving transgression past the Herculean straits. Virgil provides a *terra promessa* on earth and one beyond. When the Sybil calls Palinurus' wish to enter the second a "dread desire," it is to establish a barrier known to Dante who cautioned humanity through Virgil. All of Palinurus' being and action in the crucial episode are variants of the contention of will and destiny.

Ungaretti's sestina is a reprisal of Palinurus' own retelling that builds upon that account. Insofar as it exists for us, the life of Palinurus is to be understood as perpetual mutation. His country of static felicity would be the end of change, and he receives a part of it: not repose in Elysium, but the end of change in death and then in the choice of his petrified emblem. The transformation, "Ma nelle vene gia impietriva furia," includes the rock of Palinurus within the sweep of the single episode, thereby including the end of change within the completed poem. Palinurus' immortalization as stone, which could embody for Christian readers the vanity of earthly striving or the search of the promised land on earth, is to be contrasted with Aeneas' condensation into himself of change in its essence. What is more to be dreaded, the *ferm voler* toward false Promised Lands or the contest with supernaturally determined fate?

It is his perfect fidelity to the *object* of the voyage that breaks Palinurus. The ocean in ceaseless movement serves as a metonymy for navigation itself, involving Palinurus in a contest that is not "central" to the constructive behavior and successful completion of the voyage of Aeneas. The voyage is a category of existence and of action, both a means and an obstacle. Insofar as it is a means of discovery, form must be recovered from it, a directionality that navigation alone does not provide. The point of departure may be typologically the same (a fatherland) and different (a new land) from the point of arrival. Here the degrees of linearity and cyclicity would vary according to a "pagan" or "Christian" framework, for Aeneas' point of arrival is markedly different from his starting place, whereas the exodus from Egypt, or the poet's search for the country of innocence projects a condition of arrival at another, better place. To reread Palinurus through the filter of that difference must confer another meaning on his peripherally sited experience.

Reinvented by Ungaretti, of course, the focus of the metaphor shifts to him. The old trope of the sailor, the ship of the soul, and the morass of the body, comes to embody impossibility, the kind that could be reversed only by the wild projection of a Petrarchan-Orphic adynaton that is not forthcoming: the impossibility of causing change in things petrified (as opposed to tropes), of returning from the underworld or from the "first death" to speaking life. Explicating the sestina, Ungaretti clarifies the poet's position as beyond hope:

> Va, al timone della sua nave, Palinuro in
> mezzo al furore scatenato dall'impresa cui
> partecipa, l'impresa folle di raggiungere un
> luogo armonioso, felice, di pace: un paese
> innocente, dicevo una volta.
>
> (Ungaretti 1950: 17)

_____

(At the helm of his ship, Palinurus goes, in the midst of the unchained fury of the undertaking in which he participates: the mad enterprise of reaching a harmonious happy place of peace: an innocent country, I once said.)

But Aeneas' yet undiscovered Rome is the promise made to the human soul of a consistency and centrality that would be clear of poetic dreaming or of improvement by the recapitulating memory. Aeneas himself is the missing quantity.

The classical connections are present — that of silence with unreason and of voice with hope, which lead to the image dispersed throughout the narrative of sleep as cession of being. The value of memory emerges when it is wakeful, that of Aeneas remembering his ship and substituting for his helmsman. At the same time the center of the poetic universe is memory, finding its poetic reality the infinite and infinitely repeatable.

The sea erodes Palinurus' strength and reduces him to the thing nearest an emblem: the trap that logically and temporally precedes it. Analogously, the semblance of the star is the "nearest" thing to its presence. As the "augural eye" of the god watches over the chaos, we are reminded of the physical proximity of transcendence and that it is both the perpetrator and the instrument of negation, of Palinurus' destruction as a human being. The starry waves are enflamed with his own fire, the poet says. Through mystery or caprice, the god hovers just above; the Promised Land is in view when Palinurus falls. The helmsman and the poet are just one stage short of their goal, in a state of perpetual vergency. Tracing this contiguity relation is the sestina-scheme itself, infinitely commemorating its centerlessness and approximating repose.

Fingere in both Latin and Italian includes, although in different proportion, the conceptions of pretense and of form. Cast into the midst of turmoil, the Palinurus in the narration of the sestina immediately appears as part of the "feigned" or "formed" emblem that later comes to be understood as constituting the worship of the made object. Composed of words arranged in the mind, formed and constituted as a poem, his figure wavers among the strophe's syntactically orphaned lines, their ductility susceptible of many regroupings. Words instantaneously find their harmonics: *accordando* (line 12), for example, conveying the secondary sense of concordant sound and connecting the term, in turn, to *echi remoti*, including its own distant meanings, and to *afonc* "non-sonic." Only in dreams and illusion can this art appear as "virgin" (Virgilian?). The sleeping angel, who seems to outline a composite figure of the arts and sciences not alien to the phantasms of Dantean dreams, has the value of a siren, stimulating Palinurus to desire for knowledge. Fragments of other mediating voyages come to the surface, other conspiracies of flattery and

fury. Falling from his ship, Palinurus knows the irretrievability of
his hope of rest (Senza più dubbi . . .), whereas the reader has
long before this point experienced the lack of logical inference and
conclusion in the narrative. But emerging from the waters larger,
more defiant, Palinurus evokes others already dead and grown titanic
in death, *per strenua fedeltà*; Dante's Farinata degli Uberti for one:

> . . . el s'ergea col petto e con la fronte
> com'avesse l'inferno in gran dispitto.
>
> (*Inf.* X, 35-36)

(He drew himself up with his chest and his brow, as if he held the Inferno in great contempt.)

In his character of monument to human energy, the heretic Farinata towers above his companions. He is remembered further as a
challenger of theological order and his second "burial" in Hell is the
precedent for the moment of uprising we read of. In Ungaretti fall
and challenge appear as mutual conditions: "Erto più sù più mi
legava il sonno." Each is finally encased in stone, neither destined in
his way to pass the Siren's reefs of proffered, then retraced "knowledge." As a poem, neither is mortal.

His defiance of the elements brings Virgil's Palinurus sufficiently
on high to know his loss:

> vix lumine quarto
> prospexi Italiam summa sublimis ab unda.
>
> (*Aeneid* VI, 356-357)

(on the fourth dawn / High on a wave, I glimpsed Italy.)

Più su d'onde, Ungaretti remembers, at the moment when the waves
collaborated with his own effort, Palinurus became the emblem of
non-mortal fury. Compressing Virgilian experience, the reinvented
Palinurus need not pass through capture and torment by strangers.
His being is already dispersed at the moment of the poem's completion. From then on any imagined extension of him can never re-
assemble it (*vanità!*).

Represented as an *emblema di pace,* in the irony of stony peace
and quiet, he could hardly be more divided from the unceasing drive
of his quest. Passing into fixity, Palinurus as a narrator severed from
his avowed identity loses the vital element of his figurality. In Virgil
the rock is denoted by his name, a "language symbol" (Morris 1971:
76 f.). It is a name that designates without describing, not recognizable as a trope.

In Virgil, Palinurus begs to be made whole with his body. In

Ungaretti he knows himself to be an emblem, knows the bond between the physical representation and the speaking subject eternally severed. Only the condition of poetry relieves him from a state of contention, reactivating the old journey and, in consequence, the living trope that subverts closure. In Virgil, Palinurus was satisfied. But now Ungaretti begins again the trajectory of figural language, the sailor compelled to seek his object, gradually becoming detached from his self.

The sestina makes its order out of contextually determined waves of recurrence. An outer ring of contiguity relationships circumscribes Ungaretti's poem, that of the precursor's voice. Now conventionality follows upon Palinurus' awareness, threatening figurality with the final closure of emblem. In turn, the emblem can be undone again and its parts freshened to new life only by the new trope in the new poem, whose initial phase is always to reflect contiguity relations.

With the advent of metaphorical relations, increasing the quotient of figurality in the trope, comes the submersion of the narrow iconic relation. For the figure demands that its receiver find contexts outside the realm of direct entailment. The search for the complete figure ends, if divorced from the textual locus, in the attenuation of figurality as the figure becomes generalized. Analogously, the search for the complete reading propels language further into the petrified status of emblem—an abbreviation of great generalizing power, but one that continuously attenuates the relation between the physical representation and the object "originally" depicted, now become opaque as stone.

This final identity seems weighted by closure, of the same kind that erects monuments to memory. In the living subject, memory can never be exhausted; therefore it testifies *in extremis* to completion. Death is the sine qua non for the completion of memory. That same necessity accounts for the quotient of communicability within language (as "dead metaphor"). To recover innocence means to disperse intelligibility. Palinurus' *ferm voler* allegorizes the attempt to pass beyond that limitation. The necessary self-forgetfulness that moves him and perpetuates his fall, the abandonment of boundaries, segment by segment and word for word, are at the same time necessary cargo for the ship moved by poetic fury. Petrarch laments in a much-translated sonnet:

Passa la nave mia colma d'obblio.

(CLXXXIX, 1)

(My ship passes, charged with forgetfulness.)

Linear motion toward a receding object kept perpetually in sight is countered *in* the poem by the potential infiniteness of the object and its infinite susceptibility to repetition, in cycles.

This sestina with its palimsest of subtexts makes constant appeal to memory—as poetic form, as cultural history, as return to the place of origins. That Ungaretti sought to reenter poetic tradition reactivates the recurrences of the sestina, in a way that goes far toward the guarantee of nonpetrification, for its discourse is in a sense anchored to cyclical movement. For Palinurus, memory is abandonment to the illusion of pastness in the present, and it impedes awareness of the encroachment of Sleep. That kind of peace is a siren, fatal to all manner of helmsmen and heroes. For outside the poem we know and recognize the triumph of linear progress, although we cannot understand it. And out of that final phase of negation, there can appear in poetry the constitution of its world, the construction of another degree of reality that recapitulates and encompasses memory. The acceptance of negation is only a beginning—but a crucial one.

The analogy of Palinurus' journey to poetry is, of course, incomplete and has to be. We know how poems formally end, and view them at least provisionally from a place of repose and permanence. We are capable of taking in stridge the near-approximation of language sounds to their signata and denotata and of still delivering and receiving our messages with some sufficiency. The desire to do it perfectly would correspond to Palinurus' rise and fall, the elevation of the aesthetic object to the sole object. The warning against such measures is pragmatically directed to poets over warriors. Nearness of the Promised Land—that of Rome, or the Bible, or the terminus of all desire—may amount to no more than a trick of perspective, and ultimately determines nothing. This wisdom is built into the sestina as form, which nevertheless extends its perpetual invitation to try again.

Ungarettti accepted it only once. Whereas ship-allegory tended, as I observed, to serve as introductions to poems, his poem is a leavetaking. Memory in the living is only provisional, partial closure, always leaving the open door, making images of detachment, absence, and loss. At the core of Ungaretti's Palinurus and of Virgil's, there is the non-Aeneas, opposing the one who did pass the siren's reef and attained the promised land, and who knew detachment from aesthetic experience—action as negation. For the poem, negation can consist partially in detachment from the precursor, which is preceded by recognition.

Then the beginnings of poetic life would be a liberation from the prison of self-abandonment, with all of the implied paradoxes. Where Palinurus' energy begins to degenerate and the disintegration of his person takes over is the place of oneiric domination, the phase where metaphor changes to emblem. But the reduced quantity of energy is in turn the source of reconversion, is at once regress and rebirth. Palinurus dies of fidelity to a telos subverted by the same gods who saw Aeneas safely to Rome, and nothing knowable explains this mystery. What the gods sent to Palinurus is what concerns us: the process of his "dispersion" via madness and illusion. No adynaton but the framed privilege of speaking beyond death opens to him, but it is sufficient to demonstrate how in poetry the reduction of energy can initiate a reversible process—even the entropy of tropes.

Chapter 8

Epilogue

At the heart of interpretation, there persists the apparent contradiction that a poem affirms itself as a whole and an absolute, and at the same time belongs to a system of complex historical and cultural relations. For many readers, the major obstacle to the credibility of literary theory as an enterprise is that it seems to throw the specificity of the individual poem into question and to subordinate it to overarching patterns of likeness. Interpretation tends to describe the coherence of a whole so as to expose immanent meaning; explanation grasps this whole as itself part of ever larger wholes. The question of the compatibility of these approaches has endured in recent critical debate.

"Structural criticism," as one of its most responsible practitioners has written, "is a contradiction in terms: criticism seeks to interpret a poetic work, while structuralism, for its part . . . implies an interest in impersonal laws and forms, of which existing objects are only the realizations . . . Nor is there a structuralist interpretation that is better as such than other methods—exegesis is to be assessed according to its coherence, not according to its truth in an absolute sense" (Todorov 1971: 34).

This statement may now be understood as going both too far and not far enough. On one hand it helps to document the practice of structural criticism as we experience it in the majority of cases (although manifestos are still far more easily available to us than their implementation). Structure, we are often told, is content grasped in its material organization. Yet even as calls for a "science of literature" abate, the use of linguistic, or more properly the "linguistics" metaphor that dutifully scrutinizes literature as a sign system, courts the danger of making the discovery of conventions and assumptions that enable poems to have meaning actually synonymous with the omission or avoidance of cultural particulars. This is an aspect of the human quest for unity and centrality, expressed as the quest for pure synchrony. In many guises, we have seen it before.

The structural criticism described by Todorov presupposes a lasting opposition between the need to study the varieties of poetic experience and the need to convey their common unity or to formulate a theoretical framework. It posits conditions of meaning that subsist entirely on internal relations. As Todorov characterizes "structuralist interpretation," it is an analogical rendering of atemporal structures of mind. Since history is unable to establish *controllable* relations among things, we are led to ask what atemporal structures underlie cultural phenomena. Reading a poem always adds to the variety of its signifiers, and this feat is more easily demonstrable than the attainment of some ultimate signified. But immediately two capital differences block the linguistic analogy: First, literary works with respect to language possess a narrowed range of reference; second, literary works do not themselves undergo material transformation, whereas language endlessly constructs anew. A reading that does not discover another "sense" may be seen as tantamount to an exact repetition of the text itself. Borges' Pierre Menard, who rewrote every word of *Don Quixote,* is the perfect reader of this type (we must hope, an impossibility).

The fullest use of language is made in lyric, which most overtly depends on verbal resources, so much so that an essential condition of poetic language is "its lack of naïveté, its constant self-consciousness. Language means by signs; art means by designs" (Miles 1972: 44). Meaning, function, and significance are therein convertible into rhythm, music, and form: "To effect that conversion in all its dynamism," writes the poet John Hollander (1975: 38), "must come to engage the fullest concerns of poetics." This is admirable as far as it goes in its stress on the dynamic, as well as in its refreshing lack of mournful overtones. For the rule of language over poetry has often seemed like a tyranny of inert material over creative inspiration, and in consequence, often has "inspiration" been allowed the run of the whole terrain of poetry. To accept and welcome the double-articulation of language as Hollander does is to accept a given only as a point of departure.

The attempt to identify and decipher codes cannot function without reference, for the relation between codes is contingent, diachronic, and open-ended. Even fragmentary historical data help to uncover the active, logical, and affective senses with which a poem is charged. In turn, if such components of a poem as national language, regional variants, and "value"-style (i.e., such qualifications as *gravis, levis,* and *medius* for that of medieval poems) are interdependent, they can only be discussed with reference to texts. If atemporal structures can exist, still the world at any moment is the product of their interaction within a dynamic of change. It probably is impossible to eliminate the analyst's ideological system from his arena; this too is a given. We sometimes do not know "if the text is recited by flesh-and-blood characters or lent by a clever ventriloquist to puppets invented by himself" (Lévi-Strauss 1965: 128; trans. mine). "Grammars" of a particular literary form, period, or of a poet's works rarely select for study poems with an extensive semantic dimension (as evidenced by attempts with folk poems and narratives). The more subtle a fiction, the more the analysis must deal in detail with semantics.

The hermeneutic circle, a continuous movement between the whole poem and its interior forms, and the circle of the whole of similar texts, are not concentric but tangential. To begin from the intention of studying certain characteristics common to a large number of poems, the better ultimately to reveal their individuality, is a critical procedure that takes intuition and delight for granted. Instead of rupturing the union of mind and language, of the conventional with the cognitive and affective, good analysis strives to read their lesson wholly. Therefore it is not the fact of imperfect reference that should strike us but the very ubiquity of reference, the persistence of the unconscious in the letter. Then the apparent opposition of structure and history may dissolve, to be gradually replaced by a rewriting of human history as a history of consciousness, of conceptualization. The voices of many kinds of criticism have to be heard. If such an undertaking leads to some kind of critical Esperanto, that may be a necessary occupational hazard.

Unquestioning obeisance to a purported unity of form and content and to assumptions of the coherences defining the verbal icon only uncovers the alienation between speech and truth. The question of the linguistic specificity of poetry has been provocatively raised, since the troping nature of poetic language occasions an exposé of

235

the bad faith common to all linguistic codes. "Behind the assurance that valid interpretation is possible," writes Paul de Man (1973: 25), "stands a highly respectable moral imperative that strives to reconcile the internal, formal, private structures of literary language with their external, referential and public effects." But the idea that the necessary gap between intention and poem is the most appropriate matter for exclusive concentration actually displaces meaning from poetic content (hence is itself metonymic). Taking into account the cautionary value of de Man's statement, meaning still cannot be transferred to an extrinsic point beyond language, for a poem has an implicit discourse that can continue, or integrate, as well as contradict discourse with explicit external reference. "L'expression, c'est la présence en quelque sorte sensible du signifié dans le signifiant, lorsque le signe éveille en nous un sentiment analogue à celui que suscite le sujet" (Expression is the somehow sensible presence of the signified in the signifier, when the sign arouses in us a feeling analogous to that aroused by its subject [Dufrenne 1963: 72]).

The investigation of poems as signs calls for another kind of reconsideration, one that has to do more precisely with the semiotic analysis of language structure and deals directly with the problems of form as content, which has been a central concern of this book. Since I have worked under the assumption that Hjelmslev's fundamental articulation of the interrelation of form and content is a necessary point of departure for literary analysis, I will briefly summarize it here:

Following Saussure, Hjelmslev (1970: 36-38) defined *langue* as a form that mediates between two aspects of substance, the things we talk about and the acoustic tokens we use as sign-vehicles. He couched the question in terms of a series of strata (cf. Andersen MS):

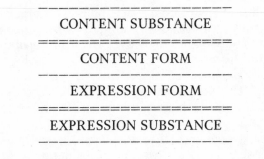

CONTENT SUBSTANCE

CONTENT FORM

EXPRESSION FORM

EXPRESSION SUBSTANCE

In Hjelmslev's conception the strata are essentially of the same rank, hence the relations between them are symmetrical. We now know (thanks to Andersen MS), however, that his conception is in need of emendation.

First, the relation between form and substance is one of inclusion. Second, the same relation obtains between expression-substance and content-substance.

The relation of inclusion that holds between expression-substance and content-substance is defined as such by the fact that language encompasses the content-substance of all other human sign systems. All other signs can be translated into linguistic signs, *including the forms of language,* and that is the reason that there can be meta-linguistic discourse (talk about language). The expression-substance of language is included in the content-substance, because all the different aspects of expression-substance can be topicalized as speech.

The relation between content-form and expression-form (which Hjelmslev defined as "solidarity") is in his conception as presented in the diagram essentially static and bidirectional. Now, if we understand the structure of language as a deductive system, in which semiotic relations have the nature of an explanatory hypothesis (if X, then Y), then any given complex of content-entities has a corresponding complex of expression-entities. Each of the relations is defined by a rule of inference (the interpretant) that transforms structures of one kind into structures of another kind.

Therefore the traditional way of conceiving of an utterance (or a poem) and its meaning as somehow simultaneously present should be revised to show explicitly the asymmetric, unidirectional, and transitive character of content-substance and expression-substance, and of content-form and expression-form, as shown in the following diagram (Andersen MS):

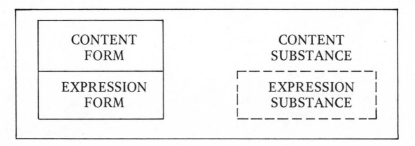

Once the asymmetric structure of the relations is understood, we are in a position to examine the form-content relation in poetry in a new light. All of the elements that enter into the definition of a poem, such as the sestina, and which differentiate it from other species of poetry, constitute its form. Everything else not part of this form but belonging to an exhaustive description of it is related to the form as substance. In the same way as in the whole of language, the form or poetic definition of a poem contracts a part-whole relation to the content. The content includes the form. To speak of the form, then, is necessarily to speak of the cardinal aspect of content.

The fundamentally dynamic and unidirectional relation between content-form and expression-form that gives definition to poetry also has particular implications for the sestina. Just as in natural languages, the sestina displays with particular clarity the nonexistence of strict synonymy and the frequent occurrence of homonymy. Strict synonymy does not exist since there is always an unequal factor between two near-synonymous expressions: Just as it is logically impossible for a single cause to have alternative effects, all other things being equal, so a single signatum cannot be joined to several signantia. On the other hand, just as different causes can have identical effect, the possibility is present that "different content entities are assigned identical expression entities" (Andersen MS). This goes to the core of the sestina's chiefly metonymic system of rhyme-words. My analysis of the sestina has demonstrated that the relation between its content and its expression is indeed dynamic and asymmetrical.

References

References

Abernathy, Robert. 1967. "Rhymes, Non-Rhymes, and Antirhyme," in *To Honor Roman Jakobson*, I. 1-14. The Hague: Mouton.

Alonso, Damaso. 1961. "La poesia del Petrarca e il Petrarchismo," *Studi Petrarcheschi*, 7:73-120

Ammons, A. R. 1965. *Corsons Inlet: A Book of Poems*. Ithaca: Cornell University Press.

Anglade, Joseph (ed.). 1919-20. *Las leys d'amors:* Manuscrit de l'Académie des jeux floraux. 4 vols. Toulouse: Privat.

Andersen, Henning. MS. "Language Structure and Semiotic Processes." To appear in *Semiotik* I, ed. T. Borbé.

Antona-Traversi, Camillo, and Zannoni, Giovanni (eds.). 1889. Francesco Petrarca, *Canzoniere*. Milan: Carrara.

Ashbery, John. 1956. *Some Trees*. New Haven: Yale University Press.

————. 1975. *Self Portrait in a Convex Mirror*. New York: Viking Press.

Auden, W. H. 1932. *The Orators: An English Study*. London: Faber & Faber.

————. 1937a. *On This Island*. 2nd ed. New York: Random House.

————. 1937b. *Poems*. New York: Random House.

————. 1962. *The Dyer's Hand and Other Essays*. New York: Random House.

————. 1967. *The Enchafèd Flood, or, The Romantic Iconography of the Sea*. New York: Random House.

Bartholomaeis, V. de. 1907. "Du rôle et des origines de la tornade," *Annales du midi*, 19: 449-464.

Beach, Joseph W. 1957. *The Making of the Auden Canon*. Minneapolis: University of Minnesota Press.

241

Beck, Jean-Baptiste. 1908. *Die Melodien der Troubadours*. Strassburg: Trübner.

Bellorini, Egidio (ed.). 1929. Francesco Petrarca, *Le Rime*. Turin: UTET.

Bergson, Henri. 1972. "La perception du changement," in *Mélanges*, 888-910. Paris: Presses Universitaires Françaises.

Bernheimer, Richard. 1952. *Wild Men in the Middle Ages: A Study in Art, Sentiment, and Demonology*. Cambridge: Harvard University Press.

Bertoni, Giulio. 1917. "La sestina di Guilhem di Saint-Grigori," *Studi Romanzi*, 13: 31-39.

————. 1927. *Poesie, leggende, costumanze del medio evo*. Modena: Orlandini.

Bolinger, Dwight. 1950. "Rhyme, Assonance, and Morpheme Analysis," *Word*, 6:117-136.

Bouissac, Paul. 1976. *Circus and Culture: A Semiotic Approach*. Bloomington, Indiana University Press.

Bühler, Karl. 1934. *Sprachtheorie: Die Darstellungsfunktion der Sprache*. Jena: G. Fischer.

Burke, Kenneth. 1966. *Language as Symbolic Action: Essays on Life, Literature, and Method*. Berkeley: University of California Press.

————. 1969. *A Rhetoric of Motives*. Berkeley: University of California Press.

————. 1970. *The Rhetoric of Religion: Studies in Logology*. Berkeley: University of California Press.

Capelli, Luigi (ed.). 1906. Francesco Petrarca, *Le traité De sui ipsuis et multorum ignorantia*. Paris: H. Champion.

Carrara, Enrico (ed.). 1953. Francesco Petrarca, *Rime e Trionfi*. Turin: UTET.

Cassirer, Ernst. 1955. *Language and Myth*. New York: Dover.

————, and Kristeller, Paul O. (eds.). 1948. *The Renaissance Philosophy of Man*. Chicago: University of Chicago Press.

Castor, Grahame. 1964. *Pléiade Poetics: A Study in Sixteenth-Century Thought and Terminology*. Cambridge: Cambridge University Press.

Cavalli, Gigi (ed.). 1958. Lorenzo de' Medici, *Tutte le opere*. 3 vols. Milan: Rizzoli.

Chaytor, Henry John. 1945. *From Script to Print: An Introduction to Medieval Literature*. Cambridge: Cambridge University Press.

Cody, Richard. 1969. *The Landscape of the Mind: Pastoralism and Platonic Theory in Tasso's Aminta and Shakespeare's Early Comedies*. Oxford: Clarendon Press.

Connell, Dorothy. 1977. *Sir Philip Sidney: The Maker's Mind*. Oxford: Clarendon Press.

Contini, Gianfranco. 1946. *Un anno di letteratura*. Florence: Le Monnier.

————. 1951. "Preliminari sulla lingua del Petrarca," *Paragone*, 16:3-26.

———— (ed.). 1965. Dante Alighieri, *Rime*. Turin: Einaudi.

————. 1973. *Varianti e altra linguistica*. Turin: Einaudi.

Corbin, Henry. 1957. "Cyclical Time in Mazdaism and Ismailism," in *Papers from the Eranos Yearbooks*, III, 115-172. New York: Pantheon Books.

Curtius, Ernst R. 1953. *European Literature and the Latin Middle Ages*. New York: Harper Torchbooks.

Damon, Phillip. 1961. *Modes of Analogy in Ancient and Medieval Verse*. Berkeley: University of California Press.

Davidson, F. J. A. 1910. "The Origin of the Sestina," *Modern Language Notes*, 25:18-20.

Derrida, Jacques. 1967. *De la grammatologie*. Paris: Seuil.

Diez, Friedrich C. 1883. *Die Poesie der Troubadours*. 2nd ed. by Karl Bartsch. Leipzig: J. A. Barth.

Di Girolamo, Costanzo. 1976. *Teoria e prassi della versificazione*. Bologna: Il Mulino.

Dubief, Henri. 1963. "Mallarmé et Pontus de Tyard," *Revue d'Histoire Littéraire de la France*, 63: 119-121.

Dufrenne, Mikel. 1963. *Le poétique*. Paris: Presses Universitaires de France.

Durling, Robert M. 1965. *The Figure of the Poet in Renaissance Epic*. Cambridge, Mass.: Harvard University Press.

————. 1976. *Petrarch's Lyric Poems*. Cambridge, Mass.: Harvard University Press.

Eliade, Mircea. 1954. *The Myth of the Eternal Return*. New York: Pantheon Books.

Empson, William. 1964. *The Structure of Complex Words*. 2nd ed. London: Chatto & Windus.

Farnsworth, William Oliver. 1913. *Uncle and Nephew in the Old French Chansons de Geste: A Study in the Survival of Matriarchy*. New York: Columbia University Press.

Ferrero, Guiseppe G. 1935. *Il petrarchismo del Bembo e le Rime de Michelangelo*. Turin: Edizioni de "L'Erma."

Ficino, Marsilio. 1576. *Opera*. Basel: Henricpetrina.

Forster, Leonard. 1969. *The Icy Fire: Five Studies in European Petrarchism*. Cambridge: Cambridge University Press.

Foucault, Michel. 1966. *Les mots et les choses: Une archéologie des sciences humaines*. Paris: Gallimard.

Fowler, Alastair. 1975. *Conceitful Thought: Interpretation of English Renaissance Poems*. Edinburgh: University of Edinburgh Press.

Fowler, Roger. 1971. "Linguistics and the Analysis of Poetry," in *The Language of Literature: Some Linguistic Contributions to Criticism*. London: Routledge & Kegan Paul.

Frank, István. 1955. *Répertoire métrique de la poésie des troubadours*. 2 vols. Paris: Champion.

Freccero, John. 1959. "Dante's Firm Foot and the Journey Without a Guide," *Harvard Theological Review*, 52:245-281.

Friedman, John B. 1970. *Orpheus in the Middle Ages*. Cambridge: Harvard University Press.

Friedrich, Werner P. 1966. "Martin Opitz: Literary Pioneer, Renegade Diplomat, Weathervane in the Eye of a Storm," *Journal of Medieval and Renaissance Studies*, 4:120-178.

Garin, Eugenio (ed.). 1952. *Prosatori latini del Quattrocento*. Milan: R. Ricciardi.

Girardi, Enzo N. (ed.). 1960. Michelangelo Buonarroti, *Rime*. Bari: Laterza.

Gombrich, Ernst. 1972. *Symbolic Images: Studies in the Art of the Renaissance*. New York: Phaidon.

Gramont, Ferdinand de. 1872. *Sextines: Précédées de l'histoire de la Sextine dans les langues dérivées du latin*. Paris: Lemerre.

Hall, Kathleen M. 1963. *Pontus de Tyard and his Discours philosophiques*. London: Oxford University Press.

Harrison, T. P., Jr. 1930. "The Relations of Sydney and Spenser," *PMLA*, 45:712-731.

Hill, Raymond D., and Bergin, Thomas G. (eds.). 1973. *Anthology of the Provençal Troubadours*. 2nd ed. 2 vols. New Haven: Yale University Press.

Hjelmslev, Louis. 1961. *Prolegomena to a Theory of Language*. Madison: University of Wisconsin Press.

————. 1970. *Essais linguistiques*. 2nd ed. Copenhagen: Nordisk Sprog- og Kulturforlag.

Hollander, John. 1975. *Vision and Resonance*. New York: Oxford University Press.

Hopper, Vincent. 1938. *Medieval Number Symbolism: Its Sources, Meaning, and Influence on Thought and Expression*. New York: Columbia University Press.

Jakobson, Roman. 1959. "On Linguistic Aspects of Translation," in *On Translation*, ed. Reuben A. Brower, 232-239. Cambridge, Mass.: Harvard University Press.

————. 1960. "Closing Statement on Linguistics and Poetics," in *Style in Language*, ed. Thomas Sebeok. Cambridge, Mass.: MIT Press.

————. 1971. *Selected Writings*, II: *Word and Language*. The Hague: Mouton.

Jeanroy, Alfred. 1913. "La 'sestina doppia' de Dante et les origines de la sextine," *Romania*, 42: 481-489.

————. 1934. *La poésie lyrique des troubadours*. 2 vols. Toulouse: Privat.

Kalstone, David. 1965. *Sidney's Poetry: Contexts and Interpretations*. Cambridge, Mass.: Harvard University Press.

————. 1977. *Five Temperaments*. New York: Oxford University Press.

Kaske, R. E. 1971. "Sì si conserva il seme d'ogne guisto," *Dante Studies*, 89:49-54.

Kristeller, Paul O. 1943. *The Philosophy of Marsilio Ficino*. New York: Columbia University Press.

Kurylowicz, Jerzy. 1975. "Metaphor and Metonymy in Linguistics," *Esquisses Linguistiques*, II, 88-92. Munich:Fink.

Lacan, Jacques. 1966. *Ecrits*. Paris: Seuil.

Lanz, Henry. 1968. *The Physical Basis of Rime: An Essay on the Aesthetics of Sound*. New York: Greenwood Press.

Laumonier, P. 1923. *Ronsard poète lyrique: Etude historique et littéraire*. 2nd ed. Paris: Hachette.

Lausberg, Heinrich. 1971. *Elemente der literarischen Rhetorik: Eine Einführung für Studierende der klassischen, romanischen, englischen und deutschen Philologie*. 4th ed. Munich: Hueber.

Lebègue, R. 1955. "La Pléïade et les beaux-arts," *Atti del Quinto Congresso internazionale de lingue e litterature moderne*, 115-124. Firenze: Valmartina.

Lévi-Strauss, Claude. 1962. *La Pensée sauvage*. Paris: Plon.

————. 1965. "Riposte a un questionario sullo strutturalismo," *Paragone*, 182:125-128.

Levy, Emil (ed.) 1883. *Der Troubadour Bertolome Zorzi*. Halle: Niemeyer.

Lewis, C. S. 1975. *Studies in Words*. 2nd ed. Cambridge: Cambridge University Press.

Lopez Estrada, Francisco. 1948. *La 'Galatea' de Cervantes: Estudio crítico*. La Laguna de Tenerife: Universidad de La Laguna.

Macksey, Richard, and Donato, Eugenio. 1972. *The Structuralist Controversy: The Languages of Criticism and the Sciences of Man*. Baltimore: Johns Hopkins Press.

Man, Paul de. 1973. "Semiology and Rhetoric," *Diacritics*, 3/#3:27-33.

Marques Braga, Manuel. 1953-57. António Ferreira, *Poemas Lusitanos*. 2 vols. Lisbon: Livraria Sá da Costa.

Marti, Mario (ed.). 1961. Pietro Bembo, *Opere in volgare*. Florence: Sansoni.

Martinet, André. 1967. "Connotations, poésie et culture," in *To Honor Roman Jakobson*, II, 1288-1294. The Hague: Mouton.

Mauro, Alfredo (ed.). 1961. Jacopo Sannazaro, *Opere Volgari*. Bari: Laterza.

McClelland, John (ed.). 1967. Pontus de Tyard, *Les erreurs amoureuses*. Geneva: Droz.

Merwin, W. S. 1952. *A Mask for Janus*. New Haven: Yale University Press.

Miles, Josephine. 1972. "Forest and Trees: Or the Sense at the Surface," *New Literary History*, 4:35-46.

Minturno, Antonio Sebastiano. [1564] 1971. *L'arte poetica*. Munich: Fink.

Morris, Charles. 1971. *Writings on the General Theory of Signs*. The Hague: Mouton.

Nelson, William. 1963. *The Poetry of Edmund Spenser: A Study*. New York: Columbia University Press.

Neri, Ferdinando. 1951. *Letterature e leggende: Raccolta promossa dagli antichi allievi con un ritratto e la bibliografia degli scritti del maestro*. Turin: Chiantore.

Paris, Jean. 1969. "Gargantua: La mode, la rupture," *Change*, 4:160-180.

Parry, Adam. 1957. "Landscape in Greek Poetry," *Yale Classical Studies*, 15:3-29.

Paterson, Linda M. 1975. *Troubadours and Eloquence*. Oxford: Clarendon Press.

Pattison, Walter. 1952. *The Life and Works of the Troubadour Raimbaut d'Orange*. Minneapolis: University of Minnesota Press.

Pazzaglia, Mario. 1967. *Il verso e l'arte della canzone nel De vulgari eloquentia*. Florence: La Nuova Italia.

Pellegrini, Anthony L. 1953. "The *commiato* of Dante's Sestina," *Modern Language Notes*, 68:29-30.

Poggioli, Renato. 1975. *The Oaten Flute: Essays on Pastoral Poetry and the Pastoral Ideal*. Cambridge: Harvard University Press.

Ponte, Giovanni (ed.). 1968. Francesco Petrarca, *Opere*. Milan: U. Mursia.

Poulet, Georges. 1961. *Etudes sur le temps humain*. Paris: Plon.

Pound, Ezra. 1952. *The Spirit of Romance*. Norfolk, Conn.: J. Laughlin.

———. 1954. *Literary Essays*. Ed. T. S. Eliot. Norfolk, Conn.: New Directions.

———. 1957. *Selected Poems*. New York: New Directions.

Preminger, Alex (ed.). 1965. *Princeton Encyclopedia of Poetry and Poetics*. Princeton: Princeton University Press.

Riesz, János. 1971. *Die Sestine: Ihre Stellung in der literarischen Kritik und ihre Geschichte als Lyrisches Genus*. Munich: Fink.

Robertson, Jean (ed.). 1973. Sir Philip Sidney, *The Countess of Pembroke's Arcadia (The Old Arcadia)*. Oxford: Clarendon Press.

Roche, Thomas P., Jr. 1974. "The Calendrical Structure of Petrarch's *Canzoniere*," *Studies in Philology*, 71: 151-172.

Roubaud, Jacques. 1969. "La sextine de Dante et d'Arnaut Daniel," *Change*, 2: 9-38.

Saville, Jonathan. 1972. *The Medieval Erotic Alba: Structure as Meaning*. New York: Columbia University Press.

Schafer, R. Murray (ed.). 1977. *Ezra Pound and Music: The Complete Criticism*. New York: New Directions.

Sébillet, Thomas. 1932. *Art poétique françois*. Paris: E. Droz.

Shapiro, Marianne. 1973. "Petrarch, Lorenzo il Magnifico and the Latin Elegiac Poets," *Romance Notes*, 15:172-175.

———. 1979. "Figurality in the *Vita Nuova*: Dante's New Rhetoric," *Dante Studies*, 97: [to appear].

Shapiro, Michael. 1976. *Asymmetry: An Inquiry into the Linguistic Structure of Poetry*. Amsterdam: North-Holland.

Shapiro, Michael, and Shapiro, Marianne. 1976. *Hierarchy and the Structure of Tropes*. Bloomington: Indiana University.

Smith, Barbara H. 1968. *Poetic Closure: A Study of How Poems End*. Chicago: University of Chicago Press.

Smith, J. C., and de Selincourt, E. (eds.). 1957. *The Poetical Works of Edmund Spenser*. London: Oxford University Press.

Spears, Monroe K. 1963. *The Poetry of W. H. Auden: The Disenchanted Island*. New York: Oxford University Press.

Spenser, Edmund. 1852. *The Poetical Works*. Vol. 4. London: Pickering.

Spitzer, Leo. 1944. *L'amour lointain de Jaufré Rudel et le sens de la poésie des troubadours*. Chapel Hill: University of North Carolina Press.

———. 1946. "Note on the Poetic and the Empirical 'I' in Medieval Authors," *Traditio*, 4:414-422.

Staiger, Emil. 1951. *Grundbegriffe der Poetik*. 2nd ed. Zurich: Atlantis.

Tabourot, Etienne. 1603. *Les bigarrures et Touches du seigneur Des Accords*. Paris: Richer.

Todorov, Tzvetan. 1971. "The Place of Style in the Structure of the Text," in *Literary Style: A Symposium*, ed. Seymour Chatman, 29-39. New York: Oxford University Press.

Toja, Gianluigi (ed.). 1960. Arnaut Daniel, *Canzoni*. Florence: Sansoni.

Trissino, Giovanni Giorgio. [1529] 1969. *La Poetica*. Munich: Fink.

Turner, Victor. 1968. "Myth and Symbol," *International Encyclopedia of the Social Sciences*, X, 576-582. New York: Crowell, Collier and Macmillan.

Ungaretti, Giuseppe. 1950. *Vita di un uomo, V: La terra promessa*. Milan: Mondadori.

Valéry, Paul. 1958. *Oeuvres complétes*. 2 vols. Paris: Editions de la Pléïade.

Van der Leeuw, G. 1957. "Primordial Time and Final Time," in *Papers from the Eranos Yearbooks*, III. 324-350. New York: Pantheon Books.

Warnke, Frank J. 1972. *Versions of Baroque: European Literature in the 17th Century*. New Haven: Yale University Press.

Weinberg, Bernard F. 1961. *A History of Literary Criticism in the Renaissance.* 2 vols. Chicago: University of Chicago Press.

Wellek, René. 1955. *A History of Modern Criticism: 1750-1950.* New York: Yale University Press.

Wetherbee, Winthrop. 1972. *Platonism and Poetry in the Twelfth Century: The Literary Influence of the School of Chartres.* Princeton: Princeton University Press.

Weyl, Hermann. 1952. *Symmetry.* Princeton: Princeton University Press.

Whorf, Benjamin. 1950. "The Relation of Habitual Thought and Behavior to Language," in *Four Articles on Metalinguistics,* 25-45. Washington, D.C.: Foreign Service Institute.

Wilkins, Ernest H. 1951. *The Making of the "Canzoniere," and Other Petrarchan Studies.* Rome: Edizioni di Storia e letteratura.

Williams, Oscar (ed.) 1977. *The New Pocket Anthology of American Verse,* rev. Hyman Sobiloff. New York: Washington Square Press.

Wimsatt, William K. 1954. *The Verbal Icon.* Lexington: University of Kentucky Press.

───── (ed.). 1972. *Versification: Major Language types; Sixteen Essays.* New York: Modern Language Association.

Zingarelli, Nicola (ed.) 1963. Francesco Petrarca, *Le Rime.* Bologna: Zanichelli.

Zumthor, Paul. 1972. *Essai de poétique médiévale.* Paris: Seuil.

Indexes

Index of Subjects

Index of Names

253